THE PERSONALITY OF SHAKESPEARE

THE PERSONALITY OF

SHAKESPEARE.

A VENTURE IN PSYCHOLOGICAL METHOD

by Harold Grier McCurdy

KENNIKAT PRESS
Port Washington, N. Y./London

PREFACE

IN THE following pages I have presented a type of study which is not customary either in psychology or in literary criticism; and therefore, although I have tried in the body of the text to make clear my assumptions, my procedures, and the tentative and experimental quality of the whole enterprise, I think that the reader may want to have a few words of explanation in advance.

First of all, as the subtitle indicates, I am concerned with exploring a method. The method derives from the theory of personality projection. It is quantitative in part, but its operation depends, as everything in science does, upon a human observer and assessor. I make no pretense to an impossible objectivity. I find, however, that respect for method does encourage impartiality, and encourages also the tracing out of consequences whether they seem commonplace or odd. The reader who has no patience with my apparatus may hold that its uselessness is demonstrated by the commonplace results and its faultiness by the odd ones. I naturally hope that other readers will adopt the more tolerant attitude that a method which yields commonplace results (and is thereby somewhat validated) may be allowed to suggest novelties which can be treated at least as hypotheses for further investigation. A certain minimum of daring is required in any scientific effort.

With regard to the personality of Shakespeare, I should like to make it plain that I have not attempted to be comprehensive and final. I do not see how we can be comprehensive and final with regard to any personality. Here, in studying Shakespeare, I have been deliberately fragmentary, limiting myself to a mere handful of questions. In particular, I have not tried to analyze the plays as artistic wholes in their entire complexity, but have only traced out a few general characteristics and a few patterns, which I have called "themes," occurring in more than one play. My analysis has focused on the dramatis personae and their interrelations. The reader may wish to argue that Shakespeare from first to last was expounding a political and moral philosophy, known to him in the abstract but given to the world in concrete parables, and surely he is free to do so; but I myself am interested in the concrete parables. I tend to think of personality as a unique set of personal relations, and I express this tendency both theoretically and in my choice of the dramatis personae as my primary units of analysis. I do so without meaning to imply that the abstractions of philosophy, politics, economics, religion, or what you will are valueless, either in themselves or in the study of Shakespeare. It just happens that the terms of my inquiry are different.

It may be asked whether it might not have been better for my purposes to capture a living author who could have been brought into the clinic and vivisected with the whole kit of psychological tools. There are reasons for considering this alternative less desirable than it appears to be. Besides, as far as I was concerned, it was impossible. But why Shakespeare? Among the many determinants of my choice, I will list three. In the first place, I was interested in Shakespeare; in the second, since the theory of projection is intimately bound up with the theory of dreams, and dreams are more like plays than any other form of literature, the Shakespearean plays appeared to be suitable material to work on, and all the more so because they extended fairly uniformly over a considerable period of their author's life; and, finally, I thought there might be some advantage in bringing into the arena of open debate, where no one who has ever read a Shakespearean play would feel excluded, some of the problems which concern psychologists today.

I know that there are people (it is perhaps truer of Shakespeare specialists than of others) to whom the very thought of a psychological approach to Shakespeare is disturbing. I hope that it will be taken as a reassurance, rather than as a sign of perversity in myself, that I admire Shakespeare's art increasingly and "doe honour his memory (on this side Idolatry) as much as any."

It is a pleasure to thank Harry K. Russell for reading and patiently criticizing two drafts of the manuscript, as well as for other offices of friendship. A number of other critics whom I should like to thank must remain anonymous. My wife, Mary Derrickson McCurdy, helped me with the line count of several of the plays, and has been my chief support and a most reliable critic during the whole period of the work.

The four text figures were drawn by William Hubbell, through the courtesy of the Institute for Research in Social Science at the University of North Carolina.

The text and line numbering of the Globe edition have been followed in the quotations from Shakespeare.

HAROLD G. McCURDY

ABBREVIATIONS

AC	*Antony and Cleopatra*
AWEW	*All's Well That Ends Well*
AYL	*As You Like It*
C	*Coriolanus*
CE	*Comedy of Errors*
Cy	*Cymbeline*
H	*Hamlet*
1 HIV	*King Henry IV*, Part 1
2 HIV	*King Henry IV*, Part 2
HV	*King Henry V*
J	*King John*
JC	*Julius Caesar*
L	*King Lear*
LLL	*Love's Labour's Lost*
M	*Macbeth*
MAAN	*Much Ado About Nothing*
MM	*Measure for Measure*
MSND	*A Midsummer Night's Dream*
MV	*The Merchant of Venice*
MWW	*The Merry Wives of Windsor*
O	*Othello*
P	*Pericles*
RII	*King Richard II*
RIII	*King Richard III*
RJ	*Romeo and Juliet*
T	*The Tempest*
TC	*Troilus and Cressida*
TGV	*The Two Gentlemen of Verona*
TN	*Twelfth Night*
T of A	*Timon of Athens*
TS	*The Taming of the Shrew*
WT	*The Winter's Tale*

CONTENTS

CHAPTER 1. ORIENTATION

1

ONE OF THE earliest of Shakespeare's biographers, Nicholas Rowe, after piecing together the external features of the great dramatist's life out of the scraps of information which he and the actor Betterton had been able to collect, tersely comments: "The Character of the man is best seen in his Writings." [1]

Whatever Rowe's epigrammatic statement may have been intended to mean in 1709, at this distance in time it appears as a special case of a general principle which modern psychologists are disposed to take seriously. Clinicians and personality theorists more and more direct their attention to literary or quasi-literary productions—reports of dreams and daydreams, stories made up in response to such inducements as the picture cards of Murray's Thematic Apperception Test, [2] and the like—in the hope of increasing their understanding of individual human nature. Although the prevailing temper of these studies is psychoanalytic, as one would naturally expect from knowing the kind of influence exerted by Freud, occasionally the investigator is primarily a statistician or experimentalist; [3] and now and then some concern is evinced for the purely methodological problems entailed by such a principle as that briefly expressed by Rowe.

The conception of an intimate relation between the personality (or character) of a man and the products of his imagination, of which dramatic literature is one example, probably has wider currency now than it formerly did. But if we should venture to depict

1. Quotation from Edmund K. Chambers, *William Shakespeare: A Study of Facts and Problems*, 2, 269. Chambers gives large extracts from Rowe. The whole account is conveniently found in Pierce Butler, *Materials for the Life of Shakespeare*, but without the original capitalization.

2. See H. A. Murray *et al.*, *Explorations in Personality*.

3. For example, B. F. Skinner, "A Quantitative Estimate of Certain Types of Sound-Patterning in Poetry," and G. Udny Yule, *The Statistical Study of Literary Vocabulary*. Though neither of these studies is, strictly speaking, concerned with personality, both of them imply the concept and enrich it.

a temporal drift from Rowe's day to the present by locating a dot on a graph opposite 1709, as determined by his pronouncement, and another considerably higher up opposite 1953, as determined by contemporary clinical practice, and then joining these points by an upward-slanting straight line, we should be grossly misrepresenting the history of Shakespearean scholarship, or, for that matter, the history of psychology, which is far from showing any such steadily mounting interest either in individual personality or in such complex, typically human products as imaginative literature.

Not until the 19th century was there a clear manifestation of the desire to interpret Shakespeare as a human personality through the medium of his literary work. The most notable example during the century was Edward Dowden's *Shakspere: A Critical Study of His Mind and Art*, published in 1875. Its thesis was that a valid impression of the inner nature of Shakespeare and of his development during the period of his maturity can be gained by taking his plays in chronological order and considering every dramatic voice with which he speaks as truly originating in himself. Dowden's fully conscious intention "to connect the study of Shakspere's works with an inquiry after the personality of the writer, and to observe, as far as is possible, in its several stages the growth of his intellect and character " [4] was carried out with skill and judicious moderation; and though, as frequently charged, he was too much under the sway of the sentimental idealism of his generation, when Victoria was queen and Tennyson was poet laureate, his book has continued to be readable and influential. An essential characteristic of his method was his attitude toward Shakespeare's dramatic personages. He wrote:

> The complex nature of the poet contained a love-idealist like Romeo (students of the *Sonnets* will not find it difficult to admit the possibility of this); it contained a speculative intellect like that of Hamlet. But the complete Shakspere was unlike Romeo and unlike Hamlet. Still, it is evident, not from one play, but from many, that the struggle between "blood" and "judgment" was a great affair of Shakspere's life; and in all his later works we observe the effort to control a wistful curiosity about the mysteries of human existence. And therefore, I say, a potential

4. (1880?), p. xiii.

Romeo and a potential Hamlet, taking these names as representative of certain spiritual tendencies or habits, existed in Shakspere. Nor do I identify Shakspere with Prospero; although Shakspere's temper in the plays of the last period is the temper of Prospero. It would not be easy to picture to ourselves the great magician waited on by such ministering spirits as Sir John Falstaff, Sir Toby Belch, and the nurse of Juliet.[5]

The last sentence in this quotation implies that a true conception of Shakespeare must leave room for these grosser elements in his personality, incongruous as they may appear by the side of that element which is Prospero. The comprehensiveness of the scheme is admirable.

Dowden was no historic freak. Even Dryden, whose name would hardly seem to many modern critics to belong in the same company, was anticipating him in 1668 when he called Shakespeare "the man who of all modern, and perhaps ancient poets, had the largest and most comprehensive soul." [6] For by these words Dryden was not merely praising Shakespeare as pre-eminent; he was meaning also that "All the images of Nature were still present to him," and that "he needed not the spectacles of books to read Nature; he looked inwards, and found her there." [7] It must nevertheless be admitted that Dryden, though the sense of his words (if taken Neoplatonically) is harmonious with Dowden, is still at some distance from Dowden's position. To reach that position it was necessary to live in a time illuminated with the consciousness of human personality, as Goethe among others had helped Dowden's time to be, and after the analysis, appreciation, and enthusiastic applause of Shakespeare's creatures had come to full tide. Morgann, Lessing, Goethe, Schlegel, Hazlitt, Lamb, Coleridge had all prepared for the new voyage of discovery. With Hazlitt, indeed, the enterprise is virtually launched. For he, in addition to developing an excited appreciation for the personal qualities of the Shakespearean characters and for the circumstances of place and action which make them come vibrantly alive, was diligent in reminding his audience that their power to be and act came from their creator.

5. *Ibid.*, pp. xiii f.
6. "An Essay of Dramatick Poesie." Quoted from F. E. Halliday, *Shakespeare and His Critics*, p. 278.
7. *Ibid.*

Dryden's old phrases take on a new sound from being vigorously associated in Hazlitt's discourse with "Shakespeare's mind." For example, in 1818 Hazlitt was saying in his *Lectures on the English Poets:* "The striking peculiarity of Shakespeare's mind was its generic quality, its power of communication with all other minds—so that it contained a universe of thought and feeling within itself, and had no one peculiar bias, or exclusive excellence more than another. He was just like any other man, but that he was like all other men. . . . He not only had in himself the germs of every faculty and feeling, but he could follow them by anticipation, intuitively, into all their conceivable ramifications, through every change of fortune or conflict of passion, or turn of thought." [8] He goes farther yet, he carries us nearly the whole way to Freud, when he says: "The poet may be said, for the time, to identify himself with the character he wishes to represent, and to pass from one to another, like the same soul successively animating different bodies. . . . As in our dreams we hold conversations with ourselves, make remarks, or communicate intelligence, and have no idea of the answer we shall receive, and which we ourselves make, till we hear it: so the dialogues in Shakespeare are carried on without any consciousness of what is to follow, without any appearance of preparation or premeditation. The gusts of passion come and go like sounds of music borne on the wind." [9]

Yet, though Dowden's book was preceded by much preparatory work and came as a natural expression and logical consequence of a long critical development, it was very soon disowned in some quarters as a misbegotten progeny of the feverish Romantic imagination, and from the beginning of our century has served as a warning example to the self-respecting literary critic. One of the later attempts in the Dowden tradition was A. C. Bradley's 1904 lecture, "Shakespeare the Man," printed in his *Oxford Lectures on Poetry* in 1909. In spite of his great eminence, the taint of morbidity has been suspected in Bradley also. Other expressions of the wish to mingle speculative biography with interpretation of the plays have been regarded as even more atrocious; and it has been deemed best

8. Quoted from Halliday, p. 310.
9. Halliday, pp. 311 f.

by many of the modern school to eschew biographical and psychological attitudes toward Shakespeare altogether.

It is possible that some of the reaction noted here was due to the
apparition of psychoanalysis on the literary scene. In particular,
Freud's footnote on *Hamlet* in his book *Die Traumdeutung* at the
turn of the century and the better-known elaboration of it in Ernest
Jones' article "The Oedipus Complex as an Explanation of Hamlet's
Mystery" in 1910 were calculated to disturb the sensibilities of
scholars brought up in libraries rather than in psychiatric wards,
and still in contact, no matter how protestingly, with the well-
mannered Victorian ethos. If this was what psychologizing led to,
then clearly one had better specialize in antiquarian research into
Elizabethan stagecraft, the literary sources of Shakespeare's plots,
the details of legal documents and topical allusions, and avoid the
foul fiend. At any rate, the reaction set in, and the most assiduous
and rewarding Shakespearean scholarship of the past forty or more
years has been largely in nonpsychological or even antipsychologi-
cal directions.

While there can be no doubt about the historical fact of a violent
recoil from biographical and psychological interpretations of the
works of Shakespeare, nor much about where the scholars have
been carried by it, it is not entirely clear what it was they found
to recoil from. Perhaps it was mainly license—the license of the
imagination itself. Concern with biography has not vanished; but it
has expressed itself in the painstaking search for documentary evidence, no matter how minute, and in dry ingenious argument there-
upon, rather than in such free-flowing reconstructions as those of
George Brandes and Frank Harris. Concern with psychology has
remained; but it has shrunk away from Shakespeare himself to a
consideration of Elizabethan psychological theories or of the psychic processes of theater audiences, whether modern or Elizabethan. (I refer here of course to Shakespearean specialists, not
psychoanalysts.) Moreover, behind some of the most cautious pre-
occupations of the period one may detect the earlier motives; thus,
for example, the attempt to settle the chronology of the plays has
gone on, fulfilling still the desire of those like Gervinus and Furni-
vall and Dowden to be able to follow the course of development

of Shakespeare's personality. Yet the powerful recoil is undeniable. Was it that the imaginative reconstructions of that personality which had begun to emerge were simply too unattractive, too abhorrent, to be tolerated?

The new attitude may be partly attributed to sheer cautiousness, to a wise distrust of extrapolations far beyond the real evidence. It is an expression in the special area of Shakespearean scholarship of the growing spirit of scientific positivism. But the peculiar violence of the reaction seems to require further explanation, especially in view of the intemperate explosions of some of those who stood for meticulous and immaculate detail. Consider Kittredge, who roundly rapped out in 1916: "Of all the methods and ideals in the study of Shakespeare's dramas, the most desperately wrong is that which seeks, exclusively or principally, to read the riddle of personality—to discover the man in his works." [10] One finds, on reading a page or two farther, that Kittredge, in spite of his previous truculent remark, is not really rejecting the theory of Dowden and his kind as wrong in itself, but is condemning the enterprise to which it leads as wrong morally, as "presumptuous beyond all limits of permissible audacity." [11] It is the deadly sin of intellectual pride that he is inveighing against. But should not one deduce something more from such words as these? "Unquestionably the man is there; the real Shakspere is somehow latent in his plays: but how is one to extract him? For if he lurks somewhere in the heart of Othello, so likewise he lurks somewhere in the brain of Iago: if Hamlet is Shakspere, so also is Claudius, and so are Banquo and Fluellen, Falstaff and Prince Hal, Benedick and Hotspur, Dogberry and Mark Antony, Polonius and Touchstone and Lear and Rosalind, Dame Quickly as well as Cleopatra and Cassius, Pistol and Osric as well as Ulysses and Prospero and Caliban. All are authentic, all are genuine, all are sincere—I use the regular jargon, the consecrated cant-words so full of sound and fury. Each, therefore, contains some fragment of Shakspere's nature, or registers some reaction of his indiosyncrasy. That is most certain. But how shall we tackle this stupendous problem in biochemistry?" [12] Kittredge

10. *Shakspere*, p. 46.
11. *Ibid.*, p. 47.
12. *Ibid.*, pp. 47 f.

makes his points, and very important points they are, too. Admittedly. But is there not a point which he does not make? The dreadful logic which he is exposing to ridicule would have us believe that Shakespeare, great as he is, contained elements of stupidity, vice, and weakness, as well as all that is noble. To a worshiper the conclusion is painful. Perhaps it was so to Kittredge. Suppose that a dreamer has related a grossly immoral dream, regarding it as a strange episode thrust upon him by powers beyond his control, and then is reminded that, after all, the dream is his own, and might conceivably have some connection with his past experience and present desires. For the dreamer the change of focus produces a kind of shock. To acknowledge a close relation between Shakespeare's dramatic characters and what he himself was produces in the mind of one drawn to him in admiration and in a sense identified with him a shock of very much the same order. To be sure, it may also produce new insights; but not while one is in the state of shock.

C. J. Sisson, in his British Academy lecture of 1934, "The Mythical Sorrows of Shakespeare," appears like Kittredge to have been laboring to throw off a suffocating incubus. Tracing the biographical mode of scholarship back through the years and locating its most malevolent offshoots in the Romanticism of the 19th century, especially in such writers as Hallam, Dowden, Swinburne, and Brandes, he complained bitterly of the tendency to attribute to Shakespeare the stormy emotions displayed by some of his characters and to derive these emotions from personally significant events, such as deaths in his family. He continued on into the 20th century, discovering serious flaws in even such a model of scholarly probity as Sir Edmund Chambers. Yet the final curious result of his destructive career through the ranks of the biographically minded was not, as one might expect, a total renunciation of all such interests, but the setting up of a preferred portrait and history of his own making, by which his hero is cleared of the bias of every human passion except the patriotic ("the cruelty of anarchy was a thought that haunted the poet like a nightmare" [13]), and not a trace of sex or depression is left in the author of *Timon of Athens* and *Troilus and Cressida* to trouble the sleep of the British people. The mar-

13. *Proc. Brit. Acad.*, 20, 27.

morealizing, wish-fulfilling nature of this astonishing production should be plain to the plainest. It is an important fact, as evidence of a renewed sympathy among present-day Shakespeare scholars with what interested their Victorian predecessors, that Sisson himself in 1950 acknowledges that his academy lecture of 1934 was too extreme, notes a "brilliant essay leading far in the opposite sense" [14] by J. D. Wilson, and concludes in a conciliatory mood: "The pendulum, swinging from pole to pole, from Lee to Brandes, is gradually settling to rest in the centre, and few would now accept the full lyrical interpretation of the plays, or deny to them their reflection of the growth and the increasing maturity of the poet's mind through which experience was transmuted into art as in a crucible." [15] Is it an ironical twitch of the pendulum that 1951 witnessed the publication of Harold C. Goddard's *The Meaning of Shakespeare*, where lyrical interpretation takes on a new dimension of fullness?

Doubtless the study of Shakespeare will continue for ages to come, and the pendulum will continue to swing, and will develop new and eccentric motions which we cannot now foresee; but its excursion in one direction at least appears to have reached its extremest point in a statement by J. W. Mackail, made, like Sisson's, in 1934. After laughing at the "inverted pyramids of purely conjectural biography" [16] and refusing to let "precarious inferences be regarded as reconstituting either the outward incidents or the spiritual experiences of Shakespeare's life," [17] he delivers the ultimate blow to those who attempt to look through Shakespeare's writings to the man himself, in these words: "In the volume of his plays and poems, as was admirably said by W. H. Page, in a remarkable speech at Stratford-on-Avon when he was American Ambassador to England, 'each of us finds the whole world of action and emotion mirrored. Especially does he find all his own moods and potentialities, his own dangers, audacities, escapes, failures and triumphs. He could write his own innermost biography from Shakespeare.' His own, yes; but not Shakespeare's." [18]

14. In *Shakespeare Survey 3*, p. 9.
15. *Ibid.*
16. In Harley Granville-Barker and G. B. Harrison, *A Companion to Shakespeare Studies*, p. 8.
17. *Ibid.*
18. *Ibid.*

"His own, yes; but not Shakespeare's." Unless the blow is simply lethal, nothing could be more provocative. Here is the final challenge to all biographers and psychologists of personality; for, if Shakespeare is not being set entirely apart by Mackail from the rest of the species, in complete idolatry, this mocking echo is a denial of the possibility of knowing other minds at all, or at least of knowing them through their imaginative productions. At the same time if it does imply that Shakespeare is a species all to himself, a being *sui generis* as St. Thomas Aquinas makes each of the angels, then a great part of the scholarly labor relating him to his contemporaries and showing the derivation of his dramatic works from earlier literary sources has likewise been sheer vanity and waste. Taken as given, the sentence is the *ne plus ultra* of all investigation and debate. As such, it must be allowed to stand, grimly reminding us of the mere relativity and profound lonely subjectivity of everything we call knowledge.

2

In the meantime, while the Shakespearean scholars have battled with their stubborn problems, and, no less vigorously, with one another, the psychologists, off in another part of the field and largely unaware of the turmoil around Shakespeare, have been developing theories, attitudes, and even special technical devices for clinical use, which have throughout assumed that knowledge of other minds, or at least of other personalities, was entirely possible, though doubtless exceedingly difficult. In the course of this development, as previously remarked, literary and quasi-literary materials have gradually come to occupy a focal area in the thought of clinicians and personality theorists. Indeed, there is reason to prophesy that literary criticism and the psychology of personality will eventually coalesce.[19] In my opinion, the union would be a fruitful one. Regardless of that, however, it is certainly a necessary part of the present discussion, as prelude to the analytical work on Shakespeare's plays which is to follow, to consider some aspects of recent psychological theory and practice. The relevance of these aspects should be apparent from their nature.

19. One piece of evidence is that the Modern Language Association has given rise to a Conference on Literature and Psychology, which publishes a newsletter and is otherwise active.

For fifty years the most important influence in the area of personality study has been Sigmund Freud. The chief reservoir of his ideas is *The Interpretation of Dreams,* which, in the original German under the title *Die Traumdeutung,* appeared in 1900. From this source have flowed many commentaries on literature, among them two significant essays by Freud himself—"Der Dichter und das Phantasieren," and "Der Wahn und die Träume in W. Jensens 'Gradiva.'" [20] Largely from his reflections on the dream, which he called "the royal road to the Unconscious," [21] Freud developed his elaborate personality theory, in which, to put the matter very simply, the human individual is seen as an unstable balance of forces, designated, topographically, the Id, the Ego, and the Superego. The dream is a representation of this complex interaction, though, for practical purposes of interpretation and in the original formulation, it is regarded more simply as the fulfillment of a wish. It is indeed by grasping this guiding thread of wish-fulfillment that Freud manages to work his way through the labyrinthine complexity of the dream; but, emphatically, he considers the structure of the labyrinth, too. To speak less metaphorically, Freud does not rest content with the enunciation of the basic original formula: he modifies it by saying that the dream is an *attempted* wish-fulfillment, and that the materials of experience out of which it is constructed and the wish which energizes and shapes it are combined and presented in such a way that often its origins and its meaning are hidden from the dreamer, so that finally one must admit that the dream is a *disguised* attempt to fulfill a wish.

Freud regards the common daydream and the stories produced by writers from the same point of view. He is more confident of his principles, however, when dealing with the naïve varieties of imaginative literature. When he approaches the great works of art he begins to waver, because he appreciates the self-consciousness and deliberate use of source materials involved in their creation.

20. These essays may be found in Freud, *Gesammelte Schriften,* Vols. 10 and 9, respectively. There is a translation of the former, as "The Relation of the Poet to Day-Dreaming," in *Collected Papers,* Vol. 4.

21. In his lectures on "The Origin and Development of Psychoanalysis," which may be found in J. S. Van Teslaar, *An Outline of Psychoanalysis,* Freud says (p. 46): "Interpretation of dreams is in fact the *via regia* to the interpretation of the unconscious, the surest ground of psychoanalysis."

Yet, for all this wavering, it is clear that a novel or drama is for him fundamentally the same as a dream. It therefore logically follows that such productions can be subjected to a similar analysis. But here a problem arises. It stems from one of the most original and valuable features of the Freudian method—his requirement, namely, that the dreamer should provide free associations in connection with the items of the dream. Out of the information thus emerging, which is emotionally bound together rather than merely random, the specific personal meaning of the details of the dream and their combined purport may be determined (by a synthesis of the kind an archaeologist might perform on the fragments of an ancient ruin which he wished to reconstruct), and the interpreter may pass beyond shrewd guessing to something plausibly like knowledge. Taken strictly, the rule precludes the interpreting of a dream or story when the individual responsible for it is not available for questioning, which is usually the case with famous authors. It is for this reason that Freud once declined to interpret a dream related by Descartes.[22] But he was not consistent. He found that there were many dreams so much alike from person to person that they could be roughly interpreted without asking for the dreamer's comment; and even in *The Interpretation of Dreams* he already ventures on bold interpretive remarks on the works of Sophocles and Shakespeare. His handling of Jensen's novel *Gradiva* is thoroughly surprising: instead of taking the whole as equivalent to a dream, as the theory dictates, he busies himself with interpreting the dreams of the fictional hero, as if he were a real person with a complicated mental structure of his own and as if the rest of the material in the novel were his free associations. The same tendency is seen in his treatment of the Hamlet problem. Freud in these instances is apparently falling victim to the illusion of reality which the author usually desires to impose on his reader. If we seek to explain this behavior (disregarding Freud's own frankly confessed desire to find some illustrative material in support of his theories outside of the psychoanalytic consulting room), we must take account of the necessities of the Freudian method: if free associations cannot be found in one place, they must be found in another. Also,

22. "Brief an Maxim Leroy über einen Traum des Cartesius," in *Gesammelte Schriften,* Vol. 12.

it was against Freud's usual practice to regard a dream's total structure as significant; he preferred to break it up into parts and to examine each of these parts in isolation. Not the drama of the manifest dream, but the latent dream, interested him—the underlying memories and wishes which got expressed, often distortedly, in the manifest dream. Both the reliance on the dreamer's free associations, then, and the atomistic approach which he favored combined to prevent him from considering the public dream of the literary artist as a revealingly meaningful whole.

Difficulties inherent in Freud's method and confusions in its application must not be allowed to obscure his influential central ideas. One among these is that the dream, regardless of how chaotic it may look or how remote from the dreamer's daily concerns, really has meaning in terms of the dreamer's wishes and total personality structure, that is, that it expresses those wishes and that structure. The insight that dreams may express wishes is a very ancient one, asserted and illustrated in the writings of Plato, Artemidorus, Tertullian, Gregory of Nyssa, and others,[23] though it remained for Freud to bring virtually all dreams under the wish-fulfillment category. But the idea of the dream as a representation of the entire personality structure is far more evident in Freud than in his predecessors. Even in him the idea appears more as a suggestion than as a thoroughly worked-out principle. It has been more deeply explored by his divergent followers, Jung and Stekel, who were more inclined than he to dwell on the manifest dream and treat it as a whole.[24]

Another central idea is projection. In its narrower sense it is applied to those cases where a person perceives his wishes or feelings as emanating from someone else. For example, the paranoid individual, in the delusional belief that others hate and persecute him, discovers his own hostility reflected back to himself. In a mild form such projection occurs generally. Projection in a wider sense applies to any endowment of objects with qualities belonging to oneself. Now, the elements of a dream are the bearers of the wishes and

23. For a brief summary, see my paper on "The History of Dream Theory."
24. All psychoanalysts interpret symbolically, but Jung and Stekel especially, in their different ways, envisioned the dream as a dramatic whole and concerned themselves much less with the network of associations which the dreamer is capable of producing than did Freud.

feelings of the dreamer, and their interaction may accordingly be regarded as corresponding to the dynamic interaction of the emotional tendencies in the individual. Thus considered, the dream is the duplicate by projection of the personality structure, or some part of it. It is in this sense (which is near to that of projective geometry) that the clinician speaks of a child projecting his conflicts into a drawing or story or doll play or dramatic play with other children; or of an adult projecting his emotional patterns into a T.A.T. story, or, more abstractly, into his reactions to a Rorschach ink blot.

This important principle of projection, with its implication of a direct correspondence or isomorphism between the projected material and the projecting personality, is usually employed with some vagueness of meaning. Vagueness in this case has two merits: it wards off too positive conclusions about the personality under examination; and, secondly, it encourages the investigator to continue dealing in complexity and dynamic wholeness, instead of sinking faintheartedly to a preoccupation with measurable trivialities, mere spots and specks of numbers, and thus surrendering before the immensely complex microcosm of individual human nature. I say this without irony. Ultimately, however, the concept will have to be examined much more critically than it has been during the past few years during which projective tests or techniques have proliferated so rapidly. In fact, I shall try in the present study to use it with some rigor and in a fairly definite sense, perilous though that may be.

The truth of the matter is that when we attempt to close in on the central issues of personality our subtlest concepts blunder unaccountably, our special devices bend and collapse absurdly in our hands. Perhaps any final success is forever beyond us; and yet it is possible that a revision of strategy might help our enterprise. Much of the concern of modern psychologists, especially in the clinic, is with areas of human behavior and with questions of method which have for a long time interested literary critics. Without thinking of themselves in any such light, psychologists are actually engaging in a kind of literary criticism when they study dreams and phantasies; and it is only by a very artificial separation of formal literature from the stories they hear daily from individuals who make no pretense of literary ambition that they can remain insensible to the similarity between their task and that of the literary critic. The resulting insulation is unfortunate for both, and especially for the psychologist. If one addresses oneself to understanding the dream of a client in a private consultation and succeeds in arriving at an interpretation which appeals to both, one is tempted to pause there, satisfied, untroubled by the critical reconsiderations which could not be avoided if the material were public property, as the works of a great dramatist are, and exposed to the interested attention of others whose biases are different and whose learning, sensitivity, and intellectual power are more than equal to one's own. It is a scientific duty, and a precious opportunity as well, to bring psychological questions and procedures fully into the open by applying them to such public matters as novels, poems, and dramas. Under favorable conditions the knowledge of particular individuals and of personality in general should be enhanced.

It is in an adventurous spirit of discovery, and not of dogma or controversy, that the present study of Shakespeare has been undertaken. It would be ideal, if it were possible, to lead the reader along the same zigzag track followed by the investigator. False starts and abandoned hunches might then be seen as the points at which error was avoided, or, unhappily, committed; and the exact reasons for certain conclusions might be adequately perceived. But that is more than the reader could bear or the writer accomplish. In fact, it seems advisable to begin by discussing some questions and ideas which arose in part during and after, rather than before, the analysis of the plays which will be reported in later chapters. The discussion will deal partly with general theory of personality, partly with special problems of method; and there will be some anticipation of matters dealt with more painstakingly later on.

CHAPTER 2. ON SOME QUESTIONS OF THEORY AND METHOD

1

PERSONALITY WILL BE taken in the present context to mean a personal world. We may think of it as being narrow or wide, as containing few or many parts, as having any degree of complexity; but in every case it obviously must involve something—whether a pervasive quality or some peculiar element or a special organization—by which it merits the appellation "personal." It is just this aspect of the matter which it is most difficult to conceptualize.

In the main, the traditional theory of personality has been dualistic. Two components are separated: the soul and the body. The soul, as defined by Descartes, is thinking nonextended substance; the body is nonthinking extended substance. Similar definitions can be found much farther back; for instance in the Socratic discourses of Plato, especially the *Phaedo*. Several consequences flow from this particular analysis. The soul is simple, that is, it cannot be analyzed any more than it can be disintegrated; it is, except for a miraculous intervention by God, immortal, and it is accessible to understanding by intuition alone. Also, since it is simple and nonextended, it cannot be sensorially perceived any more than it can be analyzed. The Humian dismissal of the soul (supposing that this is what he meant by the "self") on the ground that it could not be observed—i.e., was not a part of sensory experience—is therefore irrelevant. Yet the soul is not to be understood as a logical construct. It is not a form of words but a form of being; and indeed in the usual dualistic view it is indispensable as a cause of certain phenomena, such as human logical activity, ethical striving, purposive acts, and so on. The body, on the other hand, is eminently divisible; it is a complexity both for the senses and in abstraction. Furthermore, while the body is an object for the soul, the soul is not an object for the body, and scarcely or not at all for itself. But only that which is an object can possibly be analyzed.

When, therefore, the study of personality was undertaken by scientists, it very soon and nearly always resolved into an analysis of the body. The soul was forgotten, and the relation of the body to the soul was forgotten, especially since it was recognized from the outset that here was a mystery. The analysis of personality became largely anatomy of the body; and it has often been true that text-books of psychology, where one would naturally look for a discussion of personality, have been nearly indistinguishable from text-books of human or animal anatomy and physiology. The brain and the rest of the nervous system took over the sensory and rational faculties of the soul; the glands and muscles did service for desire and the will, and to some extent shared with the nervous system the honor of the cognitive functions.

Today in psychological circles we notice some retreat from this radical physicalism, but the retreat largely brings us back to some-thing like the Humian phenomenalism; and this kind of outlook is no more likely to discover the soul than the other. In short, any kind of analysis, whether it makes use of scalpels or of discriminations without instruments, can only discover a field of operations where there is something extended and compound; but the soul, by defini-tion, is neither. It could enter into an analysis, of course, as one of the analytic units; but if the analysis proceeds by continual appeal to sensation, this cannot happen either, because the soul is not ca-pable of being sensed, just as it is not capable of being divided. It might be inferred by an intuitive leap from sensory data and it may be treated as a cause of sensory data, but it cannot be constructed out of such data nor take its place alongside them. It must remain a mystery, therefore, and its relations with everything else must remain a mystery. But science does not deal in mysteries. The soul is necessarily dropped from the discussion. This leaves us, as pre-viously noted, with the body—which can be analyzed in various ways.

The simplest approach to analysis of the body is the frank ana-tomical, with scalpel and measuring instruments in hand. In this case, one regularly chooses some other body than one's own, and usually a corpse. This kind of analysis has been cultivated for a long time now, and the results are the standard reference material of medical libraries. Comparison of modern anatomical sketches with those of the Middle Ages proves immediately that the advance along this path has been very great.

Not until comparatively recent times, however, did anatomy become physiological. This required the study of living bodies, and it remained for such 19th-century pioneers as Bell, Magendie, and Bernard to get very far with that. Here again much progress has been made. Physiological analysis is so refined, it deals with such elusive entities, it is so evidently close to life itself, that it is not surprising that the shrinking domain of the mental philosophers of the old days was invaded very broadly and deeply by the physiologists. Thus Pavlov, at the beginning of the present century, discovered that the methods which he had been applying successfully to the study of digestion could be transferred with little apparent change to the study of the higher mental processes, or, as he preferred to call them, the higher cerebral processes. His attack bid fair to displace the old mental philosophy entirely. Indeed, when American psychologists, much attracted to his investigations, tried to join forces with him, he warned them in vigorous terms that he was not a psychologist, that he had nothing to do with the psyche—a statement which must have surprised some of the psychologists, only dimly aware of the history of their professional name.[1] In spite of that, the Pavlovian method and his concepts, along with various kindred ideas, made steady headway in this country. Such native students of physiology as Cannon took all emotion as their province. Moreover, Watson, the behaviorist, denounced as scientifically uninteresting or unreal those more ghostly topics which did not capitulate at once to the new approach. Everywhere along the line the representatives of the older psychology, who used introspection as a chief device, beat a retreat.

Nowadays, when psychoanalysis and its derivatives have made some impression on psychological thinking, the characteristic reaction of American psychologists, especially the laboratory workers, has been to attempt to translate some of the less reputable mentalistic concepts of Freud and his followers into the language

1. I. P. Pavlov, Letter addressed to H. S. Langfeld in 1929. Facsimile and comment in the *Amer. Psychol. 2* (1947), 210 f. Pavlov says, "I am no psychologist," doubts that he can interest American psychologists, and states that his work is "pure physiology . . . not psychology."

of Pavlov—the language of reflexes—unless, as in many instances, the whole psychoanalytic literature has been rejected outright as chimerical.

A somewhat less characteristic reaction, perhaps now on the increase, has been to drop the anatomy and physiology of the body and take up again, with certain changes, the method of introspection. This has occurred chiefly among the clinical psychologists or theorists with an interest in the whole human being. The clinical psychologist, because of the nature of his work and sometimes in spite of his theories, is almost compelled to accept the statements of his patients about various outwardly unobservable matters as corresponding to realities, though these realities may not be accessible to the scalpel and not readily importable into the conditioning laboratory. In this way, some psychologists have been reintroduced to the fascinating realms of imagination, of feeling and emotion, and of value thinking. Only, now, these realms are studied as it were from the outside. The clinicians do not primarily report on their own experiences, as the introspectionists of the past did; rather, they report on the introspections of their patients, endeavoring to record as fully and accurately as possible, and to stimulate a maximum production and a maximum communication of mental content. The world of experience thus opened up is overwhelmingly rich; but it is doubtful whether it, any more than the corpse or the living body, can yield any evidence of the presence of a soul. It is not likely that the masters of this new kind of analysis will contradict the old-style analysis of Hume in any such fundamental respect.

The study of Shakespeare's plays which will be attempted here belongs in this new tradition of psychology. The plays will be looked upon as documents revealing the personality of the author, as material of the same kind though of lower artistic order is regarded in the clinic; and the assumption of this attitude will be taken as an opportunity for finding out something about Shakespeare, though no less important is the desire to explore the limits of usefulness of a method. But it is important, in stating this aim, to have it clearly understood that the method, as indicated, is inherently incapable of reaching into the innermost sanctuary of the soul. The method can have absolutely nothing to do with the soul, whether one wishes to believe in the soul or not. From the point of view of soul theory, it can only deal with the soul's environment, the elements and events which surround or emanate from it. In our skeptical age, when everything supernatural is virtually passé, it may seem needless or even indecent to mention the subject; but I do so to avoid any misunderstanding.

Another question which is far beyond the scope of the method is the fascinating but difficult one of how Shakespeare came to be the great artist that he was. Psychological theories about the genesis of the artistic impulse and the passion for technique which marks the artist are, generally speaking, in a very backward state. It has frequently been argued, however, that one condition of artistic achievement is some gross personality defect. If this were indeed true, it would manifestly be dangerous to draw inferences regarding human personality in general from a study of the personality of one of the greatest of all artists. But is it true?

Plato long ago decided that dramatic writers were as inferior as philosophers were superior. In his ideal republic they would not have been allowed to exist. There were several ways, to his mind, in which their activity told against the perfect political order. For one, they were forever telling stories about the gods which tended to undermine religion and corrupt morals. For another, they introduced an intolerable amount of variety and pleasure into the lives of people. And for a third, they required actors; and this meant that some people had to give up their normal role in the state to adopt temporarily some other and probably less decent one. Plato considered that playing a part—pretending to be a woman when one was a man, or assuming the role of a criminal, or the like—could only disturb the unity of the personality and bring about its corruption. It was dangerous to falsify one's nature, even in play; dangerous to adopt for a while the values and the behavior of another person. The dramatist himself, accordingly, by projecting his thoughts into a variety of persons, often immoral or defective, was demonstrating the unhealthiness of his own nature.

Many times in the history of the Western world has the Platonic attitude been aroused. Poets and actors have frequently been under a cloud. Often, though the theater was put up with and it was allowable to write fiction, it has been thought disreputable for women

to engage in theatrical or literary activities. More than once the
theater has fallen under ban. During Shakespeare's lifetime, and
afterward, the Puritans of England fought against the stage as
against the Devil. Milton had to write an eloquent appeal against
the censoring of books; and censorship of novel and drama, in the
interests of morality, is an abiding fact in one great ecclesiastical
organization down to the present, as well as a sporadic feature of
national politics.

From the standpoint of state and church, then, the imaginative
writer appears as diseased in mind or prone to be. Writers themselves have concurred in this view. Dryden popularized a phrase
about genius being near-allied to madness, and W. H. Auden has
recently requested (perhaps for the sake of incubating artists) that
every child should have as much neurosis as he can bear.[2] Scientists
and psychiatrists have agreed. It is a widely held current theory
that the writer is more than ordinarily burdened with a sense of
guilt over an unresolved Oedipus complex; but in the recent articles
and books of Edmund Bergler this theory is discarded as crediting
the writer with entirely too much maturity. According to Bergler,
the writer is a contemptible form of masochist who is attempting
by his fictional output to deny a diseased and pitifully infantile attachment to his mother.[3]

Yet, in spite of the hypnotic eloquence with which the case is
often presented, the theory of the special degeneracy of the writer
has little or no evidential support. It probably belongs with the
mythology of the moral and physical inferiority of the whole class
of the intellectually gifted, which Terman has so effectively dis-
proved.[4] At any rate, it is not a theory to be trusted blindly; and
there is no good reason for taking Shakespeare as an outstand-

2. Auden and MacNeice, *Letters from Iceland,* p. 206.

> "I hate the modern trick, to tell the truth,
>   Of straightening out the kinks in the young mind,
> Our passion for the tender plant of youth,
>   Our hatred for all weeds of any kind.
>   Slogans are bad: the best that I can find
> Is this: 'Let each child have that's in our care
> As much neurosis as the child can bear.'"

3. *The Writer and Psychoanalysis.*
4. The writings of Lewis Terman and his associates are widely known. His

ing specimen of abnormality. What has sometimes been charged against a writer as an abnormality (and there are traits in Shakespeare which have a dark look) turns out on further inspection to be nothing more than the conspicuousness of what is common in the population. As to what makes the difference between persons in their ability to tell a dramatic story, to give it verve and artistic finish, one guess is perhaps as good as another. It is mine that we have to do here with a preferred mode of social approach rather than with the basic structure and dynamics of personality. It is not so much that the stories told by a great author are different from those told by others; but just that they are better told, so that it is easier to follow them and be absorbed in them. The stories may be different, too; but it is not this which gives them their artistic distinction.

.2

If we look at the plays of Shakespeare as though they were magnified views of the interior of his personality, just as we might look microscopically into the interior of a water drop or an earthworm, we see that this interior swarms with many different components —or, to speak more plainly, dramatic characters. Some eight hundred are individually named, and there are various unnamed supernumeraries. If these characters appeared as spheres, like oil globules in living tissue, it would be evident that the smaller spheres were much more numerous than the larger ones. The proportions would be found to vary somewhat from view to view (i.e., from play to play), but the relationship in general would be that exhibited in certain tables and graphs of the next chapter. In sum, the components, when ranked according to their volume (i.e., the space they occupy in the plays, as determined by a count of their speech lines), tend to fall into a geometrical progression such as one might find for the frequency of various levels of energy in a physical system.

Now, if the personality of our author were an unchanging system totally and accurately reflected in the plays, we should find

---

The Gifted Child Grows Up is a convenient recent summary of an important phase of his work.

the same form of distribution maintained from one play to the next. Very roughly speaking, this is so; though, as will be explained later, the mood of the play seems to have something to do with certain variations. But in another respect there are very important differences from play to play: the various positions in the distribution are not occupied uniformly by characters having the same or similar properties. The top character is not a stereotyped hero, the second a stereotyped villain, the third a stereotyped heroine, and so on down the line. For instance, to get down to particulars, the top character is sometimes male, sometimes female; and there are other qualitative differences besides. It will be argued subsequently that the qualities are not so diverse as to require us to speak of as many different kinds of top characters as there are plays; we can to some extent classify them and so bring them under a smaller number of categories. Nevertheless, the top-ranking Shakespearean characters are quite diverse as compared with those of some other authors. To illustrate by referring to a case where it is possible to be precise, the top-ranking characters in all four of the novels of Charlotte Brontë are so very much alike that we may regard them as virtually one character.[5] To be able to make the same statement about the top-ranking characters of Shakespeare we should have to move to a very high level of abstraction —so high, indeed, that most of their individual qualities would disappear and we should succeed in fusing them together into one chiefly by virtue of the fact that they are all human. It must not be concluded, however, that there is no way of relating these characters meaningfully to the author himself: they are, for example, predominantly of his sex, and they tend to grow older along with him.

The immense variety of components is one of the significant features of Shakespeare's personality. Such internal differentiation argues for a corresponding ability to distinguish finely between one person and another in the world around him. This in itself would lead one to think that his relations with others would have been marked by subtle and appropriate nuances of response, and that on the whole the relations because of that, even though

5. See my article on the Brontës.

there is evidence of a fairly high degree of suspiciousness in him, would have been ingratiating, as indeed the tenor of contemporary remarks about his sweetness and gentleness tends to confirm. Sensitiveness to the differences between people is bound to have some good effect on social relations. As a commentary on this reasoning may be mentioned a recent study of the drawings of the human face produced by patients from a psychological clinic.[6] The patients comprised two groups—those who succeeded and those who failed in establishing warm emotional relations with their therapists. Although there was no difference between the groups in respect to intelligence, they significantly differed in their drawing, the more sociable (and therapeutically more benefited) producing faces of a finer human quality.

The various characters in the plays represent as many behavioral possibilities in the author. He fills up their forms and acts through them with varying degrees of energy, or, to speak more exactly, for varying periods of time. The quantitative differences indicate perhaps the extent to which the various parts can be sustained by him, but they do not necessarily tell us which of these parts, or whether any of them, will be acted out on the stage of life. What governs the emergence of these potentialities into actuality? There are several possibilities. One is that the governor is the soul, not appearing among the dramatic characters at all but pulling the strings and even creating the puppets themselves *ex nihilo*. Another is that some specific one from among the dramatic characters corresponds to the governing force; and something like this is what is meant when the author is identified by the reader with one of the characters. A third possibility is that the author is represented by the whole collection in interaction; and that any behavioral outcome will be a kind of compromise between the various potential roles present, just as a vector of forces is developed in a physical system by the interaction of components so that the system as a whole operates in a direction not given in any single component. For example, a crowd of people may gradually move in a certain direction, although the movements of individuals

6. Fiedler and Siegel, "The Free Drawing Test as a Predictor of Non-Improvement in Psychotherapy," *Jour. Clin. Psychol.*, 5 (1949), 386–389.

in the crowd may be varied and to some extent contrary to the crowd's movement. This last possibility is the one which will receive the chief emphasis in the present analysis. It is merely a hypothesis, however, and under the most favorable conditions for testing it might prove invalid. The behavior of any totality under analysis may very well be or come to be under the influence of factors outside the collection; for instance, the movement of a swarm of gnats is not simply a function of the combined individual movements as seen within the boundaries of the swarm, but owes something also to whether a gust of wind strikes it—the wind which cannot be predicted from the constitution of the swarm or the interactional pattern. In short, we must allow for the fact that systems are rarely or never completely closed or completely autonomous.

While adopting as a heuristic principle the proposition that it is the whole collection rather than a single character which reveals the personality's behavior tendencies, we may without inconsistency devote much of our attention to the top character; for it is this character, as a rule, which most broadly interacts with the others. The bulk of the character and the extent of his relations with others are connected facts. The fate of a top-ranking character, therefore, fairly well sums up the tendencies of the whole collection. The character is a lover, let us say. Is he allowed, in interaction with the other characters, to attain his goal of union with the woman of his choice? If so, it should probably be judged that the author suffers no particular inner inhibitions, of a finally effective kind, in that direction, and might very well prove to be an adequate lover. If not, the opposite judgment would be indicated. Or suppose that the top character is a vengeful or grandly violent hero. How does he succeed? It will be argued in a later chapter that Shakespeare, because of the restraint or defeat of such characters in his plays, must himself have held back from the fulfillment of vengeful plans or impulses against his fellow townsmen.

Examples of the general soundness of such an approach can be picked up almost at random from the psychoanalytic literature. Angel Garma, in an article which happens to come to hand at the moment, tells about a man who dreams: "I show my fiancée some fire. She is nervous but I keep calm." [7] In this little drama we note that the action of the dreamer is met by opposition, in the form of his fiancée's nervousness. Without any further information we can see that the dreamer experiences a slight check in his dream and might infer that a comparable inhibition would affect his real day-by-day relations with his fiancée. Garma tells us that the accompanying material indicates that the act of showing fire to the woman represents his sexual desire for her. On this basis, our inference can be made more specific. The same man had another dream in which the relationship in question was treated more openly but still with the same general outcome. He dreamed: "I am lying with my fiancée and I am sexually excited. I want to have intercourse with her, but it is then eight o'clock in the morning and the maid comes in to pull up the blinds. This is annoying to me." [8] Here again there is evidence of sexual inhibition, which in very truth existed, as the analyst tells us. Now, according to our guiding proposition, a full appreciation of the dreamer's personality state would involve exploring the whole set of components and relationships exhibited in the dreams. Yet by fixing attention upon the main character (in this case identified without much doubt with the dreamer's ego) we come to the apparently correct conclusion that he is fated to do things with his fiancée which are not entirely satisfactory; showing her fire, or desiring intercourse with her, is followed by some event—nervousness in the woman, the interference of a maid—which points to the dreamer's lack of power to carry through his intentions. Reasoning in the same way, we should note that Romeo, the principal character in his play, comes to sexual defeat through Juliet's death and his own, and conclude that this represents sexual inhibition in the author. And when the plays are taken all together, and the *Sonnets* and erotic poems, and what little is known of Shakespeare's biography touching upon the question, the conclusion seems plausible. (The comment here on *Romeo and Juliet* is not meant to detract from the beautiful spiritual intensity of the passion between the two lovers; but the consummation and continuance of their love in sexual union are denied

7. "The Traumatic Situation in the Genesis of Dreams," *Internat. Jour. of Psycho-Analysis,* 27 (1946), 135.
8. *Ibid.,* p. 137.

them by death, as all through the play their sexual attraction is ridiculed or violently opposed by other characters.)

If, then, one knows how to pick out the right character, one can gain some insight into the author's central tendencies by noting the desires and fate of just this one. If we could be sure that the top-ranking character was closest to the author's ego, we could say without hesitation that Shakespeare at the time of *Romeo and Juliet* was principally aware of the opposition to his sexual urges, while the chief element of the opposition lay at a lower energetic level than the urges themselves as embodied in Romeo. Thus, the opposing Capulet ranks low. But later on, at the time of *The Tempest,* the impression would be that the accent had shifted. For there, though Prospero is hardly Capulet all over again, it is principally he who puts obstacles in the way of young love, as in the past it was Capulet; and this opponent, or rather regulator, of sexual love, is the top character and presumably the central element now in Shakespeare's personality. Furthermore, when we consider Shakespeare's age and circumstances at the two periods, such interpretations look reasonable. Our illustration serves to bring out the point, however, that exclusive concentration on the main character may result in overlooking the developmental possibilities in the personality. A personality which contains a Capulet component in low degree early in life may contain it in higher degree later on. There is a sort of conservatism even in the greatly varied personality of Shakespeare: things prominent in late plays have often appeared in some lesser degree of prominence before. Some trends, as will be shown, have a long history within the series of plays—suggesting both the persistence of certain basic organizations and their gradual evolution.

The question, so continuously troublesome, of which of the various characters should be singled out as performing that function within the total play which the dreamer's recognized self performs in his dream is really only a phase of a much broader one. Where, in general, do the characters come from? The answer cannot possibly come from a study of the plays alone. We need to know the psychological laws of the processes by which anything like a dramatic character arises in the personal world at all (and our knowledge is certainly scanty); and for the origin of a particular character we need to know its individual history. Even with the help of the author himself we should find it impossible to trace the history of every one.

Yet some general reflections may be useful here. All of us who have paid any heed to our dreams know that some of the dream actors are recognized by us as persons with whom we have associated in everyday life. We recognize them from their appearance, and sometimes from their names. Then there are those interesting borderline cases where the dream actor seems to be a blend of several persons whom we know. So far, so good. These actors originate in real persons in our real external historical environment. They are copies of them, or, as a primitive thinker might say, they are their souls straying loose from their bodies. The actions in which they engage, however, may often be quite different from any we have actually witnessed. This is very difficult to account for, if we want to drive every mental event back to an exact counterpart in our waking commerce with the external world. But there is more and worse. Among the dream actors there are frequently some whom we do not recognize at all, except generically as human or animal or whatnot. These have as much apparent vitality as the others. What can we do with them? We can assume, of course, that our memory has failed us, or that it has made use of persons who were once real enough in our waking experience but not clearly tagged for future reference.

Jung has felt compelled to go farther afield in explaining such dream actors. He supposes that we have access to great stores of racially acquired memories which may on occasion rise above the conscious threshold. The strangers in dreams might therefore originate at a deeper historical level than that occupied by the conscious individual. In particular he stresses the *anima* (in the male) and the *animus* (in the female)—counterbalancing forces which exercise restraint over the dominant conscious self and sometimes overwhelm it. Strictly speaking, the anima (or animus) antedates history; it is a fundamental property of life which makes certain aspects of history possible, such as the worship of Aphrodite and the Mother of God, or the dangerous fascination of witches—who in a modern American movie would appear in the form of a variety of beautiful but evil temptresses. But the anima "is conservative, and clings in a most exasperating fashion to the ways of earlier mankind. Therefore, it likes to appear in historic dress, with a predilection for Greece and Egypt." [9] Perhaps a suitable example from Shakespeare would be Cleopatra, though the saintly Isabella of *Measure for Measure* might also qualify because of the corrupting sexual power which she exerts. Jung's theory on these points is in close harmony with medieval demonology; and, indeed, not only Jung but also Freud has countenanced demonology as a type of theory which genuinely laid hold on psychic facts.[10] For it is an indubitable fact that our consciousness is invaded at times by seductive or threatening figures for which we cannot give a clear historical account. Of course, exactly the same thing can be said of our regular commerce with the world around us. We daily meet people whom we have never seen before, who have no history as far as we are concerned, and who may be decidedly unlike any others whom we have known. Occasionally it happens that the encounter is so disturbing that we want to doubt the reality of the stranger. Everywhere there is some suspicion of the stranger, some tendency to brush him aside or fear him, and now and then a readiness to identify him with the Devil. The phenomenon of the stranger is not confined to the dream. Our greater puzzlement over finding him there than in the world of waking experience may be due to our assuming that in the intimacy of our own minds, when we close our senses in sleep, nothing should occur except what is familiar, since there is no proper way for the unfamiliar to get in. Is not coming upon a stranger in our private living quarters far

9. *The Integration of the Personality*, p. 78.

10. Jung and Freud are not demonologists in the medieval sense; but they admit the value of the demonological theories in revised form. For example, cf. Jung, *op. cit.*, and Freud, "A Neurosis of Demoniacal Possession in the Seventeenth Century," printed in *Collected Papers*, Vol. 4. Freud's viewpoint is expressed in these words (*op. cit.*, pp. 436 f.): "Despite the somatic ideology of the era of 'exact' science, the demonological theory of these dark ages has in the long run justified itself. Cases of demoniacal possession correspond to the neuroses of the present day; in order to understand these latter we have once more had recourse to the conception of psychic forces. What in those days were thought to be evil spirits to us are base and evil wishes, the derivatives of impulses which have been rejected and repressed. In one respect only do we not subscribe to the explanation of these phenomena current in mediaeval times; we have abandoned the projection of them into the outer world, attributing their origin instead to the inner life of the patient in whom they manifest themselves."

more shocking than coming upon one in the street? But to accept
the same kind of freedom for our minds as for the external world
means that we must admit that persons can appear there without
benefit of a previous introduction through the senses. That again
is close to demonology.

We might leave it at that, if it were not for a characteristic result
of Freud's investigations. He found, and it is comparatively easy
to repeat his finding, that if one only patiently attends to his
thoughts many a strange unattached drifter through the dream
world becomes, as a matter of fact, identifiable. If this is true in
one case, it might be true in all. We do not know that it is true,
because even after lengthy examination many dreams retain a
residue of the nonhistorical. But those cases which finally yield up
their identity to our persistent questioning throw some doubt on
the genuine nonhistoricity of those which do not. Books, of course,
are one source of some of the obscurer items. It is this line of
thought which, in spite of all that may be suggestive in Jung, persuades most students of Shakespeare that behind his characters
there are historical persons, contemporaries of his, such as a Mary
Fitton to account for Cleopatra, or a Ben Jonson to account for
Ajax. There is more disagreement about the actual details than
about the principle.

The fact remains, whatever principle we favor for explaining the
characters, that within the plays themselves they perform without
any embarrassment about the mystery of their origin. In Shakespeare for the most part the characters are human, and their relations with one another do not ordinarily transcend the humanly
possible. Poetic fiction, let it be noted, does not have to stay within
such limits. Spenser, Marlowe, and Milton, though near to Shakespeare in time, were very far removed from him in their poetic output. Spenser in *The Faerie Queene* introduces us to a number of
persons who might have had some trouble in passing for Elizabeth's
loyal subjects; Marlowe brings the Devil on the stage; and Milton
gives us both the Devil and God along with a host of angels and
demons in *Paradise Lost*. We must regard it as a part of Shakespeare's distinction from others that his characters are usually
human. He is not any the less overwhelming for that. In fact, his
closeness to human nature, his unshrinking expression of human

emotions and motives, gives us as much to tremble at as if he had called up the legions of Hell. He teaches us that no devil or natural force can compare with the innocent-looking human being for violence, that no god has lovelier moments. He forms tempests and clear peaceful sunlit or moonlit weather out of a welter of human voices; he hurls us about or charms and calms us by meteorological forces composed entirely of human beings.

If one deduces from the plays of Shakespeare that the human personality is essentially a society of human persons, one is perhaps going too far beyond the limits of his data. The proposition holds for Shakespeare but not necessarily for others. There may be human personalities in which the components are on a higher or lower level of existence: people who are menageries of animals, others who are wide celestial spaces filled with angels. This is not mere random talk. Children sometimes give the impression of being animal menageries; and some identification with animals is common among civilized men, at least playfully, while among primitives the identification may assume the dignity of a religious ritual. On the other side, there are the saints; or, to come a little lower, there is such a personality as that of Rilke, full of angels and spirits and holy persons.

I repeat, it is a part of the uniqueness of Shakespeare that he is so thoroughly, and variously, permeated by humanity.

3

At this point in the discussion it will be useful to explore more fully the notion that personality is basically a social system.

We may begin by considering the process of introjection, as it is called by the psychoanalysts. By this process the perceived objects of the external world are taken into the memory system and continue acting within the personal world when they have vanished from the external. It is not supposed that they have to continue to act in their originally perceived form. A deconcretization ordinarily takes place, so that the voice of the forbidding parent, for instance, becomes merely a silent principle of conduct, the sight of the smiling, approving face becomes a glow of confidence, and so on. But on certain occasions, as in dreaming or in hallucinatory states, the original object may be pretty solidly restored as a perceptual thing. This return of the introjected object in perceptual form may even enable it to be put back into the external world as a part of the total environment. Such reintroduction of mental contents into the environment is covered by the psychoanalytic term projection. By introjection and projection the individual's relations with the external world are accumulated, maintained, and variously transformed, as parts of his own personality.

Theorists like Melanie Klein and W. Ronald D. Fairbairn, who are especially interested in the development of the ego, have devoted themselves to examining these processes systematically. Klein emphasizes the maternal breast as the first environmental object to be introjected, and she supposes that the quality of this object as introjected—whether it is primarily satisfying or frustrating—has much to do with the future development of the individual. At a later stage the baby is capable of taking in larger segments of his environment, and then whole persons can be introjected with their various qualities. One of the current points of debate in the working out of introjection theory is the instinct question. Fairbairn wishes to dispense with the Freudian instincts, Klein thinks it necessary to retain them. Fairbairn's guiding principle is that "both structure divorced from energy and energy divorced from structure are meaningless concepts." [11] He appeals to the recent developments in theoretical physics. No longer, he says, is the universe thought of as "a conglomeration of inert, immutable and indivisible particles to which motion was imparted by a fixed quantity of energy separate from these particles." [12] And he argues that there is no justification for continuing to think in such terms in psychology. His introjected objects, therefore, are not pushed about by the instinctual energies; they are endowed with their own energy from the start, and just as in the social world there is an interaction of energetic structures, so in the internal personal world. There is no need here to enter into the details of Fairbairn's system of thought, beyond noting that, like Klein, he supposes that the external object can be split into a good and a bad object by the per-

11. "Object-Relationships and Dynamic Structure," *Internat. Jour. of Psycho-Analysis*, 27 (1946), 36.
12. *Ibid.*

ceiver—which is the corollary of the concept of ambivalence. Both Fairbairn and Klein stress the importance of the introjection process in the formation of personality, and Fairbairn lays particular emphasis on the original energetic nature of the introjected objects, from which it follows that they must be capable of interaction.

Putting aside the question of the baby's untutored, primitive reactions to his first object, the breast, it must be apparent that many of the interactions occurring among introjected objects within the personality system should correspond to common social interactions. Let us examine briefly some typical psychoanalytic dynamic terms. There is, as an important example of intrapsychic process, *repression*. This process, by which elements within the personality which are repugnant to other elements are put out of conscious circulation, has its parallel in various techniques of restraint exercised by society over certain of its members: imprisonment, exile, curtailment of free movement, censorship. In fact, Freud has very often compared the psychic processes, such as repression, to various kinds of interactions between persons in society. Thus, not only is repression spoken of by him as censorship, but he likes at times to speak of a censor guarding the entrance to consciousness. Or take the process of *identification*. Here the parallel is with such social processes as sexual union, cannibalism, and perhaps the merging of one business corporation into another. The *complex* is like a closely knit group of friends, a clique, a band of gangsters. The *superego* consists in large part of the introjected parents in their role as authorities, judges, punishers. It is especially in connection with this psychic dynamism that the concept of introjection was first developed.

Not only do parallels exist between the processes going on in society and those going on within the individual, but the two sets of processes interact. Consider, as a commonplace example, the case where a girl is attracted sexually to a boy but resists his advances because the image of the mother (not the original mother herself) intervenes. Or consider the case where a stranger is mistaken for a friend—the internal object here being projected and fused with the external. Klein avers that "from the beginning object relations are moulded by an interaction between introjection and projection, between internal and external objects and situations." [13]

Ideally, then, besides a sociology of external society, we should have one of the internal society which constitutes personality, and a third applying to that interaction between individual and society which involves both internal and external objects.

Important as the psychoanalytic contributions to the theory of personality are, there appears to be one signal omission: attention to the hierarchical arrangement of the personality components. The most adequate treatment of this theme, to my mind, is found in the personality theory sketched by McDougall. In the selection to be quoted here he uses the term *monad*, taken from Leibniz, instead of his more customary term *sentiment*, to stand for the basic unit of personality. The term, incidentally, with its implication of organized and autonomous life, is especially appropriate in the context. McDougall writes:

> Without stopping to ask whether a monad can be perceived as a material object, whether it is capable of phenomenal representation as some part or feature of the bodily organism as it appears to us in sense-perception, or to the anatomist or histologist, let us assume that a monad is an ultimate reality, a being that exists and is active in its own right; that the normal human personality is essentially a society of such monads, living in harmonious co-operation in virtue of the integration of them all in one system. Let us also assume that a monad is, potentially at least, a thinking striving self, endowed with the faculty or power of true memory; and that different monads are of very different degrees of development: some, being relatively undeveloped, exercise the powers common to all in a relatively simple and rudimentary fashion; others, being highly developed, exercise the same powers in a developed fashion.
>
> We regard, then, the normal human personality as an integrated system of such monads; and the integrated system takes the form of a converging hierarchy. At the head of the hierarchy is the supreme monad which each of us calls "myself." And the integration of the system consists in the subordination of the monads of each level of the hierarchy to those of the next higher level. Complete integration according to this plan gives to the supreme monad control over the whole system. A close

13. "Notes on Some Schizoid Mechanisms," *Internat. Jour. of Psycho-Analysis,* 27 (1946), 99.

analogy obtains between such a system as I am sketching and such a social hierarchy as the Roman Church or an army in the field.[14]

As mentioned, the term monad used here is virtually equivalent to the term sentiment. The latter term, in McDougall's usage, stands for an energic element of the personality derived from the emotional and conational commerce of the individual with his environment. In his view objects of experience are invested with emotional qualities by their relation to the subject, and then are stored up as permanent, energetic, and directive parts of the personality. There is thus some kinship between his doctrine of the sentiments, which he traces to Shand, and the more recent development of introjection theory by the psychoanalysts. The chief reason for quoting the above passage was not to note this similarity, however, but to bring out McDougall's views on the interactional organization of the personality.

McDougall's comparison of the personality with highly organized social structures is illuminating, but it misses the point that some monads (sentiments), as well as being at the center of interconnecting lines of communication and control, bulk larger than others. A comparison which includes relative bulk along with communication and power level is that with cities in an integrated nation, where, as Zipf has demonstrated, the population sizes fall into a harmonic series.[15]

McDougall argues that there must be a dominant member if unity is to exist within the personality system.

> If a unitary personality is to be achieved, the various sentiments must be brought into one system within which their impulses shall be harmonised, each duly subordinated to the higher integration of which it becomes a member. This higher integration is what we call "character"; it is achieved by the development of a master sentiment which dominates the whole system of sentiments, subordinating their impulses to its own. . . . The only sentiment which can adequately fulfill the function of dominating and harmonising all other sentiments is the sentiment of self-regard, taking the form of a self-conscious devotion to an ideal of character.[16]

14. McDougall, *Outline of Abnormal Psychology*, p. 546.
15. Cf. *Human Behavior and the Principle of Least Effort*.
16. Pp. 525 f.

It is not his contention that integration absolutely requires the sentiment of self-regard, but that it is the most adequate means to permanent and complete integration. McDougall appears to be recommending a kind of ethical egotism, or, to use psychoanalytic terminology, narcissism. A different kind of integration would be that achieved by love for another person, which, in a way, is where we all start; or that achieved by devotion to God—a devotion found in one form in Spinoza, who saw the necessity of a permanent, unchanging object of attachment for the maintenance of true happiness, and found in another form in Augustine. The psychoanalytic terminology is not very apt in this latter instance, but, according to it, here we should be witnessing integration around a superego.

McDougall's theory was developed with the problem of multiple personality especially in mind. Partly it was a reaction to the difficulties which he detected in the traditional dualistic theory. The facts of multiple personality, he states, "negative the old simple dualistic view that regarded the personality as a conjunction of the physical structure with a single indivisible psychic being or soul; for all the arguments which led to the postulation of the unitary indivisible soul as the ground of the unity of the conscious life and of its expressions in the body require that, in cases of clearly marked multiple personalities, we should postulate a corresponding number of souls." [17] There is some weakness in this argument. In the first place, it is not quite certain that the cases reported of multiple personality demonstrate the absolute separation and independence of the various "selves" which McDougall supposes. Take the classical Beauchamp case reported by Morton Prince. I contended in a journal article [18] a few years ago that in spite of the apparent serious disorder in the personality of Miss Beauchamp there was one remarkable piece of consistency—namely, that, no matter in which of her four states she was, her life continued to revolve persistently around Morton Prince, her physician, for many years—and that the personality states which seemed so different and independent to Prince (they were less so to her friends) could

17. *Ibid.*, p. 522.
18. "A Note on the Dissociation of a Personality," *Character and Personality, 10* (1941), 35–41.

be understood well enough as manifestations of different attitudes in Miss Beauchamp toward him, now submissively loving, now stubbornly resistant. One might reasonably interpret the case not as an example of numerous personalities or souls inhabiting one body but rather as an example of the radical reordering of the personality system, depending upon the libidinal or aggressive attitude taken up by the unitary primitive self or soul. That is, it is possible to retain the theory of a unitary, single soul, even here where Mc-Dougall thought it impossible, if we only allow that such a soul is capable of reordering its personal universe, either spontaneously or in reaction to the stresses and strains of the current situation. Without maintaining that this is the only or the proper and ultimately true conception of the matter, we can see that the soul theory need not be discarded because of the Beauchamp case. The argument does not, of course, make the soul one of the components of the personality system; it simply makes the system's order depend upon this entity. The point of view is not unlike that of Newton with respect to the physical universe: he saw that the arrangement of the heavenly bodies was orderly, and that this order could be expressed in a formula relating distance and mass, but since he could not accept the notion of action at a distance as a part of his gravitational theory, he concluded that the order was maintained by the will of God, who could, as far as he knew, adopt another order equally well.[19]

A second difficulty in accepting McDougall's view on this point extends also to some remarks made by Klein and Fairbairn. Both McDougall's concept of a sentiment of self-regard and Klein's and Fairbairn's theory of an accumulation of introjected objects around the ego seem to require some kind of original nuclear self to furnish the precipitation point for these developments. Without such a subjective center it becomes difficult to speak of "objects" at all, whether these objects are to be introjected into the personality

19. There are a number of passages in Newton to this effect. I quote here from *Optics*, in Horsley's *Isaaci Newtoni Opera* (London, Nichols, 1782), 4, 263: "God is able to create particles of matter of several sizes and figures, and in several proportions to space, and perhaps of different densities and forces, and thereby to vary the laws of Nature, and make worlds of several sorts in several parts of the universe." On an earlier page he states that God is able to move the parts of the universe by His will more easily than we by ours can move the parts of our bodies.

system or are to serve as the recipients of various affective properties induced by conational responses. It is often maintained, of course, that the problem being raised here is due exclusively to an outmoded way of talking, an antique grammar that opposes subject to object in the parsing of sentences; but the problem seems to be really insurmountable as long as any interest is retained in causal relations. I find myself in warm agreement with Lundholm's criticisms of psychological systems like Köhler's or Lewin's which try to get along without a conscious subject by elaborating a field theory of dynamics.[20]

Personality is undoubtedly a multiplex unity. To try to come to final decisions, however, on the nature of the components which account for the multiplicity, and on the cause of the unity, is a supremely baffling task. The following statement of opinion must therefore be taken as only indifferently satisfying to me, though I think the distinction of "person" from "personality" is useful.

There is, to begin with and continuously, a subjective nucleus or primordial self or, to speak briefly and boldly in archaic language, a soul.[21] This is simple and indivisible. It enters into relations with other parts of the world but primarily with other souls. The community thus formed *is* the personality. Some elements of this community are more or less continuously present for the soul, namely, the elements of the body, which are of course so fused together in perception as virtually to constitute a single element. Other elements of the community, such as the enveloping earth and sky, change in various detailed qualities but not comprehensively as the soul-body combination moves about. Still other elements, namely, other persons (i.e., other soul-body combinations), are continually coming into and passing out of the perceptual field of the soul-body. The particular quality and strength of the community so composed depends upon the activity of the soul—the acceptance or rejection, the high or low valuation, the hatred and love and reconciliation or failure of reconciliation among the diverse elements—although it may often appear to the soul that it is being imposed upon or is being forced into certain decisions regarding the elements around it. The soul is thus a cause of division,

20. Cf. the critical discussion in *God's Failure or Man's Folly.*
21. See Appendix A.

of binding together, of reconciliation, as well as a sufferer, in its community.

A very notable feature of the personal community is that even the elements which have been spoken of as continually passing into and out of the individual perceptual field are or may be continuously present for the soul. I refer here to the facts of introjection. Thus it happens that the relatively permanent soul-body is always accompanied by certain elements of the wide community —especially persons—in the form of introjected objects. A mature person, therefore, never acts in reference simply to the man or woman who is bodily present at a given time, but also and simultaneously in reference to the more shadowy community of friends and enemies which accompanies him wherever he goes. This tenacious inner community is not in itself unchanging: certain elements within it rise in importance, others decline, as the years pass; and not only in importance but also in acceptability and nonacceptability to the soul. The termination of an outward social contact between one person and another rarely or never brings the relationship to a complete end. Afterward, in the privacy of the inner community the process continues, undergoing various developments. The person who made you angry receives a blow in the imagination (i.e., in the shadow community the fight reaches a climax); the person who pleased and attracted you becomes a sexual mate there. By calling it a "shadow" community I do not wish to imply any lack of importance. On the contrary, there is nothing more important. For example, a young woman suffers day and night from depression and an inability to interest herself in other people: underneath one discovers intense, persistent hatred of a dead brother whose relations with her in life were distressingly emotional; and it is not until she can work through her emotional entanglement and forgive him—forgive him, though he is dead—that she can regain her poise and her joy in living. The example is not exceptional.

Apparently there are considerable differences between persons in the degree to which they know and value their inner community; but it is a community with which everyone has to reckon, whether he knows it well or not, and even if he seeks to escape from it by resolutely turning to the affairs of the external world and making what the psychoanalysts call a flight into reality. It is particularly in this region that those events occur which are of prime importance to religion; it is here that everyone is strictly judged and rewarded; and it is the achievement of harmony here which is the highest aim of anyone who cares for happiness at all. The effort to harmonize the inner community is by no means a withdrawal from the outer: it cannot succeed indeed without affecting one's relations with the outer community and to that degree affecting the outer community itself; nor can it fail without corresponding failures in an outward direction.

The personality theory here rudely and tentatively sketched leads necessarily to the conclusion that the problems of the person and the problems of society are inextricably interwoven. In a world community afflicted by severe restrictions of intercommunication and endless displays of military power, by an inability to use natural resources except as an adjunct to war, by the desertion of principle and the surrender of magnanimous hopes, we see on a blown-up scale what it is to be a neurotic or psychotic personality divided into nonharmonious parts and benighted by ignorance. No one living in such a world can avoid some trace of the universal suffering; it does not follow, however, that everyone living in it is compelled to devote himself to disorder, to the suppression of knowledge, and to injury. Though there is much resonance between the personality and the world community, there is not an absolute circularity of relationship. There is the unpredictable emergence of creativity, and there is forgiveness—both of which, the latter only a little less unmistakably than the first, are exemplified in Shakespeare.

4

From what has been said about the personality's being a social system, and usually one dominated by human components, it naturally follows that the understanding of personality and the understanding of human society are two aspects of one great task. To speak more medievally, the task of understanding the individual man is implicated in the task of understanding Man.

If we could see all mankind as one organism, we should note that the anatomy of this organism appeared to be more or less constant from age to age. For example, there are always parents and children, and the relationship existing between them must be a fairly constant quantity in the total make-up of mankind. Such changes as do occur must occur very slowly indeed. Again, the crime rate within a society appears to be a fairly constant quantity. Presumably, almost any activity which is engaged in by any single human being will be represented in humanity at large as a constant feature of its life. To be sure, the activities will differ in relative prominence, and there may be some gradual changes. Now, an individual may be supposed to contain within himself as potential behavior all that is actual in the behavior of the species. No individual actualizes all that is potential within him; nor does he actualize all at one time what he does actualize. Though the life of the race is virtually constant in its manifestations, the life of the individual proceeds by stages, so that he comes to occupy successively some, not all, of the positions occupied constantly by some portion of the members of the race. He moves into and out of these positions (functions, relationships) without affecting them. Just as the cry "The king is dead!" is followed immediately by the cry "Long live the king!" so every position in the total organism Man is occupied in nearly unbroken fashion. Everyone, for instance, comes into the world as inevitably the child of someone, and thus participates from the beginning in the child-parent relationship, which must be one of the steadiest constants in the species. But his participation does not encompass that whole relationship at once. The child pole of the relationship is actual for the moment; the other pole is still only potential, as far as he is concerned, though it is always actual in the species. Yet so distinct is the potentiality of the other pole of the relationship that even in childhood it may be symbolically actualized in play, and it may become a full actuality at an extremely early age, as we are now and then reminded by reports of exceptionally early maternity. Usually, of course, full actualization of the parental role is delayed until late adolescence or later; and though parenthood is the norm of the race, there are cases where it is never achieved. At the stage of sexual maturity the child aspect of the relationship may still have some actuality, in memory and by virtue of a continuing dependence upon the parents; but the living quality of it as experienced by a young child can hardly be maintained or regained by the grown man or woman.

The two polar phases of the child-parent relationship are typically separated by a long period of transition. There are other polar relationships which are not so definitely age determined. Take for example the relationship of injurer and injured. There cannot be the one without the other; but the roles may be reversed very rapidly, though they need not be. Retaliation is a regular consequence of injury. It occurs very frequently in the conflicts between pairs of individuals; it occurs in the relations between groups, large and small, as in war. It has the sanction of law (which in many of its rulings appears to be based on it as a principle), and where the injury is not retaliated directly by the injured party society itself through its law agencies often completes the circuit. The injunction of Christ and of Mo Ti to give up the pattern of retaliation has had very limited appeal. But where it has prevailed, another pattern has been set up in which the injured, instead of becoming an injurer in turn, becomes a forgiver; that is, the reaction to injury continues to take the form of action of a real kind, but it is an order of action different from what initiated it and revises the relationship entirely. This transcending pattern may also be considered a constant, though a very small constant, in the total life of mankind.

The two examples cited illustrate kinds of human relationship which differ with respect to their ethical significance. The change of status within the child-parent relationship is chiefly a matter of growth and circumstance; but in the case of the relationship of injurer to injured there is a vivid question of righteousness involved, especially since the challenge of Christian teaching has come into the world.

In the plays of Shakespeare we see the distincter emergence in the course of time of the parent pole of the parent-child relationship; and we may regard this as an effect of age. But we also see in the course of time the emergence of forgiveness, or at least of the restraint of vengeance as a reaction to injury. This cannot be attributed to age; it is not a necessary consequence of aging, even in the degree that the parental role is. Some students of Shakespeare, much impressed by this emergence of forgiving behavior in his plays, have interpreted it as a sign of a profound spiritual change, a kind of conversion to a religious way of life. It seems possible. But here we may emphasize rather two phenomena which appear to be related to this change. First of all, there is some intrusion of the supernatural: in *Cymbeline*, a religious vision (though here there is a dispute about Shakespeare's authorship); [22] in *The Winter's Tale*, the message of the oracle, and other events approaching the miraculous; and in *The Tempest*, the spiritual forces at the command of Prospero. On the whole Shakespeare is certainly not a conspicuously religious writer, though his familiarity with the Bible is evident; but if we had only these plays to judge him by, we might think of him a good deal more in that way. Does the association of religious or supernatural events with forgiving behavior spring from a necessary connection? Secondly, in some of the earlier plays, where vengeance is held in check, as in *Measure for Measure* and *Coriolanus*, the ultimate restraining power is a woman—Isabella, the novitiate nun, in the first; Volumnia, the mother of the hero, in the second. Also, as will be later confirmed, in those plays where the leading character is a woman—*The Merchant of Venice, As You Like It, Twelfth Night, All's Well That Ends Well*, and *Cymbeline*—difficulties and animosities are uniformly cleared away. Finally, as will be shown by quantitative analysis in the next chapter, women, love, and life are a positively associated set of terms arrayed against men, violence, and death. It is not known whether the association is peculiar to Shakespeare, or whether it is more general, as a natural consequence of the life-bearing and life-nourishing functions of women. Certainly exceptions would be easy to find.

However it may be with others who have learned to forgive, it is evident that the lesson was not perfectly learned by Shakespeare. Not all the animosity and suspiciousness were dissipated. Once again it should be commented that whatever is constantly present in mankind at large may be expected to exist to some degree in every man. The difference between individuals is very much a matter of proportion. A man may be predominantly tough and

22. Though the authorship of *Cymbeline* as a whole is attributed to Shakespeare by Chambers, he questions whether the vision in v. 4 is not an interpolation, and states that it is generally so regarded. See Chambers, *William Shakespeare, 1,* 486.

vengeful; a trace of kindness (condemned by him perhaps as weakness) will be found in him. A man may be predominantly gentle and forgiving; there will still be a trace of cruelty and grudge bearing. The tormenting complexity of human life rests upon this fact —a fact known to Plato and St. Paul as well as to Freud.

5

From inspecting such material as a play, it is quite impossible to distinguish personality levels in the sense of levels of consciousness. We cannot justifiably speak of Hamlet as representing the conscious part of Shakespeare and Claudius the unconscious: the one is as conscious as the other. To be sure, there is conflict between them, and Hamlet has the best of it; from which one might conclude that what is represented by Claudius—betrayal, murder, incest—would be suppressed in the actual behavior of the author. The kind of struggle going on here is certainly the kind which might be supposed to occur between conscious principle and unconscious impulse. But both protagonists are really out in the open in the play, and so in the author's mind, and they are much entangled with one another—not simply set in opposition, white against black. Or again, to take an example that has more of the apparent psychoanalytic style about it: Prospero controlling Caliban. Prospero is easily taken as representing the moral ego (whether by a psychoanalyst or by a literary scholar untainted by the clinic), and Caliban the disrupting forces of the id—lust and venomous hate. But Caliban is as much an inhabitant of Shakespeare's consciousness as Prospero. What was unconscious in Shakespeare cannot have been directly represented in the plays, unless we are ready to accept the odd alternative of supposing that certain elements forced their way in while using him as their unconscious amanuensis, in the manner of a "psychic." The nature of Caliban, and his conflict with Prospero, are as much on the conscious level as anything else in Shakespeare; indeed, Prospero is inadequately defined in the drama if Caliban is left out.

The discovery of personality levels below the threshold of the author's consciousness requires very bold interpretation. A recent psychoanalytic study by Ella Freeman Sharpe, sensitive and really admirable in its *genre*, though sure to disturb the uninitiated, will serve as an example. She writes: "In *King Lear* I found revealed a child's massive feelings and phantasies, evoked by conflict of emotions associated with actual traumatic events in childhood." [23] She deduces that among these traumatic events were two pregnancies of his mother (one "when his sphincter control was not stabilised" and the other when he was "accustomed to walk about independently"), and the discovery of menstruation. She deduces further that his reaction to the first pregnancy was rage and anal rebellion; to the second, running away from home; and to the discovery of menstruation, fear and condemnation of women as being beneath the girdle altogether the property of the fiend. A part of her evidence for this last deduction is contained in the following statement: "One of child Lear's rationalizations concerning not being allowed to stay in his parents' room was their solicitude for him. They did not want him to see the dreadful things that they did, i.e. Edmund is sent out of the room so that he shall not see Gloucester's eyes put out. Gloucester with a bandage over his bleeding eyes looks 'like Goneril with a white beard'—telling us of repressed knowledge of menstruation, bandage, and pubic hair." [24] Now, without a doubt these interpretations of Sharpe's carry us far below the surface accessible to Shakespeare; carry us, the unfriendly critic will say, into the depths of absurdity. To one who knows something of the kind of material turned up in the course of a psychoanalysis, it will not seem necessarily absurd; but it fails to convince, because it is not Shakespeare who is supplying the freely wandering associations here, as required by the Freudian method, but Sharpe. And unfortunately Sharpe does not supply the larger background of clinical experience with analogous material which might have helped persuade the reader that her speculations were better than guesswork. A great part of the analyst's thinking is itself subterranean, if not unconscious. It depends also upon general psychoanalytic theory, which the reader interested in Shakespeare may not know or may not be able to accept, though it be no more than the commonplace proposition that a favorite child, dis-

23. "From *King Lear* to *The Tempest*," *Internat. Jour. of Psycho-Analysis*, 27 (1946), 21.
24. *Ibid.*, p. 25.

placed from its favored position at appropriate stages of development by the birth of another child, will inevitably show reactions
of rage and running away. Further commentary on the methodological difficulties here (which are far from unknown in the work
of much more spiritual interpreters of Shakespeare) will be deferred to a later chapter.

If we can see our way at all to accepting the main drift of Sharpe's
inferences, then we are prepared to regard the plays in their en-
tirety as probably the working out at the adult level of various
conflicts set up early in life. Even if the particular inferences are
unacceptable, we may admit the possibility of something comparable. The understanding of adult behavior is helped at times by
locating a childhood moral problem as the point of departure for
future developments. Thus, in the case of Shakespeare, we might
easily agree that the childhood situation was such as to favor the
jealousy commonly aroused in children by the birth of other children into the family. And when we remember that a principal
theme in the Shakespearean plays is that of jealousy, and how to
the last some of his leading male characters are tortured by it, the
thing seems decidedly probable. Sharpe, however, goes far beyond this. In her opinion, it is not merely the problem of jealousy
which Shakespeare has to struggle with for years; it is the problem
of infantile sexuality, a problem which proves too much for his
mental balance at about the time of *Lear*. She states that, when he
re-emerges from the depression into which as a manic-depressive
personality he finally descends, what he achieves, as demonstrated
in *The Tempest*, is "an omnipotent mastery of his infantile sexuality." She continues: "Omnipotent mastery of sexuality by the
re-installing of the romantic ideals is not a realistic method of dealing with instinctual impulses. It is a 'revolutionary' method, not
an 'evolutionary' one. The unsolved problem remains, the ego in
alliance with the super-ego against the sexual instinct which means
a continual warfare within the psyche." [25]

These statements are made with a good deal more confidence
than I, for one, should be able to muster, and they are anything but
crystal clear; but the continual warfare within the psyche is intelligible enough. Also the presence of jealousy is conspicuous in

25. *Ibid.*, p. 29.

the plays; and Sharpe's guess that it went back to the displacement of William from his exclusive position in his parents' affection seems reasonable. On this view, he would have been sensitized to the betrayal implicit in Edmund Lambert's relations with his family long before the event of the mortgage, and would have been ready to react to his wife as a betrayer with or without immediate cause —because of his mother's much earlier betrayal of him in bringing rivals into his infantile world. But such conclusions cannot, for all their plausibility, be legitimately derived directly from the plays.

It is no answer to the problem of interpretation, the problem of carrying a play back to the heart of the playwright and finding his intention (conscious or unconscious), to remind the interpreter that Shakespeare often leaned heavily on his sources. Since he selected his sources himself, we may presume, and warped them as he pleased wherever he pleased, we may take equally as reflections of his state of mind those plays based upon Plautus, Boccaccio, Greene, or whom you will, and those which he seems to have invented without such help. It is not only at points where he has modified his sources or filled in a crevice with new stuff that his personality peeps forth momentarily; it is present all the time, even when he is making the Archbishop of Canterbury tedious by letting him mouth Holinshed on the "law Salike" or Cleopatra glorious by having Enobarbus quote North's Plutarch—in words divinely edited by Shakespeare. Winnowing what is Shakespeare's own from what as "an vpstart Crow" he took from others is in very much the same class of endeavor as separating the Conscious from the Unconscious in the meaning of his plays. The one occupation is as attractive as the other. "Why, Hal, 'tis my vocation, Hal; 'tis no sin for a man to labour in his vocation."

On the various approaches to Shakespeare and their relative merits for one interested in the nature of his personality there is room for endless critical debate. But here we may let such matters rest for a time, and direct our attention to the possibilities of a reasonably objective and partly quantitative analysis of the plays, which will attempt to put into action the assumptions, now discussed at some length, lying behind Rowe's old statement and the practices of the modern psychological clinic.

CHAPTER 3. QUANTITATIVE ASPECTS
OF SHAKESPEARE'S PLAYS

1

THE FIRST CONSIDERATION in a study concerned with the development of an author is the ascertainment of the canon and chronology of his works. Ideally we should have a pure and complete collection arranged in absolutely correct order. In the case of Shakespeare the ideal can only be approximated. This being true, the study will have to avoid questions requiring great precision and be content with broad perspectives.

A varying number of plays have been assigned to Shakespeare. The thirty-two which will be used here are taken from the list of thirty-eight given by Edmund K. Chambers on pages 270–1 of the first volume of his *William Shakespeare*. The six plays omitted are the three parts of *Henry VI, Titus Andronicus, Henry VIII,* and *The Two Noble Kinsmen,* the reason being that the extent of Shakespeare's contribution to them is very debatable.[1] Perhaps in consistency *Pericles* also should have been omitted; the general agreement, however, that the last three acts at least are nearly pure Shakespeare, and the harmony between this play and others of the presumably same period, were temptations in favor of its inclusion too hard to resist. Critical uncertainties regarding some of the other plays included have also at various times been raised; but

1. In regard to *Henry VI* and *Titus Andronicus,* I have chosen to err on the side of caution. Chambers appears to be quite doubtful of Shakespeare's full authorship of *Titus Andronicus* and the first part of *Henry VI*; he is much more certain of the second and third parts of *Henry VI*. I did make use of these plays in my 1948 article on some mathematical aspects of fictional literature. Dropping them from the list did not alter any of the quantitative features noted there to any significant extent, and, for the sake of fullness, I perhaps should have retained them here; but I wanted to avoid as far as possible the inclusion of impurities in my data, especially where they were to be treated statistically, and I judged that thirty-two plays would be an adequate if not complete sample of Shakespeare's work. As for *Henry VIII* and *The Two Noble Kinsmen,* there seems to be but little question that Shakespeare's contribution, whatever the extent of it, was that of a collaborator.

in the main they are accepted by the scholars as genuine. Though our sample cannot be regarded, then, as absolutely pure, it is sufficiently so for our purposes.

The chronology of the plays, by which I mean both the serial order and the dates, is likewise not perfectly established. In this study, however, the authority of Chambers will be accepted. It should be noted that there is actually a high order of agreement among modern scholars. For example, if the sequence of the plays as given by Chambers is compared with that given by G. B. Harrison in 1947 in his *Introducing Shakespeare* (seventeen years after Chambers' book), one finds a total of eighteen reversals for our thirty-two plays; but ten of these affect the sequence by only one position, while the maximum shift of five places occurs just once, *The Merry Wives of Windsor* being made to follow *Much Ado About Nothing* instead of following *Hamlet*. The rank-order correlation coefficient between the two lists is .986, which is about as near to the perfect 1.00 as the practical statistician ever hopes to get. The chronology appears to be accurate enough for gross temporal comparisons; beyond that we are in the region of speculation.

It is scientifically desirable to be quantitative wherever possible. Analysis which has reached that stage indicates that one is able to make clear-cut decisions which can probably be arrived at equally well by others; that is to say, it points or should point to the existence of a really sharable analytic method. Furthermore, it renders possible a mathematical treatment of the data—which opens the way to elegant description and to mathematical ingenuity in the development of scientific hypotheses. Such analysis is by no means a substitute for thought and judgment or sensitive observation; nor is it easy to see how it can be extended at all, though no doubt there are enthusiasts to make the claim, to the ascertainment and evaluation of such subtle qualities as the meanings of words or other symbols, especially when these are complicated by irony and *double-entendre*. But in its place it is very useful. These brief comments are by way of introducing Table 1, where the twelve leading characters of each of the thirty-two plays in our sample are assigned numerical values indicating their relative importance within the play to which they belong, and ranked accordingly.

The basic operation performed in developing Table 1 was making a count of the speech lines of each character. The results are presented in the table as follows. The number accompanying the character at the top of the list in any given play is the number of that character's speech lines; for the remaining characters in the list the number represents in each case the proportionate quantity of lines spoken, when compared with the number spoken by the character heading the list. For example, Romeo has 613 lines; Juliet has 88 per cent as many, Friar Laurence 57, and so on down the list. For computational purposes the top character therefore has a value of 100, since this character is always taken as the standard of comparison for the rest of the characters in any one play; but in the table, for the sake of providing essential information, the invariable index value of 100 for the top character is replaced by the number of speech lines.

It must be pointed out that the accuracy of the numerical values in the table is only approximate. The count was performed in most cases no more than once and is subject to error for that reason alone. More important, it must be admitted that defining exactly what a line is and sticking to it are operations far from easy. An interesting side light on the problem is found in G. Udny Yule's *The Statistical Study of Literary Vocabulary*, where the distinguished author is hard put to it to define for purposes of counting what constitutes a word. In making my count I took Shakespeare's pentameter line as the standard unit and gave half value for fractions, though probably not with thorough consistency. Lines of prose, though slightly longer than pentameter verse lines in the books I used, were counted as equivalent, since the reading time was about the same. Perhaps the most questionable procedure was the assigning of full value to short complete lines of lyrical verse. Once again the theoretical consideration was that such lines, often lengthened out by being sung, might be thought of as having about the same time value as the basic pentameter line. The general rule was to count every line in the play; but in some cases passages were omitted from the reckoning, as deemed appropriate to the aim of measuring the dramatically interacting characters. Considered superfluous in this sense were the narrative of Gower in *Pericles*, the Chorus in *Henry V*, and the atmospheric playlet of Christopher Sly in *The Taming of the Shrew*. On the other hand, some low-

ranking individual characters not given distinctive names, such as
the Roman citizens in *Julius Caesar,* were lumped together as constituting a single complex character: these are marked by asterisks
in the table.

The Dent Everyman's Library edition of the plays was the one
chiefly used in making the line count, though recourse was had for
a number of the plays to Hudson's *Students' Handy Shakespeare*
and the Globe edition of Clark and Wright. Some adjustment of the
count of the prose lines was attempted to compensate for differences between the editions. It is believed that all three editions
present a normal text, and differences between them are slight—
certainly not enough to produce any material effects on the outcome of the count, which for technical reasons already mentioned
cannot be impeccable, though probably the margin of error is not
seriously large. It would have been ideal to base the count on a
single standard edition, as I now realize, but circumstances at the
time (into which there is no present need to enter) prevented this
ideal solution. For the benefit of the seriously critical reader there
is included in Appendix B a discussion of the earlier count of Rolfe.

TABLE 1

RICHARD III	COMEDY OF ERRORS	TAMING OF THE SHREW	TWO GENTLEMEN OF VERONA
1592–93	1592–93	1593–94	1594–95
Speech Lines (equal 100 per cent)			
1078 Gloucester	270 Antipholus S.	577 Petruchio	380 Valentine
Per Cent of Above			
36 Buckingham	97 Adriana	50 Tranio	94 Proteus
26 Q. Elizabeth	78 Antipholus E.	37 Katharina	83 Julia
20 Q. Margaret	77 Dromio S.	35 Hortensio	52 Duke Milan
15 Clarence	56 Dromio E.	31 Lucentio	48 Launce

15 Anne	53 Aegeon	29 Baptista	47 Speed
13 Duchess York	35 Luciana	28 Gremio	41 Silvia
13 Richmond	33 Duke Ephesus	24 Grumio	19 Lucetta
12 Hastings	29 Angelo	16 Biondello	16 Outlaws *
11 Murderers *	27 Abbess	12 Bianca	14 Thurio
10 Stanley	13 Courtezan	9 Pedant	10 Panthino
6 K. Edward	13 Second Merchant	6 Vincentio	9 Antonio

LOVE'S LABOUR'S LOST	ROMEO AND JULIET	RICHARD II	MIDSUMMER NIGHT'S DREAM
1594–95	1594–95	1595–96	1595–96

Speech Lines (equal 100 per cent)

638 Biron	613 Romeo	754 K. Richard	245 Bottom

Per Cent of Above

48 King Navarre	88 Juliet	54 Bolingbroke	96 Theseus
45 Princess France	57 Friar Laurence	38 York	88 Puck
38 Armado	46 Capulet	25 Gaunt	73 Oberon
37 Boyet	44 Nurse	19 Northumberland	72 Helena
32 Costard	38 Mercutio	18 Mowbray	62 Hermia
29 Holofernes	23 Benvolio	15 Queen	56 Titania
28 Rosaline	19 Lady Capulet	13 Duchess York	53 Lysander

* Asterisks identify collective characters.

TABLE 1 (*continued*)

LOVE'S LABOUR'S LOST	ROMEO AND JULIET	RICHARD II	MIDSUMMER NIGHT'S DREAM
26 Moth	12 Prince Escalus	11 Aumerle	51 Demetrius
14 Dumain	11 Paris	9 Bishop Carlisle	46 Quince
11 Longaville	7 Montague	7 Duchess Gloucester	25 Fairies °
10 Sir Nathaniel	6 Tybalt	7 Gardener	22 Flute

KING JOHN	MERCHANT OF VENICE	1 HENRY IV	2 HENRY IV
1596–97	1596–97	1597–98	1597–98

Speech Lines (equal 100 per cent)

518 Bastard	568 Portia	558 Hotspur	553 Falstaff

Per Cent of Above

82 K. John	60 Shylock	94 Falstaff	54 K. Henry
51 Constance	60 Bassanio	94 Prince Henry	50 Prince Henry
38 K. Philip	35 Antonio	61 K. Henry	30 Shallow
32 Pandulph	31 Lorenzo	24 Worcester	27 Scroop
31 Salisbury	31 Gratiano	14 Glendower	26 Hostess
29 Lewis	26 Launcelot	13 Poins	20 Westmoreland
27 Hubert	18 Prince Morocco	12 Vernon	19 Lancaster
23 Arthur	18 Salarino	11 Mortimer	19 Northumberland
15 Pembroke	15 Jessica	10 Lady Percy	16 Lord Bardolph

12 Angier Citizens *	14 Nerissa	8 Hostess	15 Morton
11 Q. Elinor	11 Prince Arragon	7 Blunt	14 Warwick

MUCH ADO ABOUT NOTHING	HENRY V	JULIUS CAESAR	AS YOU LIKE IT
1598–99	1598–99	1599–1600	1599–1600

Speech Lines (equal 100 per cent)

383 Benedick	989 K. Henry	809 Brutus	599 Rosalind

Per Cent of Above

83 Leonato	25 Archbishop Canterbury	61 Cassius	45 Orlando
82 Don Pedro	25 Fluellen	41 Antony	44 Celia
72 Claudio	16 Pistol	16 Caesar	40 Touchstone
67 Beatrice	13 Exeter	16 Casca	35 Jaques
44 Dogberry	11 Dauphin	12 Roman Citizens *	23 Oliver
31 Hero	11 Constable	12 Portia	18 Duke
29 Borachio	9 French King	6 Decius	14 Phebe
26 Don John	7 Burgundy	5 Octavius	12 Silvius
22 Friar Francis	6 Williams	5 Messala	11 Frederick
15 Margaret	6 Boy	4 Lucius	11 Corin
14 Antonio	6 Gower	4 Marullus	11 Adam

TABLE 1 (*continued*)

Twelfth Night	Hamlet	Merry Wives of Windsor	Troilus and Cressida
1599–1600	1600–1	1600–1	1601–2

Speech Lines (equal 100 per cent)

326 Viola	1382 Hamlet	379 Falstaff	543 Troilus

Per Cent of Above

92 Olivia	39 K. Claudius	76 Mrs. Page	89 Ulysses
91 Sir Toby	23 Polonius	64 Ford	86 Pandarus
82 Clown	20 Horatio	53 Evans	49 Cressida
77 Malvolio	15 Laertes	49 Mrs. Quickly	47 Thersites
67 Orsino	12 Ophelia	43 Mrs. Ford	37 Hector
42 Sir Andrew	11 Q. Gertrude	37 Page	35 Agamemnon
40 Sebastian	9 Players *	32 Slender	35 Achilles
38 Maria	7 Clowns *	28 Shallow	28 Nestor
34 Antonio	7 Ghost	26 Host	26 Aeneas
30 Fabian	6 Rosencrantz	26 Caius	20 Diomedes
10 Captain	5 Marcellus	25 Fenton	18 Paris

All's Well That Ends Well	Measure for Measure	Othello	King Lear
1602–3	1604–5	1604–5	1605–6

Speech Lines (equal 100 per cent)

473 Helena	847 Duke	1061 Iago	682 K. Lear

Per Cent of Above

80 King	50 Isabella	80 Othello	56 Edgar
69 Parolles	38 Angelo	36 Desdemona	50 Kent
58 Countess	22 Lucio	24 Emilia	47 Gloucester
56 Bertram	19 Escalus	23 Cassio	44 Edmund
50 Lafeu	18 Provost	13 Brabantio	34 Fool
35 Clown	17 Pompey	9 Roderigo	34 Goneril
29 Diana	13 Claudio	7 Lodovico	27 Regan
25 Second Lord	8 Mariana	6 Duke Venice	23 Albany
18 First Lord	7 Elbow	5 Montano	16 Cornwall
16 Soldiers *	4 Friar Peter	3 Bianca	15 Cordelia
13 Widow	4 Gentlemen *	2 Clown	13 Gentleman

MACBETH	ANTONY AND CLEOPATRA	CORIOLANUS	TIMON OF ATHENS
1605–6	1606–7	1607–8	1607–8

Speech Lines (equal 100 per cent)

689 Macbeth	818 Antony	865 Coriolanus	826 Timon

Per Cent of Above

37 Lady Macbeth	80 Cleopatra	70 Menenius	29 Apemantus
30 Malcolm	46 Caesar	35 Sicinius	25 Flavius
29 Macduff	43 Enobarbus	34 Volumnia	23 Senators *

TABLE 1 (*continued*)

MACBETH	ANTONY AND CLEOPATRA	CORIOLANUS	TIMON OF ATHENS
20 Witches °	16 Pompey	31 Aufidius	19 Alcibiades
19 Ross	13 Charmian	31 Cominius	18 Servants °
19 Banquo	11 Soldiers °	28 Brutus	12 Poet
10 Lennox	10 Messengers °	22 Roman Citizens °	12 Lords °
9 Duncan	8 Dolabella	17 Aufidius' Servants	8 Painter
6 Murderers °	8 Menas	7 Lartius	4 Lucius
6 Lady Macduff	8 Lepidus	5 Roman Senators °	4 Strangers °
6 Hecate	7 Agrippa	5 Valeria	4 Lucullus

PERICLES	CYMBELINE	WINTER'S TALE	TEMPEST
1608–9	1609–10	1610–11	1611–12

Speech Lines (equal 100 per cent)

580 Pericles	605 Imogen	674 Leontes	629 Prospero

Per Cent of Above

29 Marina	69 Posthumus	50 Paulina	29 Ariel
26 Simonides	68 Iachimo	41 Polixenes	25 Caliban
21 Helicanus	55 Belarius	40 Camillo	23 Ferdinand
19 Cleon	47 Cymbeline	38 Autolycus	22 Antonio
17 Cerimon	37 Pisanio	31 Hermione	21 Gonzalo
17 Lysimachus	35 Cloten	31 Florizel	20 Miranda

16	27	25	20
Bawd	Queen	Clown	Stephano
15	26	21	18
Dionyza	Guiderius	Perdita	Sebastian
14	21	17	17
Fishermen °	Arviragus	Gentlemen °	Trinculo
13	15	17	17
Boult	Lords °	Shepherd	Alonso
13	13	16	7
Thaisa	Gentlemen °	Antigonus	Iris

Some readers will immediately object to this mathematical and semimechanical weighting of the characters. It will be argued that the importance of a character may have little to do with the number of lines he speaks. One vividly remembers Mercutio, Cordelia, Queen Gertrude, though they do not rank high in the table; and it is possible to have a dramatic participant like Lavinia in *Titus Andronicus* who ceases to talk because her tongue is cut out. On the other hand, it may be objected that some characters are more garrulous than important, like Polonius; or, on the contrary, that some important characters are by disposition laconic—but in Shakespeare such a character may be hard to find: Coriolanus might be expected to be of a Spartan reticence but is not. Nevertheless, if the reader will compare his impressionistic estimates with the ordering of the characters by the quantitative method, he probably will not often be seriously disturbed by what he finds. Suppose we take Cordelia as an example. Now, doubtless Cordelia contributes to the pathos of the tragedy by the tension set up between her and Lear, helps to get movement, provides a bright gentle star of contrast to Lear's titanic passion; but it is possible that her importance in the play itself has been exaggerated in the minds of some by her fame and their love for her. In general, indeed, some reflection on the quantitative relations of the characters in Table 1 may help to correct distortions introduced into our conception of the plays by the special attractiveness of some of the characters or the special treatment which they have received from actors and commentators. Or suppose that a prejudice exists, because of the great familiarity of *Romeo and Juliet,* that Shakespeare is primarily a poet-playwright of young love: a glance over the top-ranking characters in the table should produce some readjustment of that view.

Doubtless it would be well if there were some way of adjusting the weights arrived at by counting the lines to accommodate the factor of dramatic intensity, but I do not yet know how to do that. Nevertheless, just as the matter stands, as I remarked above, the reader will probably not find it often necessary to rearrange the characters importantly to bring the order of characters given in my table into line with his preferred order. However much one may be impressed by the brilliance of Mercutio it is unlikely that he will be placed above Romeo as the leading character in *Romeo and Juliet,* considered as a dramatic structure and not as a picture gallery. With regard to some other cases, as for instance the relative importance of Romeo and Juliet themselves, it must be noted that the line count may throw very little more weight to the one than to the other. In any event the line-count weight must be regarded as an approximate measure. As further defense of the line count I should like to call the reader's attention to the probability that he himself in impressionistically assessing the importance of characters is influenced by the sheer bulk of the character, as a speaker. Just as we react to the physical weight of objects which we handle, and differentiate between them, without figuring out the ounces and pounds, so here. In counting up the speech lines I have in effect simply made conscious an unconscious process.

The meaning of the character weights may be clarified by noting just what is dramatically involved. A top-ranking character is one who has had more occasion for speaking than others; and this may imply long speaking, or frequent speaking, or both—usually both. Frequent speaking usually implies contact with many other characters; and long speaking sometimes does, since if the long speech is an oration a number of other characters will be present to hear it. (Soliloquies are an exception.) The top-ranking character, then, is not simply a wordy individual but one who is present in many situations and generally in active touch with more characters than anybody else in the play. The low-ranking character is just the opposite: his contacts are fewer and less ramifying where they do occur. After all, the principal method by which Shakespeare reveals a character is through the words he speaks; and the more he speaks, the more likely he is to be involved in the living tissue of the play in its various situations, and the more complex and memorable he is likely to become for us.

But this is to consider the meaning of character weights from the standpoint of the audience or reader. Think now of the meaning from the standpoint of the author himself, of Shakespeare. The top-ranking character is the one who dominates Shakespeare's own thoughts, and the others occupy him in their varying degrees. Their ordered arrangement reveals the ordered structure of his personality. Some bundles of thought and emotion in him, which appear on the stage as the dramatis personae, bulk large; others small, and smaller. Such a monadic hierarchy is just what we should expect to find in a personality, according to Leibniz, Herbart, McDougall.[2] Our own experience teaches us that some thoughts, usually permeated with emotion and often clothed in human form, are more frequently present than others; and we should not be surprised to discover the same fact expressed in the arrangement of character weights in a play, which is not a flat indiscriminate reflection of life in general but a specific expression of a living human organism.

2

Table 1 will be used later on as a guide in the analysis of the characters and the themes of the plays. But it has some interesting properties of its own which will repay examination. We may begin with Figure 1, which presents the average distribution of character weights for the thirty-two plays and, alongside the average curve, for comparison, the extremes of the range of variation among the particular plays, in *Henry V* and *A Midsummer Night's Dream*. The figures along the vertical axis of the graph represent the scale of character weights; those along the horizontal axis, the rank positions, first rank being assigned to the character with the heaviest weight. The points indicated on the graph are connected by lines

2. All three of these authors (Leibniz being the fountainhead, in this respect) recognize levels of functioning in the mental system, and tend to think in terms of living, as opposed to material-mechanical, units, organized hierarchically in grades of power.

to assist the eye to appreciate the form of the distribution. The sum of the weights for the whole set of twelve points in a distribution is noted down beside the appropriate curve.

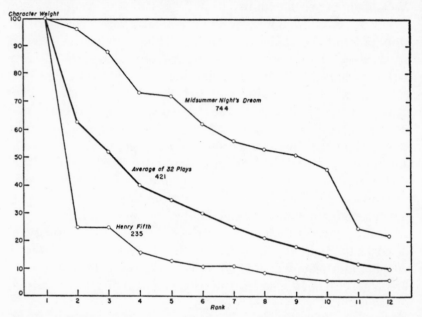

FIGURE 1. Shakespeare: Comparison of Average Character-weight Curve with Two Extreme Cases. The number shown with each curve is the sum of twelve character weights.

First, let it be observed in Figure 1 that the extremes do not reach the theoretically possible limits. The theoretical extremes would be: (A) a perfectly horizontal arrangement at the top with every character receiving a weight of 100, and (B) one in which the second character was at some very low point (signifying one line of speech, say) near the bottom of the graph and the remaining ten characters were strung out to the right on the same level. Neither of these mathematically possible extremes is actually represented in the plays, although B is more nearly approached than A. One can see, in fact, that B as a dramatic possibility is almost absurd (to be sure, it verges on the "dramatic monologues" of Browning, which *might* be rendered on the stage); but it is not so immediately obvious why possibility A, which is less nearly approached by Shakespeare than possibility B, could not be dramatically exploited. The rule seems to be—and according to our hypothesis this is a statement about Shakespeare's personality as well as about the plays—that each component, as the average curve shows, shall occupy a position different from every other one. Of course in some given individual play there may be occasional instances of equality or near equality, as illustrated in the curve for *Henry V;* but the average curve, which summarizes the tendencies of the whole collection, does not show this phenomenon. It should be noted, however, that the curves shown here are truncated, that is, they do not extend as far to the right as they could be drawn if every one of the characters in the plays was given a place; and in a play with very many characters the segment of the curve extended to the right could be expected to be virtually level.

Second, notice that the average curve has a quite graceful appearance, suggesting a simple mathematical orderliness. An elementary formulation of the arrangement of the points would be that the weight difference between them regularly decreases from left to right along the rank axis. A more precise description of the curve would be that, beginning with the second rank, every weight value is about twice as large as for the point in fourth place below it; the first point can be fitted into this scheme of relationships by supposing that two values intermediate between it and the second actual value have been omitted. This way of describing the curve has been translated into a simple exponential formula in Table 2, where it will be seen that the values derived from the formula are reasonably close to the actual empirical values.[3]

3. The formula given in Table 2 describes the empirical distribution in such a way as to bring out sharply the regular progression in the figures from the second on down, as also the distinct gap between the first and second figures—*as if* a couple of beats in the harmonic series had been skipped here. The formula was set up for me by Paul Peach, a statistician at that time located at North Carolina State College, when I showed him my data and pointed out certain of their properties in 1947. In a recent consultation with my colleague B. J. Winer I learned that the formula could be modified to fit the empirical distribution without assuming gaps by setting T_0 equal to 1.00 by definition, and for the remaining terms letting T_1 equal $K^i + 2$, K having the same value as in the table.

There is a relation between the Shakespeare distribution and that found for small groups of interacting "real" speakers, as observed by Bales, and by Stephan and Mishler. For their attempts to deal with the mathematical description of these

That the tendency of the components to fall into a geometrical progression is not peculiar to Shakespeare is demonstrated by Figures 2 and 3. In the first of these the average curve for the seven plays of Marlowe is shown, along with individual curves for *Faustus* and *The Massacre at Paris* representing extremes. (The line count, following rules similar to those for Shakespeare—except that fractions of pentameter lines were counted as units when they constituted a complete speech—was based upon the Dent Everyman's

TABLE 2

(Formula: $T_i = K^i$, where $K = .84$)

	Formula	Shakespeare
T_0	100	100
T_1	84	—
T_2	71	—
T_3	60	63
T_4	50	52
T_5	42	40
T_6	35	35
T_7	30	30
T_8	25	25
T_9	21	21
T_{10}	18	18
T_{11}	15	15
T_{12}	13	12
T_{13}	11	10

Library edition.) Though Marlowe's average curve is definitely his own, in the sense that it is different to a statistically significant degree from Shakespeare's, its general shape is of the same order; that is, it is an exponential curve.

In Figure 3 the average curves for Shakespeare and Marlowe are compared with average curves for Sophocles and Charlotte Brontë, and, in addition, curves displaying the distribution of the most frequently occurring nouns in works by Macaulay and Bunyan. Since these curves are based upon a virtually chance assemblage of data,

---

social relations, see Bales, Strodtbeck, Mills, and Roseborough, "Channels of Communication in Small Groups," *Amer. Sociol. Rev.*, 16 (1951), 461–8, and Stephan and Mishler, "The Distribution of Participation in Small Groups: an Exponential Approximation," *Amer. Sociol. Rev.*, 17 (1952), 598–608.

their general similarity should impress us as indicating a widespread and perhaps universal tendency of the human mind or personality. The very restricted range of values for the component of second rank is especially noteworthy.

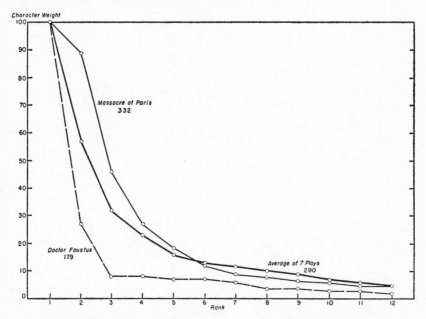

FIGURE 2. Marlowe: Comparison of Average Character-weight Curve with Two Extreme Cases. The number shown with each curve is the sum of twelve character weights.

Some explanation of Figure 3 will render it more intelligible. It was during a study of the novels of Charlotte Brontë that I first became aware of the tendency which these curves express.[4] In this case the character weights had been determined by counting the pages on which each character appeared, either as actor or object of reference. The average curve of distribution for the four novels was then constructed by the method already explained for Shakespeare; that is, the top character was assigned the value of 100 and the others values corresponding to the proportion their page frequency was of that for the top character, and the four sets of figures

4. "A Study of the Novels of Charlotte and Emily Brontë as an Expression of Their Personalities," *Jour. Personality, 16* (1947), 109–52.

were then combined. The form of this curve interested me, perhaps because I had been sensitized by reading some articles by Zipf on the harmonic series found in the distribution of human populations and certain other social phenomena. Accordingly, I looked around for another convenient sample for comparison. It occurred to me

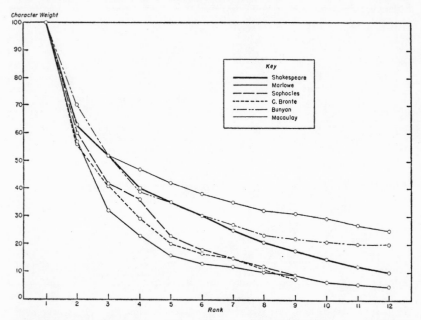

FIGURE 3. Several Authors. The curves for Shakespeare, Marlowe, Sophocles, and Charlotte Brontë represent the distribution of character weights. The curves for Bunyan and Macaulay (the upper two curves) represent the distribution of noun weights, as explained in the text.

that a suitable test choice would be the plays of Sophocles, both because they were distant in time from the novels of Charlotte Brontë and because they were in verse form in the original, which permitted an easy and accurate ascertainment of character weights by the counting of speech lines. The largest number of characters in the plays of Sophocles is nine: four plays are limited to nine characters, one to eight, two to seven, and one to six; the averages are therefore based on less than the total number of plays for the last three of the nine points, and the comparison between the two authors restricted to nine points all told. As it happens, the two curves fall very close together. It was this near coincidence which led me, in search of a still larger sample, to make the count of the speech lines in Shakespeare's plays, with the results which have been described. And finally, in order to have a contemporary of Shakespeare's for further comparison, Marlowe was chosen. It will be noticed that the curves for Marlowe, Charlotte Brontë, and Sophocles lie below the Shakespeare curve. As will be indicated in a moment the difference is reduced if only Shakespeare's tragedies and historical plays are considered.

The curves for Macaulay and Bunyan, which are the upper two in Figure 3, are based upon a different kind of data found in a previously cited publication by the statistician G. Udny Yule.[5] Yule made a count of the different nouns occurring in four essays by Macaulay and four stories or tracts by Bunyan. From his frequency tables summarizing the two authors I took the top twelve nouns for each case and translated the figures given by Yule into the form used for the other curves in Figure 3. These curves are of the same general order as the others. The somewhat different course followed by the nouns in the terminal segments of their curves might have been expected because of the fact that the number of different nouns within the sampled works greatly exceeds the number of different characters within a play or novel. But the exponential form is patent. We may therefore conclude that the nouns in connected discourse are distributed in much the same fashion as are the characters in a play or novel. Indeed, the nouns *are* the characters in an essay; the verbs are their actions.

If we may trust our random sample, our mathematical excursion has so far revealed the mind of Shakespeare as operating in a manner which, if not universal, is at least very common.

At the same time the special properties of Shakespeare's curve appear to distinguish it successfully from those of the other authors. His curve can be made to approach the others more nearly however, if, as previously hinted, only his historical and tragical pieces are considered—which may be proper in view of the tragical cast of the other authors, i.e., Marlowe, Sophocles, and Charlotte Brontë. Figure 4 presents separate curves for Shakespeare's two main classes of dramatic composition—tragedy and history on the

5. *The Statistical Study of Literary Vocabulary.*

one hand and comedy and romance on the other—and places them for comparison beside the curve for Marlowe. As one can see, Shakespeare's tragedy-history curve is decidedly nearer to Marlowe's, who is throughout tragical-historical, than is the curve for comedy and romance.

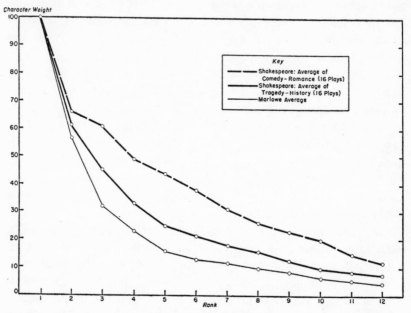

FIGURE 4. Shakespeare and Marlowe: Comparison of Two Classes of Shakespearean Plays with Marlowe's Average. The F-test differentiates the three curves at better than the 1 per cent level.

There is not enough information here to decide whether the separation of the tragic and comic curves illustrated in Shakespeare represents a general characteristic of these two types of composition and the corresponding states of mind of the author; but in Shakespeare's case at least the difference between the two curves shown in the graph is statistically significant. One way of coming to this conclusion is to take the sum of character weights for each of the plays, obtain the average sum for the two classes of play, and determine the significance of the difference between the two averages. The round average for the sixteen tragedies and histories is 358; for the sixteen comedies and romances, 483. The difference, when subjected to statistical analysis, yields an F-ratio of 8.63, indicating that a difference of such magnitude could not be expected by chance once in a hundred times. Apparently we are justified in stating that the two classes of play are based upon a genuinely different ordering of the characters. The comic class tends toward a hurly-burly of nearly equally important actors, like the members of a festive crowd as in some painting of Brueghel's; the tragic class, toward a condition in which a solitary figure muses unhappily on his fate. The social group tends to prevail in comedy; the individual in tragedy.

It was concluded in an earlier study of mine that there was, in addition to the considerable difference between comic and tragic types of play, a progressive lowering of the curve for the characters below the first with increasing age.[6] The evidence adduced there is no longer satisfactory to me. There is indeed some decline in the total weight of the twelve characters as the plays are taken chronologically, but the decline is so slight and irregular that the correlation between time and character weight is statistically insignificant. The result is the same whether the tragic and comic types are taken together or separately.

3

With the aid of the set of character weights given in Table 1 it is possible to make a crude analysis of other aspects of Shakespeare as exhibited in the plays. Since the twelve characters listed account for roughly 90 per cent of the sum total of lines in a given play (somewhat lower in the few cases where extradramatic passages were omitted from the reckoning), the distribution of any traits among them may be taken as fairly representative of the whole play. The chief problem lies in defining and allocating the traits. Here only a few dichotomies will be attempted; but even in the simple cases, such as distinguishing between male and female, questions may arise; and in less simple cases it may be really troublesome trying to decide whether a character should be categorized on one side or the other of the line. What this amounts to

6. "A Mathematical Aspect of Fictional Literature Pertinent to McDougall's Theory of a Hierarchy of Sentiments," *Jour. Personality*, 17 (1948), 75–82.

saying is that the characters do not simply possess or lack a given quality but blend qualities, even opposing qualities, in various proportions. A dichotomizing decision usually has to be determined by the presence of a quality in greater or less degree than its opposite. A salutary outcome of the exercise is an increased awareness of the complexity of many of the Shakespearean characters.

Table 3 summarizes compactly my experience in trying to use four double categories, two of them quite objective, the other two subject to considerable personal whim, though possibly no greater than found in many a psychophysical experiment. The four categories in the order of their listing in the table involved comparing male with female, lovers with nonlovers, those living throughout the play with those dying somewhere in its course, and violent characters with nonviolent. A full explanation of the table is needed to make it intelligible. The first and second columns date and name the plays in the order given by Chambers; the third, labeled *Total*, contains the sums of weights of the twelve characters in each play as individually listed in Table 1; and the fourth, fifth, sixth, and seventh, the results of subtracting the weight of characters possessing the indicated trait from the weight of those possessing its opposite and dividing by the total character weight in the play. In further explanation of the last statement let us take as an example the play *Richard III*. In the column labeled $\dfrac{M-F}{Total}$ there is an entry of 47 for this play. It was obtained as follows: Adding the weights for the male characters in the play (Gloucester, Buckingham, Clarence, Richmond, Hastings, Murderers, Stanley, King Edward) gives 203; adding those for the female characters (Queen Elizabeth, Queen Margaret, Anne, Duchess of York) gives 74; the latter sum subtracted from the former leaves 129, and this divided by the total weight 277 gives approximately .47, which is registered in the table without the decimal point. This is the procedure throughout. It is evident that the range of possible values is from 100 to −100, and that the value zero would occur if there were equality between the two numerator terms. At the foot of the five columns of measurements are given the respective means and standard deviations of the distributions, rounded to the nearest whole number to avoid any overpretentious appearance of accuracy.

TABLE 3

Date	Play	Total of 12	$\dfrac{M-F}{Total}$	$\dfrac{L-NL}{Total}$	$\dfrac{L-D}{Total}$	$\dfrac{V-NV}{Total}$
1592–93	RIII	277	47	−100	−33	30
	CE	611	44	6	100	−100
1593–94	TS	377	74	29	100	−47
1594–95	TGV	533	46	25	100	−59
	LLL	418	65	35	100	−100
	RJ	451	33	−12	−7	−8
1595–96	RII	316	82	−26	37	15
	MSND	744	49	24	100	−100
1596–97	J	451	72	−87	26	67
	MV	419	38	34	100	−71
1597–98	1 HIV	448	92	−46	36	50
	2 HIV	390	87	−100	41	20
1598–99	MAAN	585	61	−8	100	−81
	HV	235	100	−15	91	94
1599–1600	JC	282	92	−92	−26	78
	AYL	364	13	59	100	−29
	TN	703	35	7	100	−77
1600–1	H	254	82	28	−62	35
	MWW	559	40	−35	100	−49
1601–2	TC	570	83	−34	87	53
1602–3	AWEW	549	27	−43	100	−94
1604–5	MM	300	45	−34	100	−75
	O	310	59	−7	−61	41
1605–6	L	459	67	−94	16	21
	M	291	53	−100	−18	56
1606–7	AC	350	47	2	−49	41
1607–8	C	385	80	−100	53	61
	TofA	258	100	−100	22	33
1608–9	P	300	51	−25	100	−71
1609–10	Cy	513	50	−34	76	42
1610–11	WT	427	52	−14	92	−30
1611–12	T	319	83	−72	100	−45
Mean		420	61	−29	54	−9
SD		132	22	48	56	61

We may now examine the tabulated results. It will be noted that there is not a play in which the male weight falls to equality with the female; the scores range from 13 to 100, and the mean is 61. In other words, the male weight on the average exceeds the female weight four to one. It is impossible to say how much this result depends upon the natural tendency of Shakespeare's mind, since none but male actors appeared on the Shakespearean stage and the supply of those suitable for taking female parts may have had some restrictive effect on the development of female dramatic roles. It may be no more than an accident that if the *Sonnets* are divided into those concerned primarily with a man and those concerned primarily with a woman the ratio is 126 to 26, which gives an index figure of 66 to put beside the average of 61 for the plays. Comparable index figures for the three other available authors are: for Sophocles, 45; for Marlowe, 70; for Charlotte Brontë, −11. The data are too fragmentary to support any conclusive argument, but such as they are they point consistently in one direction. The figures for the three male authors are grouped high on the positive side, while that for the one female author is on the negative side and definitely separated from the others. Thus for our small sample it is true that the sex of the author agrees with the predominant sex of his or her shadow community of human figures. Should we infer that this is the rule? If we think about the ordinary social experience of people and how they are more likely to be thrown into frequent contact with members of their own sex and are more inclined to identify with members of their own sex than with members of the other, our present data are theoretically satisfying and the inference of a universal rule seems reasonable. But the data are really very scrappy; we can entertain the suggested rule only as hypothesis. As for Shakespeare himself, however, unless we suppose that the conditions of production in the Elizabethan theater warped his natural inclinations, we must conclude that his personality, so far as it can be characterized by the contents of his imagination, was strongly masculine.

In the column where lovers are set over against nonlovers the scores range from −100 to 59, with most of them on the minus side; the mean is −29. The proper inference from these data would seem to be that romance was not a leading concern of Shakespeare's; or that at least there was a great deal within his personality besides an interest in sexual love. Even if attention is confined to the sixteen plays here classified under comedy and romance, it turns out that the mean value of this index is slightly on the negative side, meaning that in those plays too the nonlovers tend to outweigh the lovers. The average value in this category for Charlotte Brontë, who was scarcely licentious, is 36, which furnishes an interesting contrast to Shakespeare's —29.

In the life-death column the scores range from —61 to 100, and the mean is 54. This figure is not far off from that of Sophocles, which is 60. But all the seven plays of Sophocles are tragedies; and it would be more correct to compare with them Shakespeare's sixteen tragedies and histories, which have an average of 10. The great tragedian of Greece loads his stage with death less than does Shakespeare, to whom in this connection the epithet "gentle Will" [7] scarcely applies.

In the column for violence and nonviolence the scores range from —100 to 94, almost from one limit to the other, and have a mean of —9. Again it is questionable whether the epithet "gentle Will" is exactly appropriate. The average is slightly on the side of nonviolence, but only slightly, and the swing from the one side to the other is very impressive. Once more it is impossible to assess the influence of stage conventions and the demands of the job of being chief playwright for a company which had to offer a varied fare to its public, but if these considerations were comfortably out of the way we should have to judge that Shakespeare was subject to decided shifts of mood, a capacity of his which must have been largely responsible for Voltaire's calling him "grand fou." [8]

What is the effect of time on the traits here examined? There is either no effect or it is too slight to be confirmed by statistical test. Specifically, if the plays are taken by five-year periods, the average values by periods are: for the sex category, 55, 69, 48, 69; for the love category, —7, —24, —46, —58; for the life category, 62, 57, 15, 74; and for the violence category, —37, —9, —2, —2. The series which at first sight most clearly promises to show a significant time trend is that for the love category; furthermore, the direction of the

7. I realize that "gentle" as used by Shakespeare and in his day meant more than "mild," but it is that implication of the word (which was also Elizabethan) which I have in mind here.

8. Quoted from Lee, *A Life of William Shakespeare*, p. 621.

trend toward a lessening of interest in sexual love seems appropriate for an aging man. But though the series is consistent and spans a fairly wide range of values, it turns out that the variation of the individual values on which the averages are based is so great that it cannot be maintained with much certainty that a regular trend is actually present. To be specific, application of analysis of variance yields an F of 1.79 which falls far short of the F of 2.95 required to demonstrate significant differences between the averages at the 5 per cent level of confidence. We must conclude, therefore, that no conspicuous change with respect to these traits occurred during the twenty years of authorship between about twenty-eight and forty-eight years of age.

On the view that the traits under investigation were after all the expressions of a unified organism, it seemed legitimate to ask the question whether they were significantly bound together in any way. The answer is partly contained in Table 4, which exhibits the degree of association between the various trait indices in terms of chi square. Two of the combinations fail to show significant association; the other four—three with chi squares of 6.12 and one with a chi square of 21.12—can be accepted as significantly associated at the 2 per cent level of confidence or better. Interpreted, the significant figures mean: that maleness and violence tend to go together; that love tends to be accompanied by life and nonviolence; and that violence tends to go with death. There is certainly nothing startling or perverse about these particular associations; they sound very commonplace. Our principle of personality projection then leads us to deduce that the organization of Shakespeare's personality did not in these respects depart from the ordinary organization of human society itself, and we become aware once more of the essential human normalcy of Shakespeare. It is well to remind ourselves that there are probably authors in whom love, for example, would be contrariwise associated with death and violence.

TABLE 4

	L—NL	L—D	V—NV
M—F	1.12	3.12	6.12
L—NL		6.12	6.12
L—D			21.12

It may be objected by some readers that the highest chi square in the table was perhaps more a function of the judgments involved than of tendencies in Shakespeare. That is to say, the likelihood of judging a character to be violent is increased by noting that he kills another character within the play, so that to some degree the estimate of violence and the estimate of death are two sides of one estimate. There is some truth in this, but not complete truth; for example, there is the play *Henry V* in which the violence estimate is very high (because most of the characters are engaging by natural inclination in war) and yet the death weight is low, and there is *Romeo and Juliet* in which the death weight exceeds the life weight (and is far above the over-all average) while the violence weight is less than the nonviolence weight. As has already been mentioned there was inevitable subjectivity in the judgments of both violence and love; but a serious attempt was made to keep the judgments of all four categories of traits independent of one another, and at the time of making the judgments there was no theory in my mind one way or another in regard to the associations to be expected among the traits. While I disclaim any intentional biasing of the results, I readily admit that it would be ideal if all judgments of traits in a study of this kind or in the clinic could be based upon the independent judgments of a number of judges.

There is another way of looking at the associations exhibited in Table 4. The points of the scattergrams on which the above chi squares were calculated showed in some cases a decided tendency to cluster; and it gradually became evident that some of this was due to the existence of the two classes of play upon which I commented previously when the distribution of character weights was under discussion. In Table 5, therefore, the data contained in Table 3 have been rearranged to facilitate comparison of the tragedies and histories with the comedies and romances. At a glance one sees that there are striking differences between the two sets of plays when grouped in this way, in part obviously to be expected, in part not so obviously. In every case the difference between one average and another is significant at above the 1 per cent level of confidence. It has already been noted that the tragedy-history average of total character weight is significantly less than that for comedy and romance. The following comparisons are even more

TABLE 5

TRAGEDIES AND HISTORIES

Play	Total of 12	$\dfrac{M-F}{Total}$	$\dfrac{L-NL}{Total}$	$\dfrac{L-D}{Total}$	$\dfrac{V-NV}{Total}$
RIII	277	47	−100	−33	30
RJ	451	33	−12	−7	−8
RII	316	82	−26	37	15
J	451	72	−87	26	67
1 HIV	448	92	−46	36	50
2 HIV	390	87	−100	41	20
HV	235	100	−15	91	94
JC	282	92	−92	−26	78
H	254	82	28	−62	35
TC	570	83	−34	87	53
O	310	59	−7	−61	41
L	459	67	−94	16	21
M	291	53	−100	−18	56
AC	350	47	2	−49	41
C	385	80	−100	53	61
TofA	258	100	−100	22	33
Mean	*358*	*74*	*−57*	*10*	*43*

COMEDIES AND ROMANCES

Play	Total of 12	$\dfrac{M-F}{Total}$	$\dfrac{L-NL}{Total}$	$\dfrac{L-D}{Total}$	$\dfrac{V-NV}{Total}$
CE	611	44	6	100	−100
TS	377	74	29	100	−47
TGV	533	46	25	100	−59
LLL	418	65	35	100	−100
MSND	744	49	24	100	−100
MV	419	38	34	100	−71
MAAN	585	61	−8	100	−81
AYL	364	13	59	100	−29
TN	703	35	7	100	−77
MWW	559	40	−35	100	−49
AWEW	549	27	−43	100	−94
MM	300	45	−34	100	−75
P	300	51	−25	100	−71
Cy	513	50	−34	76	42
WT	427	52	−14	92	−30
T	319	83	−72	100	−45
Mean	*483*	*48*	*−3*	*98*	*−62*

definitely significant: tragedies and histories are higher than comedies and romances in male weight, lower in lover weight, higher in
death weight, and higher in violence weight. While the difference
in respect to death and violence would seem to be almost inevitable
from the very conception of the two classes of play, it is less obvious
that the conception necessitates the differences in love, maleness,
and total character weight. But for Shakespeare at any rate it is
clear that the formula for differentiating tragedy-history from
comedy-romance is partly expressed in these five differences. The
next question is whether this formula was a conscious one; and the
next after that whether the admission that it was would vitiate the
theory that Shakespeare's personality was being exhibited in his
plays. The problem arises because it is often supposed that a writer
can adopt any formula whatsoever and, regardless of personality,
turn out a convincing piece of work according to the blueprint and
to order. In a more sophisticated form the theory holds that the
work of an individual author is the consequence of the literary conventions and demands of the time. Sidney Lee's interpretation of
the *Sonnets* as a cool, impersonal exercise in a very artificial current
tradition is an example of this line of thinking; E. E. Stoll's *Art and
Artifice in Shakespeare,* both in title and content, is another. For
my part, I believe on the one hand that the writer's subjection and
capacity for subjection to convention have been exaggerated, and
on the other that personality should not be conceived of as simply
what remains over after social conventions have been subtracted
but should be understood as including those conventions. As R. B.
Cattell has recently remarked: "When the individual can sufficiently discount his primary narcism he perceives, as Wells has
lucidly pointed out in *The Illusion of Personality,* that an astonishing amount of his private mental furniture is a public gift, and that
the very structure of personality is largely the result of his position
in a field of biological and social events." [9] More extended discussion of these matters will have to be deferred to a later chapter.

There is one other feature of Table 5 which deserves attention. It
was noted earlier that when all the plays are considered together
there is the hint of a steady temporal decline in lover weight but
the apparent trend does not bear up under statistical analysis. In
the present table the previously rejected trend reappears with more

9. *Personality,* p. 662.

substantiality in the comedies and romances. As a matter of fact lover weight declines in accord with the temporal order of the plays regularly enough to yield a correlation coefficient of .76, which is sufficiently high to justify acceptance of the trend, since it quite decidedly exceeds the 1 per cent level of confidence. This is not a contradiction of the previous statistical conclusion; it is merely that we seem to have extracted the trend in purer form from a selected class of plays—plays which perhaps were in general less resistant to time changes in the personality than the other class. In interpretation I can offer no more than previously: the trend, if worth accepting, does harmonize with what we should expect to happen to the sexual interests of an aging man.

CHAPTER 4. SHAKESPEARE'S
PRINCIPAL CHARACTERS

1

To COMPREHEND Shakespeare's plays as dynamic wholes means to understand the characters and their mutual relations. Ideally both phases of this task would be accomplished together; that is to say, both the personal qualities of the characters and the nature of the actions by which they affect one another would be grasped in one conception, for personal qualities are revealed in action and the action takes its meaning from the nature of the actor. In a fashion we do achieve just this kind of total comprehension when we enjoy a play as sympathetic readers or spectators. But the knowledge so obtained is difficult to communicate in a formal analysis. Nothing more ambitious shall be aimed at in this chapter than a rough blocking out of some of the major qualities of the leading Shakespearean characters, keeping always in mind the possible relevance of such information to the assessment of the author's personality.

The table of character weights (Table 1) assists us here by affording a uniform and objective kind of guidance in the selection of principal characters and giving us at the same time an estimate of how dominant they are in their respective plays, at least from a quantitative point of view.

Taking the top-ranking characters in chronological order, we have the following list: Gloucester, Antipholus of Syracuse, Petruchio, Valentine, Biron, Romeo, King Richard II, Bottom, the Bastard, Portia, Hotspur, Falstaff, Benedick, King Henry V, Brutus, Rosalind, Viola, Hamlet, Falstaff, Troilus, Helena, Duke Vincentio, Iago, King Lear, Macbeth, Antony, Coriolanus, Timon, Pericles, Imogen, Leontes, Prospero. Is it possible to discover any one prominent trait in all of these characters which would justify our concluding that as a group they represent under various names some important single component of Shakespeare's personality? I think not. Logically, then, upon our premises it must be concluded that no stable dominant element is perceptible in him. Yet it would be going too far to speak of an infinite variety here, or even of thirty-two fundamentally different components.

First of all, it may be noted that the five women have some likeness to one another. They are charming, flawless, noble; and in the dramatic structures which they dominate, hostilities and sufferings are uniformly cleared away, largely through their courage, purity, and loyalty. They are tenderness and justice, justice tempered with mercy, and Portia and Helena in particular are represented as exerting healing powers, the one legal, the other physical.

But the women constitute only about a sixth of the total. The remaining five-sixths, with the partial exception of Duke Vincentio and Prospero, must be described quite differently. For the most part they are characters whose cleverness and power are put to ignoble uses, and they are frequently thwarted, diverted from their original intentions, baffled and punished and destroyed. The lovers among them are a sorry spectacle: either they surrender their original inclination and love against their principles, or if they love willingly they run up against insuperable obstacles or conduct themselves atrociously. Of the former variety are Antipholus, Valentine, Biron, Benedick; of the latter, Petruchio, Romeo, Bottom, Hamlet, Falstaff (of *Merry Wives*), Troilus, Antony, Pericles, Leontes. Those who are motivated by the possession or desire of power—Gloucester, Richard II, the Bastard, Hotspur, Henry V, Lear, Macbeth, Coriolanus, Timon—are predominantly misanthropic and treacherous. The theme of treachery, indeed, is prominent in Shakespeare, and it has several striking incarnations, notably Iago among the top characters; but Brutus, Macbeth, and Henry V (a subtle case and disputable) are treacherous, too, although treachery is more incidental with them than with Iago, who cultivates it as a fine art. On the whole, the principal male characters exhibit noticeable weaknesses on the moral side, though gifted with much wit and energy. If compelled to sum up the very diverse qualities of these leading male characters in a single phrase, I should speak of an alert suspicious hostility.

The pertinence of the phrase may often be illustrated, if not proved, out of the mouths of the characters themselves; for Shakespeare's characters often describe themselves. In fact, Schücking regards what they say about themselves as the safest guide to correctly understanding them.[1] Thus, from the famous opening speech of Gloucester:

> I, that am rudely stamped, and want love's majesty
> To strut before a wanton ambling nymph . . .
> I am determined to prove a villain
> And hate the idle pleasures of these days.
> Plots have I laid, inductions dangerous,
> By drunken prophecies, libels and dreams,
> To set my brother Clarence and the king
> In deadly hate the one against the other:
> And if King Edward be as true and just
> As I am subtle, false and treacherous,
> This day should Clarence closely be mewed up . . .
>
> (RIII, I, 1, 16 ff.)

It is notorious that the action of the play bears out this self-description unerringly.

Antipholus of Syracuse is no such villain, but he is discontented and suspicious, saying:

> He that commends me to my own content
> Commends me to the thing I cannot get.
> I to the world am like a drop of water
> That in the ocean seeks another drop,
> Who, falling there to find his fellow forth,
> Unseen, inquisitive, confounds himself. (CE, I, 2, 33 ff.)

And later, after his first confusion by Dromio of Ephesus:

> Upon my life, by some device or other
> The villain is o'er-raught of all my money.
> They say this town is full of cozenage,
> As, nimble jugglers that deceive the eye,
> Dark-working sorcerers that change the mind,
> Soul-killing witches that deform the body,
> Disguised cheaters, prating mountebanks,
> And many such-like liberties of sin:
> If it prove so, I will be gone the sooner. (CE, I, 2, 95 ff.)

Petruchio, on his first appearance, has a senseless quarrel with his servant, and in the next moment is announcing his intention of

---

1. *Character Problems in Shakespeare's Plays, passim,* but especially p. 30.

laying hold of a wife, like a pirate boarding a ship for the sake of
the booty on board:

> and therefore, if thou know
> One rich enough to be Petruchio's wife,
> As wealth is burden of my wooing dance,
> Be she as foul as was Florentius' love,
> As old as Sibyl and as curst and shrewd
> As Socrates' Xanthippe, or a worse,
> She moves me not, or not removes, at least,
> Affection's edge in me, were she as rough
> As are the swelling Adriatic seas:
> I come to wive it wealthily in Padua. (TS, I, 2, 66 ff.)

The descriptive phrase "alert suspicious hostility" does not belong to Valentine, but more nearly to his deceitful friend, Proteus;
but it should be considered, nevertheless, that Valentine at his
setting out to "hunt after honour" is very scornful of love, which
he regards as pure folly, and at the end of the play has allied himself with a band of outlaws whose hand is against every man's,
recommending himself to them as a murderer.

Biron is a scoffer at every sort of vow, seeing in the study to which
he is pledging himself only an opportunity to increase his cleverness
to the point where he may, "having sworn too hard a keeping oath,
Study to break it and not keep my troth," (LLL, I, 1, 65 f.) and
otherwise by-pass the rules and his promises; and like Petruchio,
and like Benedick to follow, he is most charmed by a woman with
whom he can have a good fight and be forsworn in loving.

The phrase again does not fit Romeo, though he does murder his
man; nor Richard II, though he is untrustworthy; nor Bottom.

But the Bastard, Philip Faulconbridge, though his very bluffness
wins him admirers, is a bloodthirsty warrior who has no faith in the
world and who announces that he is going to make an ideal of that
which makes the world faithless—namely, money, which clinks
continually in Shakespeare:

> Since kings break faith upon commodity,
> Gain, be my lord, for I will worship thee. (J, II, 1, 597 f.)

Hotspur likewise is a fierce and high-tempered man of war,
whose whole action in the play is motivated by his hatred of the
king for refusal to ransom his brother-in-law, rightful heir to the

throne, and who accordingly turns rebel and plots with the enemies
of the English against him; and he is quarrelsome and suspicious
even with his friends, who caution him:

> In faith, my lord, you are too wilful-blame . . .
> You must needs learn, lord, to amend this fault:
> Though sometimes it show greatness, courage, blood,—
> And that's the dearest grace it renders you,—
> Yet oftentimes it doth present harsh rage,
> Defect of manners, want of government,
> Pride, haughtiness, opinion, and disdain:
> The least of which haunting a nobleman
> Loseth men's hearts and leaves behind a stain
> Upon the beauty of all parts besides. (I HIV, III, 1, 177 ff.)

He comments on his own nature when he is quarreling with Glen-
dower over a division of land:

> I'll give thrice so much land
> To any well-deserving friend;
> But in the way of bargain, mark ye me,
> I'll cavil on the ninth part of a hair. (I HIV, III, 1, 137 ff.)

Such generosity as he may possess is guarded well by suspiciousness
and a hot temper.

Falstaff, the sweet Jack Falstaff of *Henry IV*, is so well known
that quotations are scarcely needed to remind us that his occupation is theft and his natural vocation inspired lying, and that, in
the words of the prince: "But, sirrah, there's no room for faith,
truth, nor honesty in this bosom of thine; it is filled up with guts
and midriff." (1 HIV, III, 2, 171 ff.) To be sure, Falstaff's hostility
is not of Hotspur's dashing variety, but it is there—in verbal brow-
beating, if not very heroically in swordplay.

Benedick, "professed tyrant to their sex," distrusts women, and
is sharp-tongued to and about them. He sneers: "That a woman
conceived me, I thank her; that she brought me up, I likewise give
her most humble thanks: but that I will have a recheat winded in
my forehead, or hang my bugle in an invisible baldrick, all women
shall pardon me. Because I will not do them the wrong to mistrust
any, I will do myself the right to trust none; and the fine is, for
which I may go the finer, I will live a bachelor." (MAAN, I, 1,
240 ff.)

Henry V is almost as great an enigma to the critics as Hamlet; in a way, greater—because where Hamlet raises questions about the nature of his own intentions, Henry V raises them about the intentions of his creator. In short, though on the surface his personality and his behavior are such as to arouse the displeasure of the Romantics from Hazlitt to Bradley and Goddard and to repel the tougher-minded critics of the historical school like Tillyard, who finds him cold, lubberly, and coarse with his "aspect of iron," [2] or like Schücking, who cannot suppress an unexpected nausea at the "gross hypocrisy" of his relations (as Prince Hal) with Falstaff [3]— obeisance is now continually made and enjoined to the *conception* of a noble hero-king which Shakespeare is imagined to have aimed at and failed to get. But how much should we be concerned about intentions, about which it is difficult to be sure, when they are botched in the execution? If Shakespeare meant to have Henry appear the royal nobleman but spoils it a little by causing him to break the heart of a companion whom he has persuaded us to love in spite of his wickedness; if he meant to show him as the mirror of chivalry, and yet on the battlefield has him commit all the brutalities of war without restraint and fail in argument with his loyal soldiers to justify his martial cause; if he meant to give us a glimpse of a bluff, hearty, man-of-action lover and actually succeeds in giving us a brutal conqueror who lays on like a butcher in his wooing and yet never takes his politic eye off the sweet lady's dowry of cities: then perhaps we had better take just what comes up, and admit that Shakespeare, whatever he intended, produced in fact something cold, hard, hypocritical, butcherly, and treacherous, with an unpleasant habit of eloquence. We need not worry about whether this is the picture of an ideal monarch; as it turns out in Shakespeare's handling of it, the picture is of a man in armor who cares for nothing but conquest and who, steel hard as his armor, is

2. *Shakespeare's History Plays*, p. 311.

3. Especially pp. 219 and 222. Schücking, to be sure, does not conclude that the prince actually is hypocritical. Rather, he implies that we blunder, or that Shakespeare in his partiality for his hero blundered, when we get any such impression. Speaking of the notorious monologue at the end of Act 1, Scene 2, of the first part of *Henry IV*, he says: "If we were to take it literally it would stamp the Prince's character with the mark of gross hypocrisy, which was certainly not intended." Still, Schücking has to struggle hard to rid himself of the naïve reaction.

willing to sacrifice any human being or principle to get it. The question at issue is not at all one of how much we should like or dislike Henry, or how Shakespeare felt about him, but what the qualities are which produce our reactions: repulsion in some of us, as in myself; admiration in others, as in Sir Sidney Lee, who wrote: "Alone in Shakespeare's gallery of English monarchs does Henry's portrait evoke at once a joyous sense of satisfaction in the high potentialities of human character and a sense of pride among Englishmen that a man of his mettle is of English race." [4] Theoretical problems of various kinds are raised by the present considerations and will have to be discussed more at length elsewhere. But for the moment I shall simply state that, in spite of the very contradictory affective reactions produced by Henry, his nature can be epitomized not unfairly by the phrase "alert suspicious hostility," or, if that seems to dishonor him, by something comparable, like "wide-awake unsentimental aggressiveness."

Brutus is a traitor, an honorable man but nevertheless a traitor, who professes to love the man he betrays. He is chronologically the first in our list to combine a generally admirable character with a willingness to commit murder.

> This was the noblest Roman of them all:
> All the conspirators save only he
> Did that they did in envy of great Caesar:
> He only, in a general honest thought
> And common good to all, made one of them. (JC, V, 5, 68 ff.)

There is a kind of public truth in this summary of the matter; but there is a private truth, also, which is not to be overlooked. Prior to the action against the Caesar whom he loved, he became moody, indifferent to his friend Cassius, apparently misanthropic. To a criticism from Cassius he replies, in explanation:

> Be not deceived: if I have veiled my look,
> I turn the trouble of my countenance
> Merely upon myself. Vexed I am
> Of late with passions of some difference,
> Conceptions only proper to myself,
> Which give some soil perhaps to my behaviours;
> But let not therefore my good friends be grieved—

4. P. 252.

> Among which number, Cassius, be you one—
> Nor construe any farther my neglect,
> Than that poor Brutus, with himself at war,
> Forgets the shows of love to other men. (JC, I, 2, 38 ff.)

In these words there is a forecast of Hamlet, who likewise, after brooding over private and far-reaching thoughts, about which we know more than about those of Brutus, bursts into violent and bloody action—action which again involves a ruler, with others besides, particularly Ophelia and her old father. However justice may be with him, Hamlet is also technically a traitor in warring against the king. Nor does his suspicious hostility stop with the king: Ophelia experiences it in cruel degree. It should be noted that the infection of his soul, which has its professed origin in grief over his father's death and his mother's betrayal of his father, spreads out over all his relations: no human being can any longer interest him, nor anything in the world. The world and he are completely at odds; and his suspiciousness twists everything to suit his hostility—Rosencrantz and Guildenstern, properly; and poor Ophelia, most improperly.[5]

The Falstaff of *Merry Wives of Windsor* is a scurrilous buffoon who lacks the intelligence and peculiar charm of his predecessor, the companion of Prince Hal.

Troilus alters in character in the course of his play. Pictured at first as a brave, romantic young man, he becomes, after his experience with Cressida, as mad and ruthless a warrior as any in the list. He scorns the rules of chivalry which his brother Hector so nobly observes, and, calling it all fool's play, he cries:

> For the love of all the gods,
> Let's leave the hermit pity with our mothers,
> And when we have our armours buckled on,
> The venomed vengeance ride upon our swords. (TC, V, 3, 48 ff.)

Of Duke Vincentio it cannot be said that he is marked by hostility, but he is severe and in a high degree suspicious; and he has his suspicions justified in finding that his deputy Angelo is guilty of breaking the laws which the duke has imposed on Vienna—laws,

5. Madariaga, who doubts Ophelia's virginity and innocence, would consider this remark too sentimental. See his book, *On Hamlet*.

that is, against too great freedom between the sexes. He finally abates his austere judgments against Angelo and other offenders only on the plea of a woman. One offender whom he cannot pardon is Lucio—

> You, sirrah, that knew me for a fool, a coward,
> One all of luxury, an ass, a madman—(MM, V, 1, 505 ff.)

a very curious slander, which might better have been originated by one of Prince Hal's companions. Although in the end the duke stays his hand, the threat of his judgment hanging over the heads of the offenders throughout the play is dramatically more terrifying than its immediate execution could have been.

About Iago there can be no doubt. He is the epitome of envious hatred, full of suspicion and malice.

> I hate the Moor;
> And it is thought abroad, that 'twixt my sheets
> He hath done my office: I know not if't be true;
> But I, for mere suspicion in that kind,
> Will do as if for surety. He holds me well;
> The better shall my purpose work on him. (O, I, 3, 392 ff.)

Lear, in Kent's phrase, is hideously rash; and for a little plain speaking, he disowns his daughter Cordelia, and banishes Kent— after threatening to kill him on the spot. Goneril and Regan in private conversation acknowledge his gross error of judgment in driving away Cordelia, and comment:

> *Reg.* 'Tis the infirmity of his age: yet he hath ever but slenderly known himself.
>
> *Gon.* The best and soundest of his time hath been but rash; then must we look to receive from his age, not alone the imperfections of long-engraffed condition, but therewithal the unruly waywardness that infirm and choleric years bring with them. (L, I, 1, 296 ff.)

The unfilial treatment received from his daughters drives him into madness; but then he was mad before, splenetic, and lacking in judgment.

Macbeth, as he says, has only "vaulting ambition" to urge him to the first murder; but thereafter he is goaded by suspicion and fear. For Macbeth's murders haunt him. He plants spies in the houses of his potential enemies; and having got into the way of murder, he says:

> I am in blood
> Stepped in so far that, should I wade no more,
> Returning were as tedious as go o'er. (M, III, 4, 137 ff.)

In the end he is thoroughly hardened:

> I have almost forgot the taste of fears:
> The time has been, my senses would have cooled
> To hear a night-shriek; and my fell of hair
> Would at a dismal treatise rouse and stir
> As life were in it: I have supped full with horrors;
> Direness, familiar to my slaughterous thoughts,
> Cannot once start me. (M, V, 5, 9 ff.)

Antony, when we meet him at Alexandria, is changed from what he was in the past—a ferocious warrior. Nor would it be correct to say that he is suspicious or ungenerous, though traces of aggressiveness remain. His magnanimity appears in Philo's disapproving description of him, as well as in his actions throughout the play:

> Nay, but this dotage of our general's
> O'erflows the measure: those his goodly eyes,
> That o'er the files and musters of the war
> Have glowed like plated Mars, now bend, now turn,
> The office and devotion of their view
> Upon a tawny front: his captain's heart,
> Which in the scuffles of great fights hath burst
> The buckles on his breast, reneges all temper,
> To cool a gipsy's lust. (AC, I, 1, 1 ff.)

There is no meanness in him; and so he cannot be allied with some of the characters preceding.

Coriolanus, on the contrary, who is likewise the great warrior of high pride and noble bearing, is lacking in generosity just as he is deficient in sexual passion. Contempt, coldness, distrust of the motives of others are signalized by nearly every motion. All this is particularly evident in his dealings with the people of Rome.

> Who deserves greatness
> Deserves your hate; and your affections are
> A sick man's appetite, who desires most that
> Which would increase his evil. He that depends

Upon your favours swims with fins of lead
And hews down oaks with rushes. Hang ye! Trust ye?
With every minute you do change a mind,
And call him noble that was now your hate,
Him vile that was your garland. (C, I, 1, 180 ff.)

He is proud and uncompromisingly egotistic. Banished from the
Rome which he has accused of untrustworthiness, he turns traitor
to it; and then, under the influence of his mother's pleading, relents
at the last moment and dies as a traitor to the cause of Aufidius,
whom he had embraced as an ally. Because of the very nobility for
which he is admired, the dauntless heroism that has no admixture
of love and no patience with the needs of the common people, he
is thus twice a traitor.

Timon, again, is a nobleman who because of his city's ingratitude
to him betrays it. At first blandly indifferent to the defects of other
men and the limits of his own power, he becomes, upon discovering
himself in debt and out of friends, immediately misanthropic and
as thersitical as Thersites (who, incidentally, occupies a good deal
of space in *Troilus and Cressida*), and he cynically uses the gold he
happens to find in the woods to support the banished Alcibiades in
his attack on Athens, the city which has excluded them. When Alcibiades asks him who he is, he answers:

I am Misanthropos, and hate mankind.
For thy part, I do wish thou wert a dog,
That I might love thee something. (T of A, IV, 3, 53 ff.)

He rails at all mankind and every human occupation. Oddly
enough, considering that there has been no previous sign of interest
in them, he devotes a very large part of what he has to say against
the human race in defaming women, damning them all as whores
actual or potential. He instructs Alcibiades to spare no one when
he has conquered the city:

Let not thy sword skip one:
Pity not honoured age for his white beard;
He is an usurer: strike me the counterfeit matron;
It is her habit only that is honest,
Herself's a bawd: let not the virgin's cheek
Make soft thy trenchant sword; for those milk-paps,
That through the window-bars bore at men's eyes,

> Are not within the leaf of pity writ,
> But set them down horrible traitors: spare not the babe,
> Whose dimpled smiles from fools exhaust their mercy;
> Think it a bastard, whom the oracle
> Hath doubtfully pronounced thy throat shall cut,
> And mince it sans remorse: swear against objects;
> Put armour on thine ears and on thine eyes;
> Whose proof, nor yells of mothers, maids, nor babes,
> Nor sight of priests in holy vestments bleeding,
> Shall pierce a jot. There's gold to pay thy soldiers:
> Make large confusion; and, thy fury spent,
> Confounded be thyself! (T of A, IV, 3, 110 ff.)

Loathing for the human species reaches its intensest and most comprehensive expression in Timon.

Pericles is no such misanthropist, though he has cause to be; for in contesting for the daughter of Antiochus he makes the dreadful discovery that she and her father live in incest, and he must, to save his life, become a homeless wanderer to avoid the enraged king's vengeance. Later, his wife is lost at sea (in childbirth), and his daughter, placed in the hands of friends, is betrayed by the foster mother, and escapes murder only to be imprisoned in a brothel. These details are not known to Pericles in full; but when he makes his reappearance in the play, his mood of depression (which is dramatically connected with these events) is so deep that he

> for this three months hath not spoken
> To any one, nor taken sustenance
> But to prorogue his grief. (P, V, 1, 24 ff.)

We can hardly speak of hostility in him, as we can in others, but the suspicious dread of men is pronounced, and in his melancholy he withdraws himself far from them.

The ultimate in morbid suspiciousness is attained by Leontes, who wants to kill his wife, his children, and his dearest friend. As so often in Shakespeare, the ill will of Leontes originates in doubt concerning the fidelity of his woman—a doubt entirely unjust and unfounded, except in his own imagination. Paulina charges him:

> Thy tyranny
> Together working with thy jealousies,
> Fancies too weak for boys, too green and idle

> For girls of nine, O, think what they have done
> And then run mad indeed, stark mad! (WT, III, 2, 180 ff.)

He exhibits the distorted hatred of a paranoiac.

In Prospero the hatred is held in check, is mastered indeed by forgiveness; but he regards himself as the innocent victim of persecution and betrayal, and the studious cultivation of his mind has been aimed at the acquisition of magical power in order to be able to hold his enemies at his mercy and compel them to restore his kingdom to him. Also, his self-control is not perfect: the gentle Miranda's sympathy and innocent love have to be opposed to his power continually. He accuses Ferdinand (as a kind of test, to be sure) of coming to the island as a spy to win it from him, "the lord on't"; he does not neglect his opportunity to make his enemies suffer, in body and in conscience; and passion works in him strongly when he recalls the conspiracy of Caliban and his confederates against his life —so strongly that Ferdinand and Miranda are dismayed by it, and Prospero has to explain:

> Sir, I am vexed;
> Bear with my weakness; my old brain is troubled:
> Be not disturbed with my infirmity:
> If you be pleased, retire into my cell
> And there repose; a turn or two I'll walk,
> To still my beating mind. (T, IV, 1, 158 ff.)

2

Ignoring exceptions and simplifying to the utmost, with whatever exaggeration that may entail, we may think of the top-ranking Shakespearean characters as one-sixth gentle loyal women and five-sixths proud undependable aggressive men. What can we make of this? If we accept the statement as fact and contemplate it for the moment without wavering from the position that the dramas reflect Shakespeare's personality, and without making any concession to the possibility of there being various angles of reflection, plus refractive distortions, we should conclude that while Shakespeare was usually masculine in his outlook there were times at which feminine elements rose to dominance. Such a conclusion would harmonize with the homosexual trends detected in the *Son-*

nets, and with the views of biologists and psychoanalysts on the bisexuality of human nature in general. I might add that there is confirming evidence in the work of Charlotte Brontë and D. H. Lawrence.[6] In one of the four novels of Charlotte Brontë the top-ranking character is male; this is William Crimsworth of *The Professor,* the earliest of the four. Back of this fact is a history of several years of definite masculine striving by Charlotte during childhood and adolescence, when in the imaginative play with her brother and sisters she constantly assumed the role of a male hero, especially that of the duke of Wellington. In the novels of D. H. Lawrence, several times the principal character is a woman, notably Alvina of *The Lost Girl,* and in Lawrence's case there is strong evidence for a corresponding latent homosexuality of more than ordinary amount. A similar inference in regard to Shakespeare would be plausible.[7]

A basic theoretical problem arises here, however, which must not be passed over in silence. In self-analysis and in our analysis of others we find or assume a perfectly simple, unitary, conscious center to which judgments, attitudes, intentions, and actions are constantly being referred. Each one of us speaks of himself as "I" and ordinarily is aware of a considerable degree of continuity and stability in what he designates by that pronoun. Indeed, we are surprised and disturbed by any marked departure from the presumed unity of the self. "I was not myself," we say, after catching ourselves in some unusual emotion or action. We expect, we demand, an ideal unity of opinion in others from one occasion to the

---

6. See my papers on these authors listed in the Bibliography.

7. It is supposed by the psychoanalysts that, underlying the heterosexuality of the most normal people, there is always some homosexual tendency, i.e., a tendency to develop feelings and attitudes toward members of the same sex which, if unchecked, would be preparatory to sexual solicitation and intercourse. In some, who are not genuine homosexuals, this tendency is stronger and closer to the surface. The effect of this degree of latent homosexuality is to introduce a peculiar warmth and intensity into the friendly relations with members of one's own sex, and often to disturb heterosexual attachments. Paranoid complications are not unusual. Here I am drawing a parallel, for the sake of hypothesis, between certain features of the work of D. H. Lawrence, which seem to be connected with homosexual tendency in his case, and similar features of Shakespeare's work. Whether the inference which seems justified for Lawrence is also justified for Shakespeare is, of course, a matter for debate; and I mean to imply no more. It is a hypothesis which could be tested out by a systematic study of a large sample of authors.

next; and when we fail to get it we are likely to accuse them of deception, double-dealing, two-facedness, and continue to believe that in spite of the evidence there is a unitary self behind the various disguises, which is conscious of its own nature and of its fraudulence. It is this ideally conscious and causal center which we want to know when we are trying to evaluate any behavior. Was the handclasp sincere? Were the words a sneer or a compliment? Can the promise be depended upon? All such questions probe beyond the act to the actor, to the "I" which expresses itself in the act. Here I am not concerned with the ultimate truth of this conception of a unitary "I"; rather, I should like to settle (difficult or impossible as that may be) the relationship between what is so designated and the dramatis personae of the imagination.

Let us begin by considering a sort of imagination which most of us are capable of (it is realized that some individuals will not be able to recall such experiences, as Galton found to his surprise many years ago [8])—the sort which consists of reconstructing in imagery moments of the past. One visualizes, for instance, the members of his family seated around the three sides of a table in a public dining room, catches glimpses of objects on the table, of the view out the windows, of people passing or stopping in little conversational clusters, with perhaps fleeting vivid details of this and that not clearly localized; and one remembers but does not visualize himself seated on the fourth side of the table, and remembers also getting up and going to a serving table to pour a cup of coffee—remembers this largely through the visualization of other objects and a changed point of view in regard to the total scene. In such a case imagination supplies a scene and fills it with actors for the eye to enjoy (or as if for the eye) and includes oneself in the midst of it all, though not visually, both as actor and as spectator; the little fragment of a drama is organized around oneself, and oneself is the most constantly present feature of it, though not necessarily the most exciting. Now, suppose that by some extension and elaboration of this sort of thing one composed a story for publication: the "I" would naturally appear as the narrator and as such be present throughout, and now and then might join conspicuously in the action. As a matter of fact many published stories do have just this

8. Cf. *Inquiries into Human Faculty and Its Development.*

kind of structure. In such stories the top-ranking character in terms of page count would obviously be the author's "I."

But stories are not likely to be purely reproductive of the past. Even memory itself, as Bartlett has well shown, is not.[9] Both deliberately and without conscious design changes are introduced which affect details and the configuration of the whole. Among these changes the immediate properties of the narrating "I" may be importantly altered. For example, name, background history, sex, as in Charlotte Brontë's *The Professor*, may be made to diverge from what is, nonpsychologically speaking, proper to the author. By such alterations, however, we do not lose our hold on the author's "I," but merely get to see it in a different light, perhaps in a way preferred by the author, who may for example be expressing a "masculine protest" like Charlotte Brontë. A great deal of experimentation in the imagination with different possible roles in the world is done by many people, not just authors, without their "I" being lost in the process. It is common in daydreaming to bring about some desired variation—sometimes very slight, sometimes fantastically extravagant. And here we pass to the kind of imagination which is ruled over more by desire than by memory.

The daydream differs from imaginative reproduction of the past, where it differs at all, and aside from its characteristic reference to the future, by its relative freedom from reality-concern, and also at times by the greater degree in which the "I" slips away from its familiar properties. There are times when the "I" begins to take on the same independence as the other figures by which it is surrounded; that is, it begins to be a visual object, moving out into the external scene away from the daydreamer himself. Freud actually tried to distinguish between true memories and phantasies mistaken for memories on the basis of visual objectification of the self in the latter case, as opposed to lack of objectification in the former.[10] It is a doubtful criterion, if accuracy of the memory is what one is concerned with; but the fact itself is important—the fact, namely, that one can substitute for himself as center of consciousness a visual image of his body moving about in space. I am not at

9. Cf. *Remembering*.

10. Cf. his early essay (1899), "Screen Memories," in *Collected Papers*, Vol. 5, especially pp. 68 f.

all sure that the dissociation of this projected self from the self that does the dreaming is ever completely effected; but such a projected self put into a story and no longer clearly identified with the author in the role of narrator could certainly perplex the reader who wanted to pick out the author's ego from the collection.

Perhaps the dissociation comes nearest to being accomplished fully in the dream proper, the dream of sleep. Complete dissociation is surely rare; but there are dreams in which, fluctuatingly, a body recognized by the dreamer as his own acts a part without subjective accompaniment, amputated from consciousness of its own as one's hand may be when, as we say, it has "gone to sleep"—or the dreamer may be divided into an observing self and an acting self. Ordinarily, however, neither in the daydream nor in the night-dream is there such isolation of the "I" from the action as can be achieved by the writer at a stroke by the artifice of putting in place of the narrating "I" a character in every other respect the same except that he does not profess to tell the story. The playwright does this more naturally than the novelist, because of the very conditions of theatrical production; or it might be more correct to say that writers attracted to the theater are more inclined to cut the obvious subjective tie with their characters. Even in theatrical productions, however, the device of the narrating actor is not unknown. Ultimately, it is not the particular medium of presentation which determines whether the personal tie between the author and his work will remain in easily detectable form, but rather the ability or inability of the author to dissolve it and launch his characters, including the one nearest to himself as a conscious ego, into independent existence.

Extremely pertinent are the observations of Stephen Dedalus in Joyce's *Portrait of the Artist as a Young Man:*

The simplest epical form is seen emerging out of lyrical literature when the artist prolongs and broods upon himself as the centre of an epical event and this form progresses till the centre of emotional gravity is equidistant from the artist himself and from others. The narrative is no longer purely personal. The personality of the artist passes into the narration itself, flowing round and round the persons and the action like a vital sea. This progress you will see easily in that old English ballad *Turpin Hero,* which begins in the first person and ends in the third person. The dramatic form is reached when the vitality which has flowed and eddied round each person fills every person with such vital force that he or she assumes a proper and intangible esthetic life. The personality of the artist, at first a cry or a cadence or a mood and then a fluid and lambent narrative, finally refines itself out of existence, impersonalizes itself, so to speak. The esthetic image in the dramatic form is life purified in and reprojected from the human imagination. The mystery of esthetic like that of material creation is accomplished. The artist, like the God of the creation, remains within or behind or beyond or above his handiwork, invisible, refined out of existence, indifferent, paring his fingernails.[11]

Let us suppose that the artistic process has terminated in such an ideal state of separation of the work from the author: could any sign remain to distinguish what was originally closest to the author's "I" from the rest? Omitting those properties useful only to someone knowing the author first hand, I can think of two that could persist after the removal of the pronominal indicator—the amount of space occupied by the character, and the amount of his subjectivity.

Very often in novels a character is found who reflects upon himself and upon the action going on around him to a greater degree than the others do. Sometimes this property of subjectivity is about equally shared by more than one character. For example, in Charlotte Brontë's *Shirley*, which is told in the third person, there are two definitely subjective characters—Caroline Helstone, who is of the first rank, and Louis Moore, who is of the sixth. Here is a complication, to be sure; but it is not an utterly baffling one in this case; for the reader familiar with all the novels will recognize Louis as a survival of William Crimsworth, who has top rank in *The Professor* and whose connection with the novelist's "masculine protest" has already been pointed out. But when the property of subjectivity is fairly evenly distributed among many characters, as commonly happens in the plays of Shakespeare, our sign appears to fail us. Characters raised distinctly above their fellows in subjective intensity are not absent in Shakespeare (Hamlet, for instance), but the estimate of relative subjectivity is often a delicate act of judgment.

The other discriminant—the space occupied by the character—is usually present and sufficiently distinct. Unfortunately, it is, if

11. *The Portable James Joyce*, pp. 481 f.

anything, more ambiguous than the property of subjectivity. It is true that in our day-by-day experience the most constant feature of the whole complicated mass is what we call ourselves; true that in the natural direct way of telling about events this constant gives center and meaning to them; and true that when a story is written in first person form, and often when it is not, the representative of the perceiving thinking self dominates the story by the sheer quantity of its presence. The critical and disturbing thought is that it is possible that there are stories from which the author's "I" has been excluded, remaining as much a spectator of the fictional events as the reader, or in which, if present, it occupies a subordinate place. A hypothetical illustration of the latter possibility is *The Merchant of Venice,* in which Antonio, the merchant, has perhaps the best claim as Shakespeare's personal representative, if we allow ourselves to be influenced by the conventional estimates of him; for one might easily imagine the generous melancholy friend of the young Bassanio writing the *Sonnets.* Yet Antonio ranks fourth by weight. Dramatically, of course, he is very important: the function of all the other characters is defined by reference to him, even as the title of the play indicates. Then why should Portia loom so large? Is it not because she is so important to Antonio? She is the cause (through Bassanio) of Antonio's falling into the clutches of Shylock; she is the savior of his life; and she is, perhaps more importantly still, the touchstone against which the quality of Bassanio's love for Antonio is tested and proved pure. We can argue that she outweighs Antonio in just the same way that any highly interesting object which focuses our attention diminishes our self-awareness. A man desires a woman or fears an enemy or desires and fears all at the same time, and in that state of captivation by the object he forgets or almost forgets himself. (The object does not forget the self, however; the object cannot have any value except in the presence of the conscious self, whether that self is self-ignored or not.) If we conclude, then, by admitting that Antonio in this case is or could be the representative of the author's "I," the hypothesis that the top-ranking character necessarily has that function must be given up.

Locating the author's center of consciousness in a thoroughly dramatic work appears to be impossible. At any rate, it cannot be confidently held that the top-ranking character inevitably qualifies for that position. What does this admission do to the method of analysis adopted here? Virtually nothing—so long as our interest is restricted to the nature of the personality components, their relative weights, and the interaction between them. It is only when we desire to assess these components and events with reference to the author's "I" that we run into trouble. Our situation is like that of a person provided with a map showing the sizes of towns and cities, their relative positions, and the distances between them, but without knowledge of where exactly in the whole terrain he is at present located. The map still successfully reveals the organization of the area it represents; but it does not tell us how far we are from the capital city. So with the drama. We do not know how to determine with certainty the position of the author's "I," the usual point of departure for evaluating the significance of other aspects of the personality. If we are willing to take a risk, it is likely that relative subjectivity is a better criterion than relative size, though the two may coincide. Actually, the same problem faces us in assessing the behavior of the people around us every day. In which of their actions are they, to use the current phrase, ego-involved?

I do not want to slight the problem, however, by pointing to its generality. It is immediately and acutely pertinent to the task of analyzing the Shakespearean plays. There is some merit in accepting the testimony of the plays quite literally, and simply deciding, since no indubitable "I" is present in them, that when they were being generated the Shakespearean ego was in eclipse. We get the impression of a pretty consistent self speaking through the *Sonnets;* but we also get the impression that this self was capable of being very greatly dominated by its objects, as illustrated by the opening lines of Sonnet 57:

> Being your slave, what should I do but tend
> Upon the hours and times of your desire?

It may be exactly this capacity of yielding up to what is not the self that makes the complete dramatist. After all, is it not during sleep when selfhood is least clear that everybody turns into a dramatist? A loose personality structure not firmly anchored in an obtrusive ego, or a loosening up of the structure by emotional stress, may be a primary requisite for successful dramatic writing.

3

After the doubts raised by the preceding discussion, it will not be possible to accept the top-ranking character as in every case especially representative of the subjective center of Shakespeare. Is any meaning left then in the earlier statement that the nature of these characters suggested that some bisexuality of attitude existed in him? If the statement is taken as applying to the balance of male and female forces within the personality structure rather than as applying to the conscious outlook, it does have meaning still. It would be going too far to claim more.

Keeping to the same objective assessment, it may be further stated that the nature of the top-ranking male characters indicates that playing the man involved overstriving and insecurity for Shakespeare. It should be noted that nearly half of these characters meet with death. Of the fourteen who survive, nine have important connections with female characters, either as lovers or as fathers of daughters.

On the difference between Shakespeare's men and women Dowden commented: "If Shakespeare ventured upon any generalization about women, it was perhaps this—that the natures of women are usually made up of fewer elements than those of men, but that these elements are ordinarily in juster poise, more fully organized, more coherent and compact; and that, consequently, prompt and efficient action is more a woman's gift than a man's." [12] To appreciate Dowden's remark fully we must remember that it is not simply a "generalization about" with which we are dealing, however; we are dealing with dramatic persons who have arisen in Shakespeare's imagination as the actors in dreams arise, and it turns out that the men so emerging and expressing by their nature and action a part of what is in him are less efficient, less morally pure, and less capable of surviving, than the women. I am speaking still of the top characters. In abstract terms, the men are collections of principles and urges which encounter opposition of great strength in the total personality structure, while there is no such opposition, in such strength, to those principles and urges which are represented by the women, when they are dominant. Like Gloucester in *Richard*

12. P. 97.

III, the male characters are "deformed, unfinished, scarce half made up." The result of their action is generally some disturbance of the peace, some kind of tumult and destruction. It is not out of keeping with this state of affairs that Shakespeare was continually litigating, pertinaciously demanding his rights in the courts even when the monetary sum at issue was small and the debtor supposedly a friend. The trait was not peculiar to Shakespeare; his father and others in Stratford acted in the same way; but it must certainly be considered in any final estimate of his personality, and it clearly does not leave one with the impression that he was a man of long-suffering gentleness. The nature of the dominant male characters is also easy to reconcile with the traditions about Shakespeare's conflicts with the local authorities in his youth (whether or not these traditions are true) and with his probable domestic difficulties.

Finally, regardless of the connection of the leading characters with the dramatist's conscious self, it is interesting that when taken in chronological order there are some general changes in the males which suggest more than a casual association with an aging organism. Like the dramatist, the top-ranking male characters are older in the later plays than in the earlier. In the early plays they are young lovers or adventurers; in the later they are fathers and powerful rulers. In the early plays they are fiery and witty; in the later, irascible and severely grave. In the earliest plays they are without a past, so to speak, discovering themselves and plunging precipitously into life; farther along they are in the midst of life, entangled in their past and often longing for the release of death, heavy with grave concerns; and in the very last plays they are almost over the boundary into death, standing remote from life, estranged from it, in a magical illusory world, a visionary baseless fabric ready to fade away into nothingness.

4

A glance at the second-ranking characters will reveal some additional features of the dramas and, by implication, of the personality which produced them.

Listed in order they are: Buckingham, Adriana, Tranio, Proteus,

King of Navarre, Juliet, Bolingbroke, Theseus, King John, Shylock, Falstaff, King Henry IV, Leonato, Archbishop of Canterbury, Cassius, Orlando, Olivia, King Claudius, Mrs. Page, Ulysses, King of France, Isabella, Othello, Edgar, Lady Macbeth, Cleopatra, Menenius, Apemantus, Marina, Posthumus, Paulina, Ariel. It is evident immediately, though some of these characters have little less weight than those of first rank, that on the whole, with a few striking exceptions, they are not as memorable. One reason for this, apart from their lesser weight, is that in many instances they are either adjunctive extensions of the principal characters, or complements of them in the sense of opponents or sexual partners. That is to say, they complete the picture we have of the principal characters and are partly absorbed in it.

Buckingham, at first an ally of Gloucester's, later opposes him; Adriana, the wife of Antipholus of Ephesus, confusingly mistakes Antipholus of Syracuse as her husband; Tranio, the faithful servant to Lucentio, helps him to woo the mild Bianca, sister to the shrew Katharina whom Petruchio conquers; Proteus is the faithless friend of Valentine, who, forgetting Julia to whom he is engaged, attempts to seduce Valentine's beloved, Silvia; the King of Navarre is responsible for the scholarly court of celibates which Biron, though one of the members, ridicules and undermines; Juliet is Romeo's ardent fourteen-year-old sweetheart; Bolingbroke is the betrayer of King Richard II, whose throne he usurps as King Henry IV; Leonato is the grave old father of Hero and the uncle of Beatrice, who becomes Benedick's sweetheart; Theseus is the great hero, ruler of Athens, in whose court Bottom presents his tragedy; King John makes use of Philip Faulconbridge the Bastard in his war with France; Shylock is the relentless Jew whom Portia defeats at law; Falstaff (of the first part of *Henry IV*) is the licentious companion of Prince Hal and in many ways the exact opposite of the proud Hotspur; King Henry IV has already been identified as Bolingbroke, but in this play (the second part of *Henry IV*) he appears as the old father of Prince Hal and represents the duties of rulership which Falstaff helps the prince forget; the Archbishop of Canterbury praises and legally supports Henry V; Cassius is the companion of Brutus and his inciter in the betrayal of Caesar; Orlando is Rosalind's beloved; Olivia is the wealthy lady who falls in love with Viola when Viola is disguised as a page, and later marries Viola's twin brother; King Claudius is Hamlet's uncle and the murderer of his father and seducer of his mother; Mrs. Page, wooed by Falstaff, is one of the women who make a fool of him; Ulysses is the sage schemer of the Greek camp whose farsighted plans and emphasis on order contrast effectively with the shortsighted personal passions of the Trojan youth Troilus; the King of France is cured of his disease by Helena and abets her in her love for the reluctant Bertram; Isabella is the pure-minded novitiate nun who becomes the bride of Duke Vincentio; Othello is the victim and tool of Iago in the murder of Desdemona; Edgar is one of the banished men who accompany Lear in his sufferings; Lady Macbeth is the partner of Macbeth in his career of ambition and murder; Cleopatra is the fascinating sexual partner of Antony; Menenius is the mild old Roman senator who plays the role of a substitute father to Coriolanus and tries to restrain his violent impulses; Apemantus is the cynical philosopher who utters professionally the bitter opinions on mankind which Timon more passionately expresses after his ruin; Marina, who preserves her virginity and purity of mind even in a brothel, is the daughter of Pericles; Posthumus is the exiled and trustless husband of Imogen; Paulina defends Hermione against the mad accusations and murderous rage of Leontes; Ariel is the tricksy sprite who carries out the wishes of his master Prospero.

Summing up the brief sketch preceding we can say with some correctness that thirteen in the list are opposites to the principal characters, either as opponents in the sphere of action or ideationally: Proteus, the King of Navarre, Bolingbroke, Theseus, Shylock, Falstaff, King Henry IV, Leonato, King Claudius, Mrs. Page, Ulysses, Menenius, Paulina. Eleven are extensions of the main characters, in the sense of fulfilling and continuing their natures and wishes: Buckingham, King John, the Archbishop of Canterbury, Cassius, the King of France, Isabella, Othello, Edgar, Lady Macbeth, Apemantus, Ariel. Six are related to the main characters as sexual partners or as soliciting sexual partnership: Adriana, Juliet, Orlando, Olivia, Cleopatra, Posthumus. This classification leaves out two characters: Tranio, and Marina. Tranio might be forced into the first list, since he aids his master in striving for a woman who is the opposite in disposition to Petruchio's Kate, but this would surely be straining for a point; and it might not be entirely fantastic to find a parenthetical place for Marina in the list of lovers, in view of the incestuous father-daughter relationship which introduces and colors the play, and in view of the occupation which Marina nominally (but not actually) follows in preparation for the meeting with her father—a meeting which restores his interest in life. Aside from these two extremely doubtful cases, the three categories accommodate the second-ranking characters fairly well. Simplifying, therefore, we may speak of these characters as helpers or opponents or sexual partners of those in the first rank.

Does the classification work because it employs kinds of human relationship so comprehensively fundamental that going outside them is inconceivable? I believe not. Both Tranio and Marina fit into the scheme with difficulty if at all. Furthermore, they illustrate possibilities which, though not characteristic of Shakespeare, have been exploited by other writers. Tranio has a role which is essentially out of contact with that of the chief character. If this arrangement were more widely extended in the play, tense drama would of course be abolished; yet something like this disconnectedness does occur in some dreams, where everybody seems to move about indifferent to others, and also in some modern fictional works, such as the novels of Kafka and Eliot's *The Waste Land*. This schizoid modern fiction produces an effect of dreariness and pointlessness not to be found in Shakespeare's work, even when his characters are complaining of the stale, flat unprofitableness of the world. In short, vigorous interaction of some kind between the characters is a distinguishing mark of Shakespeare's dramas, not necessarily of all drama. Marina, also, illustrates a possibility which is rarely actual in Shakespeare: a nonsexual, or not primarily sexual, attachment of tenderness between parent and child, a relationship of gentle protection and interest. The relationship does occur in other cases, but only here does it implicate a first- and second-ranking character. Again, to make it clear that the possibilities are not exhausted by Shakespeare or this classification, we may note the absence of the religious attitude of worship in the relations between the characters, which could occur as humble, adoring submission in purely human relationships if no divinities were to be had. Power and sex relations abound in Shakespeare; awed loving dependence on a higher being, hardly at all. On the contrary, independence, pride which acknowledges no morally higher power than one's own will, principled action on occasion but without any sense of mystical leading, are constantly found in the Shakespearean characters. Where religion enters formally, in the habit of a friar or archbishop, it enters as a trade, possibly with a trace of goodness here and there, but without supernatural sanction and sanctity. In times of crisis, the characters let their thoughts run on death and its mystery, but little on God. At the fringe of human affairs there are ghosts, witches, fairies, shadowy pagan deities, wavering between real and hallucinated. The overwhelming spiritual vision of Dante is quite absent.

The point is that the relationships between the first and second characters are decidedly limited in variety. They are very common, very fundamental kinds of relationship, likely to arouse the sympathy and understanding of most people, and thus indicating once more the broad central humanity of Shakespeare; but nevertheless they set certain boundaries to his personality and help to distinguish him from others.

Finally, since the relations of struggle and sex have emerged in the discussion of the first and second characters, a comment is in place here on the traits of power and sensuality in general in Shakespeare.

The sensuality ranges from a sensitive delight in color and music, the color of flowers and a woman's skin, the music of instruments and a woman's voice, on to the grossest playing with sex. A mingling of sex with the frailest flowers and even with the landscape occurs. At the same time this delicious mixture is often contaminated with loathing; it is a constant problem how to shun the heaven of beauty that leads men into hell. The phraseology is from the *Sonnets*, but it would not be hard to illustrate the same ambivalence from the plays. Shakespeare is afflicted, as was Augustine, by the temptation of beauty; but he does not rage against it like Augustine, who was afraid that even the sparkling of light would carry him away from God; it is only that when he thinks of flowers he thinks of the gross names that shepherds give them (though "our

cold maids do dead men's fingers call them"), and that when he
hears the cuckoo he thinks of adultery. All poetry tends to keep this
close union between sex and the charms of natural things, but it is
not true of all that where the connection exists there accompanies
it, as happens in Shakespeare, an emotion of disgust.

As for the motif of power, it is everywhere in the plays, but more
pronounced in the later ones. Brute force and intellectual master-
fulness are incorporated in hero after hero. To be sure, one after
another these heroes come to ruin; but they are magnificent while
they last. At first the reliance of these characters is on cunning
policy and the virtues of the warrior—courage, agility, physical
strength, a commanding presence, the science of slaughter. In
Antony and Coriolanus we still have it, though flawed now by attachment to women—the grandeur of Antony whose eyes "have
glowed like plated Mars," of Coriolanus who with his grim looks
and the thunder-like percussion of his sounds made his enemies
"shake, as if the world Were feverous and did tremble." But at the
last it is the power of intellect alone which counts, the power of
magical influence over nature, as we have it in Cerimon of *Pericles*
who restores Thaisa to life, and supremely in Prospero who governs
the sea and the air as well as human beings. Cerimon speaks of
himself thus:

> I hold it ever,
> Virtue and cunning were endowments greater
> Than nobleness and riches: careless heirs
> May the two latter darken and expend;
> But immortality attends the former,
> Making a man a god. 'Tis known, I ever
> Have studied physic, through which secret art,
> By turning o'er authorities, I have,
> Together with my practice, made familiar
> To me and to my aid the blest infusions
> That dwell in vegetives, in metals, stones;
> And I can speak of the disturbances
> That nature works, and of her cures; which doth give me
> A more content in course of true delight
> Than to be thirsty after tottering honour,
> Or tie my treasure up in silken bags,
> To please the fool and death. (P, III, 2, 26 ff.)

Cerimon occupies sixth place in *Pericles,* but the great magician of
The Tempest ranks distinctly first, and his power is almost un-
limited:

> I have bedimmed
> The noontide sun, called forth the mutinous winds,
> And 'twixt the green sea and the azured vault
> Set roaring war: to the dread rattling thunder
> Have I given fire, and rifted Jove's stout oak
> With his own bolt; the strong-based promontory
> Have I made shake and by the spurs plucked up
> The pine and cedar: graves at my command
> Have waked their sleepers, oped, and let'em forth
> By my so potent art. (T, V, 1, 41 ff.)

In Prospero, the last of Shakespeare's heroes, the Baconian knowledge-power is in full activity, still carrying an aura of the black
magic of the Middle Ages, but prophetic of the attitudes and ac-
complishments which are the commonplaces of our own day. But
while we accept our own knowledge-power with complacency,
until we begin fearing that others will use it for our destruction as
we are willing to use it for theirs, in Shakespeare in this final stage
it is looked on as a means of healing and restitution, and, even so,
is by Prospero renounced, with the acknowledgment that what
strength he has of his own is "most faint." Power, manifest in various phases throughout Shakespeare's career and here at the zenith,
is surrendered as if in essence unsatisfactory. Over and over again
this proves true in the actual fate of the supermen of the earlier
plays. They fail and are defeated. But in this case instead of failure
there is renunciation by a man who perceives and accepts other
values. Or perhaps Prospero's renunciation of his power is his defeat. Where power is so perfect, defeat cannot come from outside,
it must come from inside the magic circle.

CHAPTER 5. SHAKESPEARE'S THEMES

1

SOME CRITICS PRETEND to find infinite variety in Shakespeare. Others—and with these I agree—discover a good deal of repetition. An example is Barrett Wendell, to choose one from far back when the reaction against Dowden was beginning to set in. The repetition which he finds, however, is treated by him as having no significance for the dramatist's personality. In his view it is nothing more than "economy of invention," a demonstration of the canny playwright's habit of making the most of any situation which had proved agreeable to his audiences in the past. He regards Shakespeare as first of all a shrewd theatrical businessman, sensitive to the box-office receipts, and therefore very much concerned with producing sure-fire hits; for which reason, and because the invention of plot was not one of his strong points anyhow, he was continually warming over the incidents, stories, denouements which had excited interest before. Wendell's attention to the chronology of the plays is accordingly not aimed at following the author's development as a man. In fact, he warns his readers against any biographical inclination. He writes: "At the risk of tedious repetition, it is prudent to warn whoever has not carefully watched the work of artists that no valid conclusion concerning their actual lives and characters can be drawn from even their most sincere artistic achievements. Without other evidence than is as yet before us, we cannot assert that Shakespeare thought, or believed, or cared for this ideal or that; nor yet that to have known in imagination what he has expressed he must personally have experienced certain circumstances, good or evil."[1]

The words are sensible, and one may agree with Wendell that it is unsafe to infer from the content of the plays what the writer's outward biography was: it is obviously ridiculous to suppose that because there are murderers in the plays, Shakespeare himself committed murders; and nobody fancies that Shakespeare was at the

1. Pp. 215 f.

siege of Troy because Troilus was, or rose from the tomb where
Romeo died to write about him. It is unsafe, though not quite so
ridiculous, to argue for situations in his personal history analogous
to some of those in the plays, such as a love affair with a woman
resembling Cleopatra in complexion, sprightliness, faithlessness,
and passion; which could be reasonably done without committing
oneself as to whether the woman was Mary Fitton or Anne Hathaway or some other. But it is blindness to refuse to grant that Shakespeare was immersed to a considerable depth in his dramatic productions, as experiences. In the little nutshell of a room where he
wrote out these things, he was necessarily for moments and probably for long periods more intensely aware of the dramatic action
than of anything around him in the way of furniture, London
streets, Elizabeth's Court, or other historical circumstances. Furthermore, it is questionable whether anyone, practical-minded
shareholder in the Globe or demigod, could charge his page with
such intense life without being more than word deep in what he
communicated. My argument is that the plays are, in a reasonable
sense, a record of Shakespeare's experience; not all of his experience, and not as a chronicle of events which would interest a court
of law, but as a revelation of precisely those contents, tensions,
and resolutions which are of greatest moment to the psychologist.
And we have a right to focus attention on the recurring elements
in this experience with the expectation of finding in them matters
of weight, just as in the case of recurring dreams, under which typically lie important external events and a strong sustaining emotion
in the dreamer.

2

One major theme is that of betrayal, which has both a sexual and
a political form. This has been touched on in the discussion of the
traits of the principal characters. It is prominent in its sexual form
in *Two Gentlemen of Verona, Much Ado About Nothing, Hamlet,
Merry Wives of Windsor, Measure for Measure, Othello, Cymbeline,* and *Winter's Tale.*

In *Two Gentlemen of Verona,* Proteus, the dear friend of Valentine, attempts to seduce and even to rape Valentine's sweetheart,
Silvia, simultaneously proving untrue to his own betrothed, Julia.

In *Hamlet,* what lends especial horror to the situation is that Hamlet's mother has been unfaithful to his father and has assisted her seducer, the father's brother, to murder him; so that the betrayal violates the sacred laws both of marriage and of kinship. In *Merry Wives of Windsor,* there is the jealous husband Ford who *thinks* his wife is unfaithful to him. In *Measure for Measure,* the apparently virtuous Angelo, the special deputy in whom the duke has rested all authority, takes advantage of his position to attempt to seduce the chaste Isabella, in violation of the law he is supposed to be enforcing; he is thus a traitor on all sides—to Duke Vincentio and the law, to Isabella, and to her brother whom he has falsely promised to spare in exchange for her sexual favors, and already in advance to Mariana, with whom he has broken his betrothal. But then the whole play is saturated with betrayal.[2]

The above are instances of the theme, but I want to dwell most carefully on *Much Ado About Nothing, Othello, Cymbeline,* and *Winter's Tale,* because these four plays exhibit the theme most centrally and have many points in common. They will be examined in chronological order. Their dates are approximately 1598, 1604, 1609, and 1611.

The situation in *Much Ado About Nothing* is this: Claudio is in love with Hero, daughter of Leonato; he declares his passion fervidly to Benedick, who eventually recognizes his own love for Hero's cousin, Beatrice, but is at this time a professed "atheist in love." The opening of the play thus has some resemblance to *Two Gentlemen of Verona,* where Proteus is the admitted lover, Valen-

---

2. In speaking of sexual betrayal in these plays I do not overlook the fact that sexual irregularities of various kinds are found elsewhere in Shakespeare. There is, for example, *Troilus and Cressida.* Cressida in this play does in a sense betray Troilus; that is to say, as a captive of the Greeks she continues to satisfy her sexual desires without much inhibition. But the special variety of the betrayal theme which appears in the plays just listed is not well represented in *Troilus and Cressida;* for the disposition toward frivolous promiscuity which marks Cressida is absent from the heroines involved in the betrayal theme of the other plays, even from the queen in *Hamlet,* monstrous as her behavior is, and her abandonment of her body to the enemy is in a different category from the behavior of the women in the plays I wish to examine here. In brief, I detect in the series of plays listed, and especially in the four set apart for close analysis, a pattern of relationships which is lacking in *Troilus and Cressida,* and it is this subvariety of the great theme of sexual betrayal which is studied here.

tine the determined bachelor. The plot thickens with the entrance of Don John. Superficially a reconciled brother of Don Pedro (the latter an old friend of Leonato and patron and friend of the two young noblemen, Benedick and Claudio), Don John secretly wishes to cause as much suffering as he can to Don Pedro and his friends. He plots with his scoundrelly companion Borachio to make it appear that Hero, now engaged to be married to Claudio, is carrying on a surreptitious affair with Borachio on the eve of the wedding and is in general a light wench. Don Pedro, who has assisted Claudio in his suit, and Claudio are both convinced by a contrived midnight scene that Hero is indeed debauched; and subsequently they contemptuously charge her with this looseness of conduct, publicly, at the wedding ceremony, and march out, leaving her in a swoon on the floor of the chapel. No convincing proof of Hero's innocence is immediately forthcoming, except her own disavowal of guilt; and though her cousin Beatrice, furiously loyal to her, rouses both Benedick and the overwhelmed father to defend her honor by outright challenges to their former friends, the priest advises that Hero be kept in hiding and it be rumored that she is dead of grief until the mystery of the midnight assignation is cleared up. Don John has meantime disappeared. But Borachio is caught by the blundering arm of the law, in the shape of Dogberry, and a confession is extracted from him which is communicated to Leonato. After this revelation, which is convincing to all, the faithless agents of Hero's suffering, Claudio and Don Pedro, are kept in ignorance of the fact that she is really alive and are compelled to pay humble tribute to her memory at her supposed tomb. At the end of the play the chastened Claudio, to his great astonishment, is reunited to Hero.

Much Ado About Nothing is comedy verging on tragedy. *Othello*, six years later, is a darkly tragic rendering of the same basic plot. Iago, a complete villain, is the filled-out duplicate of Don John; he is assisted by Roderigo, consciously, and by Cassio, unconsciously, in the same way that Don John was assisted by Borachio; Othello murders his innocent beloved and comes to regret it, more intensely and irreversibly but otherwise in much the same fashion as did Claudio, who exhibits some of Othello's wholehearted impetuosity; and Desdemona, innocent and gentle like Hero, is defended against Othello's charges just as the earlier heroine was defended by Beatrice. Even in the forthrightness of Emilia and in the fact that her mate is a witty cynic not altogether unlike Beatrice's Benedick, we get the impression of having witnessed these things before. The intensity and grim finality of *Othello,* however, mark a change which makes the whole play bite deeper. The readiness of Claudio to believe the worst on little evidence makes him appear merely fickle, where Othello, gradually worked into a passion of jealousy by the persistent subtlety of Iago playing upon the deepest chords of his nature, appears solid and profound, still loyal to his love while destroying the precious object of it. Iago, again, is more deliberately, directly, effectively villainous than Don John, who by comparison is a mere prankster. And the proof of Desdemona's affection for Othello is greater than the proof in the comedy; for she is his wife, not simply his betrothed, and has had to defy her father and local views of propriety to become so. It is a heightening of the tragic effect, also, that it is a trusted friend, Cassio, not an indifferent rascal like Borachio, who is suspected of sexual trespass. Iago, too, is close to Othello's heart. In every way, Othello's suspicion of his beloved is more heavily charged with emotion than Claudio's, just as it is more genuinely lethal. In one respect, however, Othello is less justified in his conclusions than Claudio: Othello goes on ambiguous hints dropped by a man whom he has offended (for Othello promoted Cassio to a position which Iago had some right to expect for himself), whereas Claudio is given a direct demonstration, as far as he can see, of the wantonness of Hero, and given it by a man unmotivated by any cause of quarrel with him. The evidence for Desdemona's infidelity is weakly circumstantial; for Hero's it is flagrantly direct. This is an important point, because it places more of the blame for the consequences on Othello; and, as will be shown, it is in line with the development of the theme in the next two examples.

Five or so years after *Othello,* in *Cymbeline*—where Imogen is in the line of succession from Hero and Desdemona, Posthumus in that of Claudio and Othello, and Iachimo in that of Don John and Iago—though the core of the plot is still the same, there are some interesting variations. Posthumus Leonatus, after marrying Imogen, daughter of Cymbeline, king of Britain, is forced into exile by the threat of Cymbeline's displeasure; but he swears to his wife before leaving,

> I will remain
> The loyal'st husband that did e'er plight troth. (Cy, I, 1, 95 f.)

Arrived at Rome, he makes the acquaintance of several gentlemen, among them Iachimo, and brags to them of the beauty and virtue of his wife. Iachimo contemptuously offers to go to Britain and seduce her, in demonstration of the universal badness of women, and lays a wager on the enterprise. Posthumus accepts the challenge, saying:

> I embrace these conditions; let us have articles betwixt us. Only, thus far you shall answer: if you make your voyage upon her and give me directly to understand you have prevailed, I am no further your enemy; she is not worth our debate: if she remain unseduced, you not making it appear otherwise, for your ill opinion and the assault you have made to her chastity you shall answer me with your sword. (Cy, I, 5, 169 ff.)

Iachimo hastens to Cymbeline's court; there, in audience with Imogen, first defames her husband, and then invites her to revenge herself on him by submitting to his own embraces. Imogen's unhesitating response to this proposal is to call out for Pisanio, the loyal servant of Posthumus whom he left as her attendant. The wily Iachimo then retracts, pretending that he was only testing her love for Posthumus, and begs her to keep a box under guard for him. She offers to keep it in her bedchamber. In this box Iachimo hides, and during the night he crawls out to take note of the details of the room, steal a bracelet from Imogen's arm, and find an identifying mole upon her breast. Armed with these credentials, he returns to Rome and easily convinces Posthumus of Imogen's infidelity. Posthumus reacts with a furious tirade against all women, his mother and his wife first, and then turns his rage against himself—against what he calls the woman's part in him.

> Could I find out
> The woman's part in me! For there's no motion
> That tends to vice in man, but I affirm
> It is the woman's part: be it lying, note it,
> The woman's; flattering, hers; deceiving, hers;
> Ambitions, covetings, change of prides, disdain,
> Nice longing, slanders, mutability,

> All faults that may be named, nay that hell knows,
> Why, hers, in part or all; but rather, all;
> For even to vice
> They are not constant, but are changing still
> One vice, but of a minute old, for one   .
> Not half so old as that. I'll write against them,
> Detest them, curse them . . . (Cy, II, 5, 19 ff.)

Following this, he sends a letter to Pisanio ordering him to kill Imogen. Pisanio, loyal to them both, will not do it, convinced that Posthumus has been deceived by slander; instead, he takes Imogen into his confidence, and after he has succeeded in calming her passionate outburst against the faithlessness of Posthumus, induces her to pretend death until Posthumus has come to his senses. This plan involves disguising her as a boy. While in disguise and living in the wilderness, she takes a potion designed by her stepmother the Queen to poison her, and falls into a coma, which is believed to be death by the outcasts with whom she has taken haven. Meantime, the Queen's son, the brutal Cloten, dressed in Posthumus' clothes and pursuing her to rape her, is killed and beheaded by one of the outcasts. The two are laid side by side on the ground, and when Imogen recovers from her stupor she supposes the body beside her, which is headless, to be Posthumus. The rapid and complicated denouement, involving a battle between the Romans and the Britons in which Posthumus, who has come along with the invading Romans, goes over to the British side and distinguishes himself by his fighting, reunites the two lovers, clears up all mysteries, and provides Iachimo a chance to confess and be forgiven.

In this play as in the two preceding ones there is still a villain; his villainy, however, is at first a kind of light-mindedness, springing from a gambling spirit and the lust of the eye, rather than from deeply engrained evil; and it yields to contrition in the last scenes. Iachimo has, indeed, a becoming gracefulness about him and a thorough artist's eye for the charming details of Imogen's room and person; his language glitters:

> The roof o' the chamber
> With golden cherubins is fretted: her andirons—
> I had forgot them—were two winking Cupids
> Of silver . . . (Cy, II, 4, 87 ff.)

Shakespeare's sensualism appears in Iachimo in its lighter forms; it is Posthumus who is gross, with his "full-acorned boar, a German one." (Cy, II, 5, 16) Also, the guilt of Posthumus is greater: he urges Iachimo on, gives him directions and a letter of recommendation, with full knowledge of his intentions. This is not true of Claudio and Othello. They are victims. Posthumus is the villain himself. In fact, Posthumus condemns himself as such, finally:

> Thou, king, send out
> For torturers ingenious: it is I
> That all the abhorred things o' the earth amend
> By being worse than they. I am Posthumus,
> That killed thy daughter:—villain-like, I lie—
> That caused a lesser villain than myself,
> A sacrilegious thief, to do't. (Cy, V, 5, 214 ff.)

By all these modulations the emphasis is shifted; guilt, and the consciousness of guilt, come to rest heavily on the victim of the betrayal.

Cloten introduces a new note, or rather a new accent; the note was already struck long before in *Two Gentlemen of Verona*. As the rival of Posthumus he is the incarnation of brutal lust, and in the wilderness he plans to rape Imogen just as the slighter Proteus does when he is in pursuit of Silvia. There is no trace of this in *Much Ado About Nothing*. There is a trace in *Othello*, for Iago states as a part of his motivation that he has designs on Desdemona's body:

> Now, I do love her too;
> Not out of absolute lust, though peradventure
> I stand accountant for as great a sin,
> But partly led to diet my revenge
> For that I do suspect the lusty Moor
> Hath leaped into my seat. (O, II, 1, 300 ff.)

Here in *Cymbeline* there is the attempt outright. It is not, admittedly, linked directly with the main plot of suspected infidelity; but it does have points of contact with it dramatically. It is in the imagination of Posthumus that Imogen is mounted by a "full-acorned boar," and it is in the garb of Posthumus that Cloten lustfully pursues her. As Iachimo is the agent of Posthumus' suspicions, so Cloten is the physical counterpart of his thoughts of rude sexual assault. To put it in another way, as Iachimo fulfills the delicate artistic sensuality of Shakespeare, so Cloten fulfills that sensuality at the more violent end of the scale; and both are knotted together, so to speak, in the convolutions of Posthumus' tormented intellect.

A year or two later comes *The Winter's Tale*. Here the fusion of betrayed and betrayer is complete; for it is Leontes, the husband, who initiates the thought of infidelity, implements it by the yeasty working of his imagination, and brings down the terrible consequences upon himself. Against the reasonings of Camillo and the impassioned defense by Paulina, he convinces himself that his friend from boyhood, Polixenes, who has been visiting with him for nine months, is responsible for his wife's pregnancy; he therefore attempts to get Camillo to poison his friend (but Camillo escapes with him to Bohemia, which further strengthens Leontes' convictions), has Hermione his wife imprisoned and condemned to death, and sends the newborn baby out in the charge of Antigonus, Paulina's husband, to expose it to death in some distant spot. The tension produced by these events, and especially the mistreatment of Hermione, so affects their young son Mamillius that he dies. Leontes has no sooner completed his self-righteous sentencing of Hermione to death than a message from the oracle at Delphi wholly undermines his jealous delusions, though for the moment he denies truth even to the oracle; but the news of the death of Mamillius which quickly follows is a telling blow, and he cries out:

> Apollo's angry; and the heavens themselves
> Do strike at my injustice. (WT, III, 2, 147 f.)

At the news the overwrought Hermione swoons, and Paulina declares that she is dead. Sixteen years later, having been kept in secret confinement by Paulina during the whole interval, Hermione is restored to Leontes; but this only after the daughter whom he had ordered Antigonus to expose—Perdita, as she was named by the shepherds who rescued her and brought her up—has returned, as demanded by the oracle. The happy ending, besides reuniting Hermione to her repentant husband, includes a reconciliation between Leontes and his old friend Polixenes, the restoration to favor of Camillo and his marriage to Paulina (her husband Antigonus was devoured by a bear after the exposure of the baby), and the marriage of Perdita to Florizel, son of Polixenes.

The singular hideousness of Leontes' conduct stems from the fact that the main basis for his suspicions regarding his wife and Polixenes is her success in prevailing upon Leontes' friend to extend his visit, on the urging of Leontes himself. He finds their friendly conversation "Too hot, too hot!" (WT, I, 2, 109) His jealousy then overflows in bitter thoughts which he soon communicates to Camillo, with the command that he put Polixenes to death. To Camillo's protests in reasonable defense of Hermione he answers:

> I say thou liest, Camillo, and I hate thee,
> Pronounce thee a gross lout, a mindless slave,
> Or else a hovering temporizer, that
> Canst with thine eyes at once see good and evil,
> Inclining to them both: were my wife's liver
> Infected as her life, she would not live
> The running of one glass. (WT, I, 2, 300 ff.)

He will not tolerate any evidence or argument which runs counter to his own fixed delusion. At first, in ordering Camillo to do away with Polixenes, he declares that he will do no harm to Hermione or her reputation; but after Polixenes' escape, he publicly accuses her of adultery and in a public trial condemns her. By the time of the trial his delusion has expanded far beyond a simple charge of adultery; the supposed infidelity has become the core of a plot of vast dimensions and malignity. His indictment of her reads:

> Hermione, queen to the worthy Leontes, king of Sicilia, thou art here accused and arraigned of high treason, in committing adultery with Polixenes, king of Bohemia, and conspiring with Camillo to take away the life of our sovereign lord the king, thy royal husband: the pretence whereof being by circumstances partly laid open, thou, Hermione, contrary to the faith and allegiance of a true subject, didst counsel and aid them, for their better safety, to fly away by night. (WT, III, 2, 12 ff.)

Nothing can prevail against the madness of Leontes, not even the word of God from Delphi:

> There is no truth at all i' the oracle:
> The sessions shall proceed: this is mere falsehood.
>   (WT, III, 2, 141 f.)

The news of the death of Mamillius is the healing thunderbolt; suddenly Leontes executes a complete about-face and confesses his own guilt:

> Apollo, pardon
> My great profaneness 'gainst thy oracle!
> I'll reconcile me to Polixenes,
> New woo my queen, recall the good Camillo,
> Whom I proclaim a man of truth, of mercy;
> For, being transported by my jealousies
> To bloody thoughts and to revenge, I chose
> Camillo for the minister to poison
> My friend Polixenes: which had been done
> But that the good mind of Camillo tardied
> My swift command, though I with death and with
> Reward did threaten and encourage him,
> Not doing't and being done: he, most humane
> And filled with honour, to my kingly guest
> Unclasped my practice, quit his fortunes here,
> Which you knew great, and to the hazard
> Of all incertainties himself commended,
> No richer than his honour: how he glisters
> Thorough my rust! and how his piety
> Does my deeds make the blacker! (WT, III, 2, 155 ff.)

The announcement by Paulina of the death of the queen, and her powerful invective against Leontes, complete the victory over his mad pride. In sorrow and humility he closes the scene with:

> Prithee, bring me
> To the dead bodies of my queen and son:
> One grave shall be for both: upon them shall
> The causes of their death appear, unto
> Our shame perpetual. Once a day I'll visit
> The chapel where they lie, and tears shed there
> Shall be my recreation: so long as nature
> Will bear up with this exercise, so long
> I daily vow to use it. Come and lead me
> Unto these sorrows. (WT, III, 2, 235 ff.)

In *The Winter's Tale* we have the summing up of all the motifs from *Much Ado About Nothing* on through *Othello* and *Cymbeline*, and in it we discover as the cause of the suffering not an idle heartless trick, as in *Much Ado*, perpetrated upon an innocent bystander, nor the machinations of a devilish villain, as in *Othello*, nor the falsehood of an unprincipled gallant and gamester, as in *Cymbeline*, but simply and only the twisted thinking of a moody, jealous husband who has no faith in anything but his own corrupted reason. There is a progression here, a bringing of the guilt closer and closer to the victim of the guilty act. In *The Winter's Tale* Leontes acts the parts of Don John, Borachio, and Claudio, all by himself; and the parts of Iago and Othello; and the parts of Posthumus and Iachimo. Only in his thoughts is his friend Polixenes a participator in the crime; there is no criminal except Leontes himself, and no crime except what he commits in the name of justice. The drama is all psychological. On the one hand there is the real world, where love and honesty prevail; and on the other there is the tormented Leontes, who on the grinding machinery of his reason tortures a horrible meaning out of it which is not there.

We must pause here to ask what the relevance of all this is to the personality of the author. Should we conclude that the development of this theme of sexual betrayal is evidence of Shakespeare's deepening penetration into the mysteries of human fate, an increase of confidence in psychical determinism, a gradual working out of the thesis that what happens to human beings is due to themselves rather than to their stars? Or should we conclude that it is not simply as an objective critic of life that he handles the theme and progressively refines it into a psychological drama, but that he does so because the poison is circulating in his own system and he himself must be purified of it? Is the theme merely a convenient text on which to hang a general commentary, or is it deeply, bitterly, his own problem? Perhaps the two alternatives cannot be cleanly separated; but to the extent that they can be, it is my opinion that the second cannot be lightly dismissed. The protocols of many a psychoanalysis, the records of clinical studies like those of Henry Murray and his associates,[3] agree in showing that sequences of stories and dreams typically cohere internally and with the serious daily concerns of their producers. In addition to this general evidence we have a few slender particulars of Shakespeare's own history to go on, which will be reviewed in their place. But if

3. Murray *et al.*, *Explorations in Personality*.

we wipe out all reference to a possible Stratford experience and insist that we know absolutely nothing about Shakespeare's domestic affairs, there still remains the fact that the theme of sexual betrayal, involving husband or near-husband and wife, is broadly and acutely present in the dramas; and the further fact that a development occurs in its treatment which might be summed up briefly, in subjective language, thus: "I was not the victim of the falsehood and infidelity of others; I suffered instead from my own self-deception."

The subjective formulation is especially fitting with respect to *The Winter's Tale*. It is true that in drama such as Shakespeare wrote all the characters are on much the same plane of objectivity, so that it is a delicate operation to single out this or that one as representing the author's particular locus of consciousness. But in *The Winter's Tale* much of what Leontes has to say is addressed to himself rather than to the other characters or even to the audience; and the impression of being in the bosom of his thoughts, as in no one else's in the play, is very strong indeed. He is not hissing to the audience, as Gloucester does, that he is a villain, nor even striking a soliloquizing pose like Hamlet; he is muttering to himself, thinking aloud almost without words, lost in his delusional dream and drawing the eavesdropping audience with him into the whirlpool. I should add that there seems to me to be much more of this kind of thing in the later Shakespeare than in the earlier. *A Midsummer Night's Dream,* for instance, is not nearly so dreamlike, so saturated with the atmosphere of the inner man, so tinged with subjectivity, as *Timon of Athens, Cymbeline, Pericles, The Winter's Tale,* and *The Tempest;* nor is there the same localization of a dreaming, thinking, mentally influencing center in it as in these late plays. And if this is a true judgment, then it harmonizes with the development of the special theme which has been under discussion here—a development withdrawing the power of action, and harm, from objects to subjects.

To summarize and clarify the preceding discussion a table is subjoined (Table 6) showing the primary relations and lines of succession among the various characters importantly concerned.

The political implications of Hermione's imagined sexual transgression appear in *The Winter's Tale* as a paranoid delusional system. In earlier plays political betrayal is itself a chief focus of evil in the dramatic action. Gloucester makes his way to power by a series of betrayals; Bolingbroke defies and against clear promises kills the king; John, as part of a political maneuver, orders the

TABLE 6

THEME: SEXUAL BETRAYAL, REAL OR IMAGINED

Date	Play	Betrayer	Betrayed	Wife or Sweetheart
1594–95	TGV	Proteus	Valentine	Silvia
1598–99	MAAN	Don John Borachio	Claudio	Hero
1600–1	H	Claudius	Ghost	Gertrude
1600–1	MWW	Falstaff	Ford	Mrs. Ford
1604–5	MM	Angelo	Vincentio	Isabella
1604–5	O	Iago Cassio	Othello	Desdemona
1609–10	Cy	Iachimo	Posthumus	Imogen
1610–11	WT	Polixenes (Leontes)	Leontes	Hermione

young Arthur killed; Henry V bears with him occasionally the burden of his father's guilt and is in his turn threatened by a Court conspiracy; Brutus and Cassius conspire against Caesar, whom Brutus professes to love, and kill him; Macbeth and Lady Macbeth kill their ruler and friend and almost father, Duncan; and so on and on. The essence of political life appears in the Shakespearean dramas as treachery. Rulers are constantly under its threat; and they have often arrived at their station by its aid.

Now, betrayal is not possible except where ties of love, or at least professions of such ties, exist. It is precisely when these ties are closest that the betrayal is most tragic. On these considerations it does not appear gratuitous that sexual betrayal should be mingled so intimately with political betrayal. In both cases there is a subversion of order in the world, and it has been frequently remarked that Shakespeare expresses little sympathy for mob action, popular revolt, and the like; even when so hateful a prince as Cloten is

killed, his princely rank is respected. It follows that when the roles
of lover and ruler are united in one person, betrayal can have the
mightiest and most hideous repercussions; for both domestic and
public disorder result. Shakespeare was not himself a prince,
though certainly energetic in application for a coat of arms, which
is a gesture in that direction; but there was a great deal of the
princely in him. Dukes, princes, kings—his plays are full of them.
It makes no difference that the theatrical conventions of the time
were thereby satisfied; a conventional posture can be a personal
one too. In the royal figures in his plays, into whom he enters most
intimately; in the persistent application to the college of heralds;
in the nature of his patronage and perhaps his friendships; even
in an indecent story told about him, which makes him out as William the Conqueror,[4] there is more than a hint of his basic sympathy with the kingly role. I do not mean to imply that there was
necessarily anything peculiar to Shakespeare in this attitude, which
may have been widely shared among his contemporaries, the times
being what they were; but I think that it was definitely present in
him, and it seems to me, though this is a point on which I stand
ready to be corrected, that the attitude is more strongly felt in his
plays than in those of most of his contemporaries. Shakespeare was,
I think, particularly sensitized, for whatever causes, to the tragic
possibility of betrayal inherent in the position of a king or other
ruler, as well as in the position of a lover; and *The Winter's Tale*
brings the double theme of betrayal to a critical focus, where it has
a subjective and highly paranoid quality.

3

A second theme which occurs very often in Shakespeare as an
important side issue, and is treated centrally in *King Lear* and
nearly so in *Pericles, The Winter's Tale,* and *The Tempest,* is the
father-daughter relationship. I have noted fourteen plays in which
the theme is prominent. The frequency and importance of this
theme in Shakespeare are all the more striking from the comparative absence of the mother-daughter relationship. Halliday has
noted this fact with something like surprise and made some inter-

4. Chambers, *William Shakespeare,* 2, 212.

esting comments on it in his book *Shakespeare and His Critics*. He disposes of the objection that the Elizabethan theater could not have handled maternal roles: "for there are plenty of examples of middle-aged and elderly women" in Shakespeare's plays; and he says: "It may be that Shakespeare consciously or unconsciously avoided the mother-daughter relationship owing to some disturbing domestic experience, and in compensation emphasised that between father and daughter instead. Or it may simply be that mothers are often dramatically a nuisance." [5] Whatever the explanation, the lopsidedness of Shakespeare's approach to the domestic scene in this respect is clear.

Table 7 presents the characters chiefly involved in the father-daughter relationship in the fourteen plays previously mentioned; as indicated by the inclusion of a list of lovers, the relationship typically forms part of a rivalry triangle. The number beside each name is the character weight; where the number is zero, however, all that is meant is that this character fell lower in weight than the twelfth character of the particular play, and so does not appear in Table 1. (The actual weight is given in parentheses.)

TABLE 7
THEME: FATHER-DAUGHTER RELATIONSHIP

Date	Play	Father	Daughter	Lover
1593–94	TS	Baptista 29	Katharina 37	Petruchio 100
1594–95	TGV	Duke 52	Silvia 41	Valentine 100
1594–95	RJ	Capulet 46	Juliet 88	Romeo 100
1595–96	MSND	Egeus 0 (17)	Hermia 62	Lysander 53
1596–97	MV	Shylock 60	Jessica 15	Lorenzo 31
1598–99	MAAN	Leonato 83	Hero 31	Claudio 72
		Antonio 14	Beatrice 67	Benedick 100
1600–1	H	Polonius 23	Ophelia 12	Hamlet 100
1600–1	MWW	Page 37	Anne 0 (7)	Fenton 25
1604–5	O	Brabantio 13	Desdemona 36	Othello 80
1605–6	L	Lear 100	Cordelia 15	King of France 0 (5)
1608–9	P	Pericles 100	Marina 29	Lysimachus 17
		Simonides 26	Thaisa 13	Pericles 100
		(Antiochus	Daughter	Pericles)
1609–10	Cy	Cymbeline 47	Imogen 100	Posthumus 69
1610–11	WT	Leontes 100	Perdita 21	Florizel 31
1611–12	T	Prospero 100	Miranda 20	Ferdinand 23

5. Pp. 197 f.

With this table as introduction, let us now examine in more detail the nature of the relations between father, daughter, and lover, taking the plays in chronological order.

In *The Taming of the Shrew* Baptista professes to be a liberal father to his two daughters. He has determined that the younger, Bianca, who has a gentle disposition attractive to men, shall not be married before Katharina, who is the shrew. He himself seems to enjoy Bianca's company more than Katharina's, and Bianca is more sweetly submissive to him. In fact, Katharina is jealous, and Baptista has occasion to chide her for her roughness to Bianca; whereupon Katharina flares up angrily. Baptista is glad enough to conclude a marriage pact with Petruchio on his first appearance, and to be rid of his mettlesome daughter.

In *Two Gentlemen of Verona* the father, the Duke of Milan, wishes his daughter Silvia to marry Thurio, and thus opposes her interest in Valentine. Fearing that she may elope, he places her in a bedroom in a high tower; and when Proteus betrays his friend Valentine to the duke by revealing his elopement plans, the duke banishes Valentine on pain of death. Later, as head of a band of outlaws Valentine rescues Silvia from Proteus, and with his sword stands off Thurio, who has come to claim her; the duke applauds his spirit, forgives him, and yields Silvia to him, saying that he is worthy of an empress' love. The courtship of Valentine and Silvia is witty and playful. The attitude of the father to the daughter at the time of the discovery of the elopement plans is embittered, is in fact a mild prelude to the wrath of Lear:

> she is peevish, sullen, froward,
> Proud, disobedient, stubborn, lacking duty,
> Neither regarding that she is my child
> Nor fearing me as if I were her father;
> And, may I say to thee, this pride of hers,
> Upon advice, hath drawn my love from her. (TGV, III, 1, 68 ff.)

The speech is aimed in part at sounding out Valentine, but may nevertheless be accepted as describing the father-daughter relationship at the moment. At any rate, it is not atypical of the Shakespearean fathers of this period.

In *Romeo and Juliet*, composed perhaps within a year of the preceding, father Capulet also finds his daughter Juliet stubbornly opposed to his plans for her, and, if he had known it, would have

been rancorously against Romeo, because of the ancient feud between the families. Capulet is an interesting study, deeply attached to his daughter and yet fretfully displeased with her when
she fails to submit unquestioningly to his will. Speaking to the
favored suitor Paris, he says, after begging him to delay his courtship two more years because she is still a mere child of less than
fourteen:

> The earth hath swallowed all my hopes but she,
> She is the hopeful lady of my earth:
> But woo her, gentle Paris, get her heart,
> My will to her consent is but a part. (RJ, I, 2, 14 ff.)

But when he finds his choice of a husband disdained by Juliet, he
goes into a rage and screams:

> God's bread! it makes me mad:
> Day, night, hour, tide, time, work, play,
> Alone, in company, still my care hath been
> To have her matched: and having now provided
> A gentleman of noble parentage,
> Of fair desmesnes, youthful and nobly trained,
> Stuffed, as they say, with honourable parts,
> Proportioned as one's thoughts would wish a man;
> And then to have a wretched puling fool,
> A whining mammet, in her fortune's tender,
> To answer "I'll not wed; I cannot love,
> I am too young! I pray you, pardon me".
> But, an you will not wed, I'll pardon you:
> Graze where you will, you shall not house with me:
> Look to't, think on't, I do not use to jest.
> Thursday is near; lay hand on heart, advise:
> An you be mine, I'll give you to my friend;
> An you be not, hang, beg, starve, die in the streets,
> For, by my soul, I'll ne'er acknowledge thee,
> Nor what is mine shall never do thee good. (RJ, III, 5, 177 ff.)

Allowance must be made for the old man's general fussiness and
irascibility, and for the comic touches in the excessive worried emotion which is characteristic of him, but the pattern remains: the
domineering father angered by a spirited daughter. The passionate
love between Juliet and Romeo, of course, sets the paternal will at
naught.

In *Midsummer Night's Dream* no sooner are Theseus and Hip-

polyta introduced than Egeus enters with his familiar father's tirade against his daughter:

> Full of vexation come I, with complaint
> Against my child, my daughter Hermia.
> Stand forth, Demetrius. My noble lord,
> This man hath my consent to marry her.
> Stand forth, Lysander: and, my gracious duke,
> This man hath bewitched the bosom of my child:
> Thou, thou, Lysander, thou hast given her rhymes
> And interchanged love-tokens with my child:
> Thou hast by moonlight at her window sung
> With feigning voice verses of feigning love,
> And stolen the impression of her fantasy
> With bracelets of thy hair, rings, gawds, conceits,
> Knacks, trifles, nosegays, sweetmeats, messengers
> Of strong prevailment in unhardened youth:
> With cunning hast thou filched my daughter's heart,
> Turned her obedience, which is due to me,
> To stubborn harshness: and, my gracious duke,
> Be it so she will not here before your grace
> Consent to marry with Demetrius,
> I beg the ancient privilege of Athens,
> As she is mine, I may dispose of her:
> Which shall be either to this gentleman
> Or to her death, according to our law
> Immediately provided in that case. (MSND, I, 1, 22 ff.)

Here we have something more serious than an old man's peevish-
ness; and Duke Theseus, while granting that Egeus may not have
considered every angle of the case as he should, upholds him, and
tells Hermia, "To you your father should be as a god." (MSND, I,
1, 47) The lovers accordingly plan to elope beyond the reach of the
Athenian law. The problem is solved, however, by the varying en-
chantments of the summer night, first dividing and then bringing
back together the pairs of lovers—Hermia and Lysander, Helena
and Demetrius—and thus ending in harmony with the original
choices of the women.

In *The Merchant of Venice* a dead father's will controls Portia in
her choice of a lover. But Shylock, the living father, has no such
power over his Jessica. He leaves her at home, bidding her lock up
tight; and she robs him both of his money and of herself, to give
them to Lorenzo, a hated Christian. In this case, too, as in *Romeo*

and Juliet, the lovers ignore the war between the two houses, Jewish and Christian. When he discovers his loss, Shylock voices in a confused jumble his concern for both his wealth and his daughter; it is half uncertain which is which. At the height of his grief he exclaims:

> I would my daughter were dead at my foot, and the jewels in her ear!
> would she were hearsed at my foot, and the ducats in her coffin!
>
> (MV, III, 1, 93 ff.)

At the trial over the pound of flesh, the sentence requires that he should settle half his estate on Jessica. The avariciousness of Shylock cannot be regarded as simply that of the traditional Jewish usurer; it is rather a trait of fathers, whose parallel is to be found elsewhere in the Shakespearean portrait gallery. The romance of Jessica and Lorenzo, though on a lower spiritual plane, has many of the qualities found in the passionate affair between Juliet and Romeo.

There is no settled opposition of the fathers, Leonato and Antonio, to their daughters' lovers, Claudio and Benedick, in *Much Ado About Nothing.* Indeed, they participate in bringing the lovers together. But after Claudio's attack on Hero's reputation, the old father is up in arms against him. Yet it is first of all his daughter whom he condemns and curses, not waiting for clear proof nor accepting her own declaration of innocence. He addresses her, lying in a dead faint at his feet, as Shylock wished his Jessica to be:

> Do not live, Hero; do not ope thine eyes:
> For, did I think thou wouldst not quickly die,
> Thought I thy spirits were stronger than thy shames,
> Myself would, on the rearward of reproaches,
> Strike at thy life. Grieved I, I had but one?
> Chid I for that at frugal nature's frame?
> O, one too much by thee! Why had I one?
> Why ever wast thou lovely in my eyes?
> Why had I not with charitable hand
> Took up a beggar's issue at my gates,
> Who smirched thus and mired with infamy,
> I might have said "No part of it is mine;
> This shame derives itself from unknown loins"?
> But mine and mine I loved and mine I praised
> And mine that I was proud on, mine so much

That I myself was to myself not mine,
Valueing of her,—why, she, O, she is fallen
Into a pit of ink, that the wide sea
Hath drops too few to wash her clean again
And salt too little which may season give
To her foul-tainted flesh. (MAAN, IV, 1, 125 ff.)

Later, beginning to be convinced of her innocence, he is as passionate in his assault on Claudio. There is no similar occasion to call forth Antonio in defense of his daughter, but he joins Leonato in defending Hero, who is his niece.

In *Hamlet* the old father Polonius, prudent to the point of foolishness, cautions Ophelia against the dangers of listening to the love-making of hot-blooded young men and commands her to have nothing to do with Hamlet. Obeying him, she repels Hamlet's advances; and when Hamlet in a state of distraction breaks into her room and gazes at her sadly without speaking, she immediately carries her terror to Polonius, who interprets his behavior as lunacy due to frustrated love. Polonius reports his observations and conclusions to the king and queen, making it clear that his daughter is strictly under his thumb; and offers to use her as a decoy to prove the source of Hamlet's madness. Hamlet, encountering the old man, takes advantage of his madness (or pretended madness) to taunt him with his senile officious concern for his daughter's virtue; and later, when Ophelia returns his gifts, he puts Polonius' cautions against love into cutting and bitter language, telling her to hie to a nunnery and avoid such knaves as himself, and have her father shut up in the house that he may play the fool nowhere else. Not long after, he kills Polonius by accident behind the arras, and damns him as a meddlesome fool. Ophelia's subsequent madness and death are permeated with her love for her father, whose death is the immediate cause of her collapse. In the father-daughter relationship here there is some anticipation of that between Lear and Cordelia.

In *Merry Wives of Windsor* not a great deal is made of the father-daughter relationship, which is a minor theme in the subplot under the horseplay of Falstaff and the two matrons; but what there is of it follows the old pattern: the father, Page, insists on one suitor, the daughter chooses another.

In *Othello* as in *Hamlet* the father's death precedes the daughter's, for at the end of the play we are informed that Brabantio died of grief because of Desdemona's marriage to the Moor. Roused out of bed by Iago and Roderigo to be told that his daughter has eloped, the old senator in the beginning of the play goes at once to bring Othello to account, sure that he must have used some magic or drug to seduce her. In a few swift passages the whole story of the courtship is detailed before the Duke of Venice, and Desdemona herself, summoned as witness by Othello, confirms his statement that she gave her love to him of her own free accord. Brabantio accepts the accomplished fact, though with breaking heart, and makes his final exit with the warning:

> Look to her, Moor, if thou hast eyes to see:
> She has deceived her father, and may thee. (O, I, 3, 293 f.)

Relations between father and daughter are summed up in the following interchange:

> *Des.*   My noble father,
> I do perceive here a divided duty:
> To you I am bound for life and education;
> My life and education both do learn me
> How to respect you; you are the lord of duty;
> I am hitherto your daughter: but here's my husband,
> And so much duty as my mother showed
> To you, preferring you before her father,
> So much I challenge that I may profess
> Due to the Moor my lord.
> *Bra.*   God be wi' you! I have done.
> Please it your grace, on to the state-affairs:
> I had rather to adopt a child than get it.
> Come hither, Moor:
> I here do give you that with all my heart
> Which, but thou hast already, with all my heart
> I would keep from thee. For your sake, jewel,
> I am glad at soul I have no other child;
> For thy escape would teach me tyranny,
> To hang clogs on them. (O, I, 3, 180 ff.)

In this case there is no rival who is preferred by the father; Roderigo, who has been a suitor, is just as unwelcome as the Moor or any man, in that role. Before the elopement, in fact, Brabantio regarded Othello as a friend; it is apparently only as a lover of his daughter that he is hideous and unwelcome to him.

In *King Lear* the father-daughter theme is central, and pathetic. Once again, at the beginning of the play, the tyrannical old father is confronted by a spirited, plain-spoken daughter; he rebukes her and disinherits her; and her lover takes her without dowry. But the focus of the conflict is shifted. It is not Cordelia's stubbornness about a particular lover which enrages Lear; it is her refusal to say that her love for him is absolute, as her hypocritical sisters have done. She says:

> Good my lord,
> You have begot me, bred me, loved me: I
> Return those duties back as are right fit,
> Obey you, love you, and most honour you.
> Why have my sisters husbands, if they say
> They loved you all? Haply, when I shall wed,
> That lord whose hand must take my plight shall carry
> Half my love with him, half my care and duty:
> Sure, I shall never marry like my sisters,
> To love my father all. (L, I, 1, 97 ff.)

Having been cast out by Lear, and rejected as a wife by the Duke of Burgundy because she now has no dowry, she is chosen by the King of France to be his queen. At the last of the play, after Lear has been disowned and maltreated by Regan and Goneril, Cordelia returns with an army from France in an attempt to save the old man and his kingdom; she finds him in his madness and proves her love for him; but in the end she is killed, on orders from Edmund, bastard son to Gloucester and pledged lover to both Goneril and Regan, and Lear dies holding her in his arms, struggling to restore her to life. Cordelia thus has an importance in this play out of proportion to her weight as an active character, though ultimately it rests more upon her significance to Lear than it does upon her own actions. It is notable that the tie between father and daughter here, as well as in *Hamlet* and *Othello,* is much closer and more vital than in the earlier plays.

In *Pericles* the father-daughter relation is displayed three times, and it is untouched by the hostile tension present before. (No doubt the evidence of *Pericles* has to be accepted with some reservation because of the uncertainty regarding Shakespeare's part in it, the first two acts in particular being supposed on stylistic grounds to have been written by someone else, though presumably under his supervision.) The play opens on the incestuous relation between Antiochus, king of Antioch, and his daughter, whom Pericles has come to woo; on making the discovery Pericles has to flee for his life. In the second case, Thaisa, daughter of Simonides, king of Pentapolis, is entirely pleasing in her father's eyes, even in her choice of Pericles as her husband; and when Pericles, fearing the royal father's anger because of her love, disclaims any courtship on his part, Simonides courteously insists on the marriage as a wholly desirable thing. As for Pericles and his own daughter Marina, it is one of the prime causes of his prolonged depression, his profound melancholy, that he has lost her; and it is his rediscovery of her which restores him to health; furthermore, he willingly approves of her marriage to Lysimachus, governor of Mytilene, who first encountered her in a brothel and was there dissuaded by her eloquence and virtue from his attempt to seduce her. At all points in this play, then, the relation of father and daughter is one of love, and at one point is openly sexual.

In *Cymbeline*, the King of Britain, whose name gives the title to the play, is so enraged with his daughter Imogen because of her marriage to Posthumus that he banishes her husband and has her penned up, exclaiming:

> Nay, let her languish
> A drop of blood a day; and, being aged,
> Die of this folly! (Cy, I, 1, 157 ff.)

It only adds to his anger that Imogen says:

> Sir,
> It is your fault that I have loved Posthumus:
> You bred him as my playfellow, and he is
> A man worth any woman. (Cy, I, 1, 145 ff.)

Cymbeline's choice for her is the brutal Cloten, her half brother. The various changes of fortune which the play unfolds end, however, in overjoyed reconciliation between the father and daughter and her husband.

In *The Winter's Tale* the familiar rejection of the daughter by the father comes even before her birth; and Leontes condemns her to death shortly after she is born. After sixteen years of grief Leontes is reunited to her when, now supposedly the daughter of the shepherd who saved her, she flees with her lover Florizel, son of Polixenes, to take refuge in her true father's Court. On this occasion Leontes, still ignorant of the kinship with her, finds his daughter so attractive that he tells Florizel, who has begged him to intercede on her behalf with his father, that he would willingly marry her himself. Paulina, who has just recently argued that out of respect for the memory of Hermione he should not think of taking another wife, reproaches him for this amorous speech:

> Sir, my liege,
> Your eye hath too much youth in't; not a month
> 'Fore your queen died, she was more worth such gazes
> Than what you look on now. (WT, V, 1, 224 ff.)

Leontes excuses his behavior by saying that he was reminded of Hermione when he saw Perdita. The scene is similar to the meeting of Pericles with Marina, but the sexual coloring is more distinct. Leontes does proceed to reconcile Polixenes to his son, and when the discovery is made that Perdita is actually the daughter of Leontes and thus of equal birth with Florizel there is no further obstacle to the match. It should be noted that when Leontes first sees the two lovers, before their story is fully known to him, he comments that they remind him of what his son and daughter would have been if they had survived.

The Tempest delineates a relationship between father and daughter which is one of perfect love. Prospero and his daughter Miranda have lived on their desert island since she was three, when he was forced out of Milan by his brother Antonio, the usurper of his dukedom. At the time of the play Miranda is fifteen. During the long period of residence on the island Prospero has cared for her in every way, and he especially commends himself on his success as a teacher:

> and here
> Have I, thy schoolmaster, made thee more profit
> Than other princesses can that have more time
> For vainer hours and tutors not so careful. (T, I, 2, 171 ff.)

He declares that he loves her above everything else in the world. Even on this lonely island she has faced dangers, which he has protected her from; particularly the lustful advances of Caliban, the monster whom Prospero has tried in vain to humanize. The love which springs up between Miranda and Ferdinand, whom the magical storm conveys to the island, has Prospero's entire approval. Although he tests the character of Ferdinand by putting him to heavy labor, he watches their love-making with pleasure and comments upon their ecstatic condition:

> So glad of this as they I cannot be,
> Who are surprised withal: but my rejoicing
> At nothing can be more. (T, III, 1, 92 ff.)

When he gives his consent to their marriage he says to Ferdinand:

> If I have too austerely punished you,
> Your compensation makes amends, for I
> Have given you here a thrid of mine own life,
> Or that for which I live; who once again
> I tender to thy hand: all thy vexations
> Were but my trials of thy love, and thou
> Hast strangely stood the test: here, afore Heaven,
> I ratify this my rich gift. O Ferdinand,
> Do not smile at me that I boast her off,
> For thou shalt find she will outstrip all praise
> And make it halt behind her. (T, IV, 1, 1 ff.)

There is none of the old tragic tension between father and daughter in this last play. Yet even Prospero thinks it necessary to warn Ferdinand not to be intimate with his daughter before the wedding.

Having now gone through the chief examples of the father-daughter relationship, we may consider the theme in a more general way. Friction between father and daughter is common in these plays of Shakespeare; and the cause is usually the willful choice of a lover by a daughter, which may anger the father either because the choice is different from the one he prefers or because the father resents rivalry for the affections of the daughter altogether. The latter variant of the cause seems to be the more basic one. The pattern is broadly this: There is an original intense affection existing between father and daughter, usually mutual; the harmony is disturbed by the daughter's becoming attached to another man; because of her new love the daughter defies the authority of the father and is rejected by him. But the father-daughter relationship does not remain at a standstill in Shakespeare; as time passes it becomes tenderer and more sympathetic. From the beginning the daughter, in the main, does not reject the father but continues to admit her allegiance to him while insisting on her right to choose a lover and leave the father if necessary; but the father is often quite absolute in rejecting the daughter. With the passing of time absolute paternal rejection ceases to be so common. Thus, if the first seven plays listed in Table 7 are compared with the last seven, one sees that in the first seven there is only one instance out of the eight cases where the father abstains from severe condemnation of his daughter (and this is Polonius, who is a doubtful exception because of his prudish and nagging counsel), whereas in the last seven there are four instances out of eight (Pericles, Simonides, Leontes, Prospero) where no such condemnation is uttered. To be sure, statistical test does not reveal this difference as a clearly significant one; but we may note it as harmonious with the impressions received from detailed analysis of the plays. Also, in the two time periods there is a reversal of the relative weights of the fathers and lovers. In the first seven plays there is no father with a weight above 83, while in the last seven there are four with weights of 100; on the other hand in the first seven plays there are four lovers with weights of 100, while in the last seven there is only one—or two, if Pericles who has a double role is included. This comparison also fails of statistical significance when put in these terms. Neither is it possible to demonstrate the impressionistically perceived reversal by the more minute process of analysis of variance, when the weights of the fathers and lovers are reduced to comparable form by dividing each weight (summed in *Much Ado* and *Pericles*) by the corresponding total weight for the play involved and making the appropriate comparisons, with the plays split into groups as before. Father weight is greater in the second period by this method of comparison as by the other, and lover weight is less, but the respective F's are only 1.66 and 1.03. Also, if the difference between fathers and lovers is taken and the two periods compared, the F of 3.56 is still short of the 4.96 required to reach the 5 per cent level of confidence. Thus the quantitative analysis leaves us in some uncertainty as to whether we should maintain that a real increase of father weight and decrease of lover weight can be said to characterize the two periods so taken. Doubtless one reason for failing to demonstrate a significant increase of father weight at least is just that the particular line of demarcation chosen is inappropriate, as will appear from the brief discussion of this point at the conclusion of Section 6.[6]

The improvement noted in the relations between father and daughter in the plays is accompanied by some sexualization of the relationship: I refer especially to Pericles, Leontes, and Prospero. Considering the shift of emphasis from lover to father in the plays (and correspondingly in the personality of the author), and considering the fact that the heroine in these relationships is uniformly a young girl in the bloom of beauty, the sexualization is not surprising. One should expect that delight in the heroine's charms would be transferred to some extent from the lover, who has a minor role, to the father, who has a major one. To use a Freudian term, the quantity of libido in the total personality of the author finds its outlet at the primary masculine focus.

Finally, the quantitative relations between the character weights of the fathers, daughters, and lovers as given in Table 7 deserve some attention. The father weights are negatively related to the weights of the lovers and the daughters, while the weights of lovers and daughters are positively related. In terms of the correlation coefficient, father and lover weights co-vary $-.73$, father and daughter weights $-.32$, and lover and daughter weights $.36$. (For purposes of these calculations three weights were employed which are entered in Table 7 in parentheses, viz., 17 for Egeus, 7 for Anne, and 5 for King of France.) Now, only the coefficient of $-.73$ for the relation between father and lover weights is statistically significant taken by itself; but the three coefficients of correlation are really organically intertwined, and when the relationships are submitted to partial correlation this fact becomes evident. Our problem is the isolation of trends of relationship where contrary trends are entangled. We can meet the problem by artificially holding constant one of the variables concerned (eliminating it, as it were, in order to purify the mixture), and then we can examine the remaining two variables in isolation. When this is done, all the correlation coefficients rise to above .90 in magnitude and become definitely signifi-

6. P. 157 f.

cant. Specifically, when the appropriate third variable is held constant, the correlation coefficient between father and lover weights becomes —.96; between father and daughter weights —.91; and between daughter and lover weights .92. As the data stand, it is hardly an exaggeration to say that these three components of Shakespeare's personality constitute a self-contained system in which the power status of each influences the power status of the other two in a very determinate way. Here once more, as with the question concerning the trait differences between tragedy-history and comedy-romance,[7] it is impossible to say to what degree this set of quantitative relations depended upon a conscious formula in the mind of Shakespeare and how much upon tendencies of which he was not aware.

4

I turn now to a third theme, which will be defined by first extracting it from *The Tempest,* where it is most unmistakable, and then tracing it in obscurer manifestations back through some of the preceding plays.

Two distinctly opposite figures of a supernatural kind appear in *The Tempest:* Ariel and Caliban. Both are servants of Prospero, but Ariel is loved by him, Caliban hated. Ariel, a spirit capable of changing form and doing anything commanded by his master Prospero, willingly does his bidding, though complaining occasionally because he wishes to be entirely at liberty. Caliban, in contrast, an ugly, evil, earthy monster, habitually greets Prospero with curses and in return is punished by him with aches and cramps; but he does the necessary heavy work around the island, such as bringing in the wood and tending the fire. Ariel is the efficient agent of Prospero's magical power; Caliban is a rebellious slave, kept in subjection by it. Their histories as well as their natures are opposite. Both were on the island when Prospero arrived —Ariel imprisoned in a pine by the witch Sycorax because he was "a spirit too delicate To act her earthly and abhorred commands," Caliban (the witch's son) roaming at large. Prospero freed Ariel from the pine, and in the beginning he took Caliban also under his care:

7. Pp. 74 f.

> I pitied thee,
> Took pains to make thee speak, taught thee each hour
> One thing or other: when thou didst not, savage,
> Know thine own meaning, but wouldst gabble like
> A thing most brutish, I endowed thy purposes
> With words that made them known. But thy vile race,
> Though thou didst learn, had that in't which good natures
> Could not abide to be with. (T, I, 2, 153 ff.)

The specific crime for which he came to hate Caliban was the at-tempted rape of Miranda; and for that Prospero isolated him on the island, removing him from his own cell where at first he lodged him and forcing him to occupy a separate cave or region of rocks. Caliban charges in turn that Prospero robbed him of the island, which he inherited from Sycorax and which he helped Prospero to explore. He continually thinks of revenge; and when the drunken Stephano and Trinculo come on the scene he conspires with them to destroy Prospero, possess his daughter, and regain the island. This plot is balked by Prospero and Ariel, who punish the con-spirators furiously.

Such dramatic figures as Ariel and Caliban naturally suggest all kinds of allegorical interpretations. It seems to me only slightly allegorical, however, to regard Caliban as connected with Pros-pero's body and its desires, and Ariel as connected with his im-agination and its powers. They are Prospero's only two servants, and they are very close to him, as body and imagination are close to every self; and in their nature and functions they fit very well into such a half-allegorical scheme. But even if it seems impermis-sible to take them out of their proper character at all, it is still clearly evident that they are a contrasting pair, and that one of them is of the earth earthy, heavy with brutal desires and physical suffering, while the other is a thing of air and fire, light, musical, a pure spirit.

It is possible to discover antecedents of these two figures else-where in Shakespeare, though perhaps only in *A Midsummer Night's Dream* is there a conspicuously similar contrast. We find in that play the opposed figures of Bottom and Puck, opposed less extremely than Caliban and Ariel but along the same dimension. Although Bottom is not the demidevil that Caliban is, he is very gross, close to the earth, ridiculous, and on being endowed at one point with the head of an ass he takes on the appearance of a thorough monster; and though Puck is not so pure and well-governed a spirit as Ariel, he is still a spirit, swift and musical, doing magical things at the behest of Oberon his master. It might be pointed out that there are other features of the earlier play which anticipate matters in *The Tempest*. For instance, there is Theseus' famous remark about poetry:

> And as imagination bodies forth
> The forms of things unknown, the poet's pen
> Turns them to shapes and gives to airy nothing
> A local habitation and a name—(MSND, V, 1, 14 ff.)

which has its counterpart in the more superb speech of Prospero's about the "baseless fabric" of the vision he has called up to celebrate the contract of love between Ferdinand and Miranda. There is a trace of the high jinks of *The Tempest* in Puck's persecution of the uncertain lovers and in the fright he gives to the companions of Bottom. We might even note that, as Theseus has a pack of hounds and routs the lovers out of the wood with his playful hunting, so Prospero uses a pack of his own in the much grimmer hunting of Caliban and his henchmen. We achieve a still closer convergence of these plays if we regard Prospero as a fusion of Theseus and Oberon, uniting in his one person the rulership of two realms, the earthly and the spiritual. Whether we permit ourselves this synthesis or not, it is evident that in *The Tempest* the two realms of being are more perfectly joined than in *A Midsummer Night's Dream*, where the fairy-governed adventures of the summer night are almost entirely separated from the transactions of the real world over which Theseus reigns. Prospero is as solidly real as anything in *The Tempest*, and yet his commerce with the spirits is a basic feature of his life. It may be said in general that the later plays of Shakespeare reveal less cleavage of waking experience from sleeping, of physical occurrence from psychic, of commonplace matter of fact from magic, than do the earlier ones; and the seamless junction of earthly and spiritual in Prospero is an example of this. There is, however, greater spiritual tension around Prospero; or rather, to keep to the allegory, there is greater tension between the earthly and the spiritual. Ariel and Caliban differ from Puck and Bottom principally in the fact that the opposition between the two members of the pair is taken less seriously in the earlier play. Both Puck and Bottom are comic figures, both amiable in their way, both faulty in their kind, and both meant for entertainment; but Ariel and Caliban are hostile extremes.

In the plays between *A Midsummer Night's Dream* and *The Tempest* nothing distinctly like Puck or Ariel is to be found; but Falstaff has some of the lineaments of Bottom and Caliban. Take away his wit but not his garrulity, and he might pass very well for something betwixt the two. Like Caliban, he is associated with drunkards and rascals, and knows the art of cursing. A spiritual opposite to him is not present in any pure form, however. There is just the faintest trace, perhaps, in the description of Prince Hal rising from the ground like feathered Mercury to vault easily into his saddle,

> As if an angel dropped down from the clouds,
> To turn and wind a fiery Pegasus
> And witch the world with noble horsemanship.
>
> (I HIV, IV, 1, 109 ff.)

But it is no more than a trace, and one has to strain to see it. The address of the prince in which, after inheriting the crown from his father, he rejects his old companion, while painting a most unpleasant picture of Falstaff, also vaguely reminds one of the situation on the magic island of *The Tempest*:

> I know thee not, old man: fall to thy prayers;
> How ill white hairs become a fool and jester!
> I have long dreamed of such a kind of man,
> So surfeit-swelled, so old and so profane;
> But, being awaked, I do despise my dream.
> Make less thy body hence, and more thy grace;
> Leave gormandizing; know the grave doth gape
> For thee thrice wider than for other men.
> Reply not to me with a fool-born jest;
> Presume not that I am the thing I was;
> For God doth know, so shall the world perceive,
> That I have turned away my former self;
> So will I those that kept me company.
> When thou dost hear I am as I have been,
> Approach me, and thou shalt be as thou wast,

> The tutor and the feeder of my riots:
> Till then, I banish thee, on pain of death,
> As I have done the rest of my misleaders,
> Not to come near our person by ten mile. (2 HIV, V, 5, 51 ff.)

But this is not Puck or Ariel; it is rather a forecast, at several re-
moves, of Prospero thrusting Caliban out of his presence to dwell
in a limited region of his island; and this is not the parallel we are
looking for.

In *Twelfth Night* Sir Toby Belch is a watered-down version of
Falstaff, and the mischievous Maria may have a streak of Puck;
but, once more, the earthy nature of the one is more obvious than
the spiritual nature of the other.

The Falstaff of *The Merry Wives of Windsor,* as the critics never
tire of pointing out, is not a continuation of his namesake of *Henry
IV,* but something much cruder, whose comical appeal, such as it
is, is mostly in the bulk of his "guts and midriff" and his remarkable
capacity for being gulled. But he clearly belongs in the Bottom-
Caliban series, and both his animality and his ancestor Bottom are
recalled by dressing him up as "a Windsor stag; and the fattest, I
think, i' the forest" for his rendezvous in the park with Mrs. Ford.

More distinctly of the Caliban breed are Parolles of *All's Well
That Ends Well* and Cloten of *Cymbeline.* Parolles is something
like Falstaff—a great garrulous liar and misleader of youth. It is
on his seconding that Bertram runs away from his wife and so
incurs the king's displeasure. Bertram himself denounces him as
"a most perfidious knave, With all the spots o' the world taxed and
deboshed." (AWEW, V, 3, 205 f.) His role lacks the comedy of
Falstaff, just as Falstaff lacks the innocence of Bottom. In short, he
is more despicable than his predecessors. And more despicable still
is Cloten. For Cloten lacks both innocence and wit, even the wit of
Parolles; he is a stupid, vicious beast. It is curious that both these
latter put much emphasis on clothes: Parolles is a dandy, whose
fantastic fashionableness is ridiculed by Lafeu; and Cloten thinks
it a clever part of his design on Imogen that he wears Posthumus'
garments. Cloten summarizes his combined villainy and silliness
in the speech in which he lays out his plans:

> I would these garments were come. She said upon a time—the bitter-
> ness of it I now belch from my heart—that she held the very garment of

Posthumus in more respect than my noble and natural person, together
with the adornment of my qualities. With that suit upon my back, will
I ravish her: first kill him, and in her eyes; there shall she see my valour,
which will then be a torment to her contempt. He on the ground, my
speech of insultment ended on his dead body, and when my lust hath
dined,—which, as I say, to vex her I will execute in the clothes that she
so praised,—to the court I'll knock her back, foot her home again. (Cy,
III, 5, 144 ff.)

Beyond Cloten it is not far to Caliban, whose gross inhuman viciousness has as one of its chief aims the ravishment of Miranda.

A series of dramatic figures, then, from Bottom—through the
two Falstaffs, Sir Toby Belch, Parolles, and Cloten—to Caliban,
reveal an aspect of Shakespeare's personality which becomes progressively more evil and bestial in appearance. To use the allegor-
izing language of an earlier paragraph, this progression indicates
a devaluation, though hardly an extinction, of the body and its
desires. It is interesting to observe the increasing quantities of lust
attributed to these characters, and the correlative loss of respect
and romantic feeling for women. Bottom shows no particular interest in Titania, the fairy queen who is magically enamored of him,
but he is not offensive in behavior, however repulsive in form; the
first Falstaff, though scarcely chivalrous or maidenly, tends to
emphasize his appetite for drink rather than for women; Sir Toby
Belch makes no direct assault, but he commits offenses against his
niece Olivia by his panderizing horseplay; the second Falstaff goes
rutting after a married woman; Parolles verbally, and verbosely,
makes an attack on the ideal of virginity; Cloten, slightly gallant
in his wooing, is bent on rape; while Caliban, finally, knows only
brutal lust, without a touch of courtesy or romance. As interesting
to observe and as important is the tightening up of the dramatic
defenses (and, by inference, the personality defenses) against the
kinds of operations which these characters perform. Bottom has
virtually free range and, though ridiculed, is not rejected (odd,
however, that it is a woman—Hippolyta—who comes nearest to
rejecting him, being much less tolerant than Theseus of his efforts
to be entertaining); the first Falstaff, after dominating or nearly
dominating the action of two plays, is rejected, to die subsequently
of a broken heart; Sir Toby, who is permitted some scope in his

horseplay, is given a sound drubbing by the man who is to become Olivia's husband; the second Falstaff is repeatedly thwarted and punished; Parolles is excruciatingly tortured and discredited; Cloten is beheaded; and Caliban is enslaved, kept under constant surveillance, and periodically racked with bodily pains. There is a rough gradation in the series toward a greater severity of control.

If now we estimate the relative bulk of these eight characters by dividing the character weight of each by the total of twelve character weights for the respective plays we get the following values, in chronological sequence: .134, .209, .256, .129, .178, .125, .068, .078. Inspection suggests an orderly decline of weight. The correlation coefficient for the weights against the temporal order is —.67, which falls just a little shy of the 5 per cent level of confidence usually required for demonstrating significance. But if Bottom is eliminated from the list, as being really too innocent to belong among his sinful and bestial successors (for it is only his earthiness, not his sinfulness—he is too pristine for that—which unites him to them), then the decline of weight with time becomes more evident and the correlation coefficient rises to —.89, which is high enough to place it at the 1 per cent level of confidence and justify us in accepting the trend as not due to accident. This particular decline harmonizes with the results of the qualitative analysis just preceding and with the view previously advanced that there is a general trend in Shakespeare toward the diminution of the importance of sexual love as the years pass.

So much for the predecessors of Caliban. But where are the counterparts of Ariel in *Twelfth Night, The Merry Wives of Windsor, All's Well That Ends Well,* and *Cymbeline?* They are nowhere to be found, unless we are content to accept the spiritual loveliness of the heroines Viola, Helena, and Imogen as tangentially indicative of what Ariel stands for; and this may be overingenious. As a distinct dramatic figure, the delicate spirit suffers an eclipse between *A Midsummer Night's Dream* and *The Tempest.*

5

The three conspicuous themes which have been examined do not by any means exhaust the dynamic content of the dramas. Exhaustiveness is not my aim; but I do feel compelled to deal with a fourth theme, that of the relation between mother and son, especially because of the somewhat dubious prominence given it by Freud in a note on *Hamlet* and by Ernest Jones in a lengthy essay. These psychoanalysts, resting their case heavily upon this one play, have stressed the importance of the Oedipus complex in Shakespeare. What evidence does the present method of analysis afford for agreeing with them? On the whole, not much. The role of mother is comparatively rare in the plays, and where it occurs it is represented by characters having relatively little weight. The women function primarily as daughters and sweethearts and wives. It is true, however, that the mothers, when they do appear, are usually mothers of sons, and in the main they exhibit a good deal of love for them; but anything like sexual reciprocation of this affection on the part of the sons is hard to find, and the peculiar triangle of Oedipal rivalry even harder. Critical examination of this and related questions will, however, be deferred to a later chapter.

Table 8 extracts from Table 1 the principal mother-son relation-

TABLE 8

THEME: MOTHER-SON RELATIONSHIP

Date	Play	Mother	Son
1592–93	RIII	Duchess York 13	Gloucester 100
1592–93	CE	Abbess 27	Antipholus S. 100
1595–96	RII	Duchess York 13	Aumerle 11
1595–96	MSND	Titania 56	foundling 0
1596–97	J	Constance 51	Arthur 23
		Elinor 11	John 82
1600–1	H	Gertrude 11	Hamlet 100
1602–3	AWEW	Countess 58	Bertram 56
1607–8	C	Volumnia 34	Coriolanus 100
1609–10	Cy	Queen 27	Cloten 35
1610–11	WT	Hermione 31	Mamillius 0

ships. The chronological order of the table will not be strictly followed in the exposition.

The Duchess of York in *Richard III* is an old woman whose principal son, the villainous Gloucester, is the tragic burden of her incessant lamentations and imprecations. She cries out against him:

> Thou camest on earth to make the earth my hell.
> A grievous burthen was thy birth to me;
> Tetchy and wayward thy infancy;
> Thy school-days frightful, desperate, wild, and furious,
> Thy prime of manhood daring, bold, and venturous,
> Thy age confirmed, proud, subtle, bloody, treacherous;
>
> (R III, IV, 4, 166 ff.)

and as he goes to his last battle she curses him and prophesies his death:

> Bloody thou art, bloody will be thy end;
> Shame serves thy life and doth thy death attend.
>
> (R III, IV, 4, 194 f.)

The abbess of *The Comedy of Errors* figures in the action primarily as the protectress of her son Antipholus of Syracuse, who flees into her priory to escape the vigorous attentions of Adriana, who, being married to his twin, has mistaken him for her husband. She lectures Adriana on the proper behavior toward a husband, and refuses to let her follow Antipholus into the priory. At the time, she is not aware that he is her son.

Titania, the fairy queen of *A Midsummer Night's Dream*, has a little boy (not an actor in the play)—a foundling whom she adopted when the human mother died. The fairy king Oberon vainly begs her to surrender the child to him. It is because of her refusal that he has her enchanted so that she compulsively falls in love with Bottom, equipped with his head of an ass.

Dramatically, the preceding mother-son relationships are rather incidental. More important figures are the Duchess of York in *Richard II* and Constance in *King John*. Both are mothers of sons to whom they are devoted.

The incident in *Richard II* which is relevant here is highly charged dramatically. The young Duke of Aumerle, the duchess' son, being involved in a plot against the usurping king Bolingbroke, is accused of treason by his father; the mother calls the father a villain for not protecting his son, and cries to Aumerle to strike him; all three then hasten to the king, Aumerle and the duchess to pray for pardon, the duke to demand that his son be punished as a traitor. The duchess is passionate and eloquent in defense of her son, and it is distinctly clear that her love for him is greater than her love for her husband. Incidentally, the familiar note of sexual betrayal is here; for the duchess suspects the duke of regarding his son as a bastard, and swears that it is not so.

In *King John* Constance is the mother of Arthur, young nephew of King John of England. In the course of a war with France John captures his nephew and has him imprisoned under guard of Hubert, who is instructed to kill him. Arthur is so young, good, and gentle that Hubert, hardened though he is, cannot bring himself to carry out the king's demand; but subsequently the boy is killed accidentally in an attempted escape. All of Constance's love is wrapped up in her son. She regards him as the rightful heir of the English throne, and when he is taken from her she dies of a broken heart. Sure that John or the hardship of prison will kill the boy, she displays grief verging on madness. Tearing her hair, she cries:

> For since the birth of Cain, the first male child,
> To him that did but yesterday suspire,
> There was not such a gracious creature born.
> But now will canker sorrow eat my bud
> And chase the native beauty from his cheek
> And he will look as hollow as a ghost,
> As dim and meagre as an ague's fit,
> And so he'll die; and, rising so again,
> When I shall meet him in the court of heaven
> I shall not know him: therefore, never, never,
> Must I behold my pretty Arthur more. (J, III, 4, 79 ff.)

To the empty phrases of Cardinal Pandulph, whose whole thought is of political influence, she scornfully replies, "He talks to me that never had a son," and goes on venting her misery in piercing tones:

> Grief fills the room up of my absent child,
> Lies in his bed, walks up and down with me,
> Puts on his pretty looks, repeats his words,
> Remembers me of all his gracious parts,
> Stuffs out his vacant garments with his form;
> Then, have I reason to be fond of grief?
> Fare you well: had you such loss as I,
> I could give better comfort than you do.
> I will not keep this form upon my head,
> When there is such disorder in my wit.
> O Lord! my boy, my Arthur, my fair son!
> My life, my joy, my food, my all the world! (J, III, 4, 93 ff.)

Constance's laments have an unusually genuine ring, and the depiction of Arthur is touchingly sympathetic.

In *The Winter's Tale*, in one brief scene, an exquisitely charming picture emerges of the relations between Hermione and her little son Mamillius. A trifle annoyed with him at first, perhaps because of his too lively attentions to her, she asks the ladies with her to look after him. A few moments later she breaks in on their conversation, and invites him to tell her a story. He offers to tell her one "of sprites and goblins." They sit down together, and when we last see him he is whispering the spooky adventure in her ear. After the mother's imprisonment by the father he loses all spirit and appetite, and on the day of the trial dies. At the news, Hermione collapses in a deathlike faint.

In *Hamlet, All's Well That Ends Well, Coriolanus,* and *Cymbeline* we are presented with mother-son relationships developed on a larger scale than in the preceding cases and involving grown men. The two of greatest emotional impact are *Hamlet* and *Coriolanus*.

The play of *Hamlet* revolves upon the death of the hero's father. It opens two months after that event with Hamlet still deeply mourning, and distressed by the fact that his mother, Queen Gertrude, has married Claudius, his father's brother, within a month of the funeral. The apparition of the father's ghost, revealing that he was murdered by Claudius and calling for revenge, brings all Hamlet's conflicting emotions to the boiling point, but does not fundamentally alter their character. Even before this occasion the turmoil of his thoughts has been expressed in a violent soliloquy:

> That it should come to this!
> But two months dead: nay, not so much, not two:
> So excellent a king; that was, to this,
> Hyperion to a satyr; so loving to my mother
> That he might not beteem the winds of heaven
> Visit her face too roughly. Heaven and earth!
> Must I remember? why, she would hang on him,
> As if increase of appetite had grown
> By what it fed on: and yet, within a month—
> Let me not think on't—Frailty, thy name is woman!—
> A little month, or ere those shoes were old
> With which she followed my poor father's body,
> Like Niobe, all tears:—why she, even she—

> O God! a beast, that wants discourse of reason,
> Would have mourned longer—married with my uncle,
> My father's brother, but no more like my father
> Than I to Hercules: within a month:
> Ere yet the salt of most unrighteous tears
> Had left the flushing in her galled eyes,
> She married. O, most wicked speed, to post
> With such dexterity to incestuous sheets! (H, I, 2, 137 ff.)

The emphasis of this passage is on the wickedness of the mother, which has two aspects: the brevity of her mourning, and her entrance into a sexual relationship which Hamlet damns as incest, as legally it was. The Ghost, when he appears, bids Hamlet to focus his enmity on the murderous uncle and leave his mother to the judgment of Heaven; but he is never quite able to do this. In what is perhaps the most oppressively emotional scene in the play, a scene sultry with ambiguous passion, Hamlet assails his mother in her bedroom, after killing the eavesdropping old Polonius, with the most vivid charges of unbridled lust. Even the interposition of the Ghost, to "whet his almost blunted purpose" of revenge, does not check the torrent of abuse which he pours down on his mother's head. Before he leaves her, he orders her not to:

> Let the bloat king tempt you again to bed;
> Pinch wanton on your cheek; call you his mouse;
> And let him, for a pair of reechy kisses,
> Or paddling in your neck with his damned fingers,
> Make you to ravel all this matter out,
> That I essentially am not in madness,
> But mad in craft. (H, III, 4, 182 ff.)

He leaves her with difficulty. Five times he says good night before he can tear himself away. It is hardly farfetched to interpret Hamlet's behavior as expressing an emotional attachment to his mother capable of generating sexual jealousy. The queen on her side consistently shows a warm motherly affection for him. On neither Hamlet's side nor hers is the love quelled by his vehement moral attack.

In the next two plays in our list the mothers are represented as attempting to guide their sons into lives of morality and honor.

The countess in *All's Well That Ends Well* supports the virtuous Helena in her suit for the love of her son Bertram, and is as anxious as Helena (after Bertram's desertion) that he return home and accept his responsibilities as Helena's husband. The nature of the attachment between mother and son is given in the opening lines, along with a reference that wakes memories of the state of affairs in *Hamlet:*

> Count. In delivering my son from me, I bury a second husband.
> Bert. And I in going, madam, weep o'er my father's death anew.
> (AWEW, I, 1, 1 ff.)

The countess gives him her blessing in parting:

> Be thou blest, Bertram, and succeed thy father
> In manners, as in shape! thy blood and virtue
> Contend for empire in thee, and thy goodness
> Share with thy birthright! Love all, trust a few,
> Do wrong to none. (AWEW, I, 1, 70 ff.)

Bertram some time after this is married to Helena, with the countess' consent and at the command of the king, whom Helena by her medical art has restored to health; and when he later runs away and sends letters back to say that he will never live with his wife, his mother is so profoundly displeased with his conduct that she exclaims, "I do wash his name out of my blood." (AWEW, III, 1, 70) The mother in this case, then, although she loves her son deeply, is not willing to tolerate his dishonorable behavior toward a virtuous wife.

In *Coriolanus* the mother Volumnia is the primal source of Coriolanus' heroic, ambitious nature and controls him as no one else can. Her attitude is well expressed in her words to Virgilia, her gentle daughter-in-law, as they await his return from battle:

> I pray you, daughter, sing; or express yourself in a more comfortable sort: if my son were my husband, I should freelier rejoice in that absence wherein he won honour than in the embracements of his bed where he would show most love. When yet he was but tender-bodied and the only son of my womb, when youth with comeliness plucked all gaze his way, when for a day of kings' entreaties a mother should not sell him an hour from her beholding, I, considering how honour would become such a person, that it was no better than picture-like to hang on the wall, if renown made it not stir, was pleased to let him seek danger where he was like to find fame. To a cruel war I sent him; from whence he returned, his brows bound with oak. I tell thee, daughter, I sprang not more in joy at first hearing he was a man-child than now in first seeing he had proved himself a man. (C, I, 3, 1 ff.)

With such a mother, it is small wonder that Coriolanus is a military hero. But he is also extremely proud, extremely contemptuous of the common people of Rome; and when he is up for the office of consul, he is so disdainful of them that they accuse him of treachery and banish him from the city. Taking leave of his family and friends, but with especial attention to his mother, he promises her:

> your son
> Will or exceed the common or be caught
> With cautelous baits and practice. (C, IV, 1, 31 ff.)

Volumnia is as angry as her son at the Roman citizens, and berates their leaders with a sharp tongue. Coriolanus, whose whole thought is of revenge, makes an alliance with his former enemy Aufidius and joins him in attacking Rome. They sweep all before them and are at the gates of the city when the Romans begin sending out envoys to beg for terms. Coriolanus refuses to listen to them—even to Menenius, who is his godfather and long-respected friend. At this critical juncture, his family come out to plead with him. His wife and little son move him, but it is his mother who has the most powerful effect, kneeling and saying:

> There's no man in the world
> More bound to's mother; yet here he lets me prate
> Like one i' the stocks. (C, V, 3, 158 ff.)

Yielding to her entreaties he makes peace with Rome; but exclaims, prophetically:

> O mother, mother!
> What have you done? Behold, the heavens do ope,
> The gods look down, and this unnatural scene
> They laugh at. O my mother, mother! O!
> You have won a happy victory to Rome;
> But, for your son,—believe it, O, believe it,
> Most dangerously you have with him prevailed,
> If not most mortal to him. (C, V, 3, 182 ff.)

On his return to his adopted city of Antium he is once again accused of being a traitor because of the terms he has granted Rome, and at the instigation of Aufidius he is assassinated. To his powerful mother, then, Coriolanus owes both great strength and great weakness.

The Queen in *Cymbeline* and her son Cloten need not detain us. The Queen evidently wants her son to possess Imogen for himself, if she is to be allowed to survive at all; but it is her own possession of the throne that interests her more, and she is ready to eliminate every obstacle which threatens her position. There is too little action between the two to define the nature of the relationship precisely, beyond noting that the viciousness of the son is backed up by the viciousness of the mother.

Reviewing the list of mothers and sons, we see that the relationship is dramatically most important in *Hamlet* and *Coriolanus*. From the point of view of rank within a play, however, no mother is more important than Constance, who is in third place. Constance's son is a young, dependent child. Nearly all the other sons in the list (the most pronounced exception is Gloucester), though not all young, are also dependent upon the mother, or at least strongly under her influence and care. This influence is not entirely well taken by Bertram and Coriolanus; Hamlet is in open rebellion; and in three other cases of grown men, the unrebellious dependency of Aumerle is made to appear disgraceful and that of Cloten evil, while in the close harmony between King John and his mother, Elinor, what chiefly appears is hardness of character and wickedness of aim in both. The general impression produced by all these cases is not one of a flourishing Oedipus complex in the author. If any such complex is present (and *Hamlet* is the best evidence), it is the reaction against it rather than submission to it which one would most logically derive from the kind of analysis attempted here, which does not pretend to reach into the repressed depths. While there is no doubt of deep or superficial motherly affection in all these cases (with the exception of Gloucester's mother), there is scant evidence of a return of affection by the son which can justifiably be called sexual, except in the one case of Hamlet, where nauseated rejection of the tendency is the predominant emotion.

6

In order to complete the examination of the foregoing theme, and to round out (but still not completely) the treatment of various family relationships, it will be well in this place to make a brief

survey of father and son relations. Table 9 presents in chronological order the fathers of sons listed in Table 1 and, alongside them,
their sons, whether these are listed among the first twelve characters or not. Coriolanus, who does not appear in this table, was left
out because the mother-son relationship between Volumnia and
him far overshadows the faintly delineated relationship between
him and his son. If he had been included, the quantitative trend
discussed on page 157 would have been still clearer than it is.

TABLE 9

THEME: FATHER-SON RELATIONSHIP

Date	Play	Father	Son
1592–93	CE	Aegeon 53	Antipholus S. 100
			Antipholus E. 78
1593–94	TS	Vincentio 6	Lucentio 31
1594–95	TGV	Antonio 9	Proteus 94
1594–95	RJ	Montague 7	Romeo 100
1595–96	RII	York 38	Aumerle 11
1596–97	J	K. Philip 38	Lewis 29
1597–98	1 HIV	King 61	Prince 94
			Lancaster 0
1597–98	2 HIV	King 54	Prince 50
			Lancaster 19
			Clarence 0
			Gloucester 0
1600–1	H	Polonius 23	Laertes 15
		Ghost 7	Hamlet 100
1600–1	MWW	Page 37	William 0
1605–6	L	Gloucester 47	Edgar 56
			Edmund 44
1605–6	M	Duncan 9	Malcolm 30
			Donalbain 0
		Banquo 19	Fleance 0
		Macduff 29	son 0
1609–10	Cy	Cymbeline 47	Guiderius 26
			Arviragus 21
1610–11	WT	Leontes 100	Mamillius 0
		Polixenes 41	Florizel 31
1611–12	T	Alonso 17	Ferdinand 23

Aegeon, Vincentio, Antonio, and Montague, of the first four
plays in the list, all show in their various ways solicitude for their
sons; but the sons do not show a corresponding care for the fathers,

and to some extent, though not by any direct attack, bring trouble and suffering to them. Thus, Aegeon undergoes various trials, including arrest and the threat of execution, while he searches for Antipholus of Syracuse who has himself gone in search of his twin brother Antipholus of Ephesus; Vincentio, after sending Lucentio to Padua to improve his education, comes to visit him and runs into sundry farcical but nevertheless painful experiences before he finds him, now married without his father's permission; Antonio, paternally concerned for his son's welfare, sends Proteus to the emperor's Court to advance his knowledge of the world—with the disgraceful consequences previously noted; and Montague, who warmly defends the son whose secrets he does not share, loses his wife because of her grief over Romeo's banishment and later has to grieve Romeo's death. Between York and his son Aumerle there are open and radical differences, and York climaxes the bitterness between them by accusing Aumerle before the king of treason. The relations between King Philip and Lewis, the Dauphin, are not exhibited; but Lewis continues his father's struggle, more successfully, against King John.

After these somewhat marginal treatments, the father-son relationship rises to central importance in the two parts of *Henry IV* and in *Hamlet*, and in later plays remains as a more serious theme than it was before.

In the very beginning of the first part of *Henry IV* the king laments the shameful behavior of the prince, and wishes that Harry Percy, the Hotspur of the north, were his son instead of Harry Plantagenet. The doubts of the king about the prince are, indeed, the *raison d'être* of both installments of *Henry IV*. The prince is under a cloud, and he has to demonstrate to his father and the world at large that he is not what he seems, but the very glory of his royal house. This he does in the first part by his heroic exploits on the battlefield, where he rescues the king from imminent death and in single combat kills Percy; and in the second part by the display of grief at his father's death, the austere acceptance of his kingly duties, and his renunciation of Falstaff and his companions, who symbolize his former licentious and shiftless ways. In the first of their two important interviews, the prince meets his father's verbal chastisement contritely and with promises of a better future:

> *Prince.* So please your majesty, I would I could
> Quit all offences with as clear excuse
> As well as I am doubtless I can purge
> Myself of many I am charged withal:
> Yet such extenuation let me beg,
> As, in reproof of many tales devised,
> Which oft the ear of greatness needs must hear,
> By smiling pick-thanks and base newsmongers,
> I may, for some things true, wherein my youth
> Hath faulty wandered and irregular,
> Find pardon on my true submission.
> *King.* God pardon thee; yet let me wonder, Harry,
> At thy affections, which do hold a wing
> Quite from the flight of all thy ancestors.
> Thy place in council thou hast rudely lost,
> Which by thy younger brother is supplied,
> And art almost an alien to the hearts
> Of all the court and princes of my blood:
> The hope and expectation of thy time
> Is ruined, and the soul of every man
> Prophetically doth forethink thy fall. (1 HIV, III, 2, 18 ff.)

In enlarging on this dismal theme, the king contrasts the prince's behavior with that of himself and Harry Percy, who energetically pursues military honors; and to all this the prince eloquently replies that he will redeem his name by killing the northern hero, whenever

> This gallant Hotspur, this all-praised knight,
> And your unthought-of Harry chance to meet.
>
> (1 HIV, III, 2, 140 f.)

He indeed betters the promise in the performance on the field of Shrewsbury; for he not only kills Percy, but he also rescues his father from the fierce Douglas. In connection with this heroic rescue there is a curious interchange between father and son which brings into sharp focus one of the charges against the prince obscurely referred to above, where he implies that he has been slandered by "base newsmongers":

> *King.* Stay, and breathe awhile:
> Thou hast redeemed thy lost opinion,
> And showed thou makest some tender of my life,
> In this fair rescue thou hast brought to me.
> *Prince.* O God! they did me too much injury

> That ever said I hearkened for your death.
> If it were so, I might have let alone
> The insulting hand of Douglas over you,
> Which would have been as speedy in your end.
> As all the poisonous potions in the world
> And saved the treacherous labour of your son. (1 HIV, V, 4, 47 ff.)

In the second part the prince is shown again in the company of his disreputable companions, endeavoring to hide under forced merriment the sorrow he feels because the king is ill. The conversation with Poins is very odd:

Prince. Marry, I tell thee, it is not meet that I should be sad, now my father is sick: albeit I could tell to thee, as to one it pleases me, for fault of a better, to call my friend, I could be sad, and sad indeed too.
Poins. Very hardly upon such a subject.
Prince. By this hand, thou thinkest me as far in the devil's book as thou and Falstaff for obduracy and persistency: let the end try the man. But I tell thee, my heart bleeds inwardly that my father is so sick: and keeping such vile company as thou art hath in reason taken from me all ostentation of sorrow.
Poins. The reason?
Prince. What wouldst thou think of me, if I should weep?
Poins. I would think thee a most princely hypocrite.
Prince. It would be every man's thought . . . (2 HIV, II, 2, 42 ff.)

How deep the skepticism runs concerning the prince's worth and trustworthiness, even after the exploits at Shrewsbury, is shown again at the bedside of the king, as he lies dying. The prince, thinking his father dead, places the crown on his head and walks out of the room. The king revives, sees that the crown is gone, and learns that it has been taken by his graceless heir. Only one construction seems possible, and the king voices it:

> Thou hast stolen that which after some few hours
> Were thine without offence; and at my death
> Thou hast sealed up my expectation:
> Thy life did manifest thou lovedst me not
> And thou wilt have me die assured of it. (2 HIV, IV, 5, 102 ff.)

And for the kingdom he prophesies general ruin under the riotous misgovernment of his son. But the eloquence of the prince is equal to this occasion, as to every other, and the king is so satisfied in the matter of the purloined crown that he sighs:

> O my son,
> God put it in thy mind to take it hence,
> That thou mightst win the more thy father's love,
> Pleading so wisely in excuse of it! (2 HIV, IV, 5, 178 ff.)

He has him sit beside his bed to hear his last confession of guilt about his own career and to advise him

> to busy giddy minds
> With foreign quarrels; that action, hence borne out,
> May waste the memory of the former days. (2 HIV, IV, 5, 214 ff.)

And then, to add a touch of counterfeit grace to his own reign, which he had vowed to devote to a crusade into the Holy Land, he has himself borne away to die in the room called "Jerusalem." The new king's rejection of Falstaff proves the reformation of his life, and his famous victory of Agincourt in *Henry V* is the resounding answer to his father's dying wishes.

The very subtle parallels between certain aspects of the prince's commerce with Falstaff and with the king—such as the mock interview in part one of *Henry IV* and Falstaff's request that the prince, who is shortly to rescue his father, should bestride his body if it fell in battle—cannot be explored here without digressing inexcusably; but it may be noted that, in a sense, Falstaff is the prince's father too. And so the prince has two fathers, a good one and a bad. But which is which only a wise man could say.

In *Hamlet*, the father of the prince of that play returns as a ghost to command his son to revenge his murder. The son shows his devotion by his deep mourning and (though the Ghost confesses to a sinful life) by praising him as the paragon of mankind, as king, husband, and father; but he has as much difficulty in actually obeying him as his predecessor Harry had in obeying his father. He inclines to a suicidal melancholy rather than to the deed of blood against Claudius. Laertes is the Hotspur of this play. His father Polonius, whom Hamlet kills without a qualm (accidentally, of course), is a wise old counselor or a counseling old fool, depending on how one takes him; and at this point at least shares in the ambiguity of the character of Falstaff. How odd it is that Falstaff, with his white hairs that ill become a jester, says to Hal, "thou art essentially mad, without seeming so" (1 HIV, II, 4, 541), while Hamlet says to his mother over the dead body of old Polonius (that "wretched, rash, intruding fool"), "I essentially am not in madness, But mad in craft." (H, III, 4, 187 f.) Is it a delayed answer? Prince Hal also killed Falstaff. The thousands of intertwining strands of the plays of this period tempt the reader into a veritable labyrinth of cross references. But to keep straight on with our more forthright analysis, it is necessary to observe briefly the relations between Polonius and Laertes. The old father, like many a father before, wishes his son well and arranges for him to travel abroad. One of the most famous of all the speeches written by Shakespeare is that in which Polonius gives Laertes his blessing as he sets forth and furnishes him with a set of maxims of conduct to carry with him, concluding:

> This above all: to thine own self be true,
> And it must follow, as the night the day,
> Thou canst not then be false to any man. (H, I, 3, 78 ff.)

The attitude of Laertes is one of full respect. When he hears of his father's death, he returns at once, armed, and makes direct for the king, with

> O thou vile king,
> Give me my father! (H, IV, 5, 115 f.)

and will not be calmed until he can discover how to avenge his death. The consequence is that the two revengers meet in a duel and kill each other and leave the stage a royal shambles, with king and queen dead beside them.

Merry Wives is an interlude. The son here is a schoolboy, William Page, who demonstrates before his mother and his tutor that he is a cleverer and more dutiful scholar than his father had given him credit for.

But with *King Lear* the theme of the father returns in force. The father of sons here is Gloucester. He has a true son, Edgar, and a bastard, Edmund. The bastard tricks his father into believing that the true son is plotting to take the father's life. Edgar therefore has to flee; but eventually he is able to render essential service to his father, who has been blinded by Cornwall with Edmund's connivance; to save his life indeed, and finally kill Edmund in a duel. As he is dying, Edmund repents all his former wickedness. Of

Edgar, Gloucester says, as he is offering shelter to Lear and his friends (among whom is Edgar, disguised as a madman):

> I had a son
> Now outlawed from my blood; he sought my life,
> But lately, very late: I loved him, friend:
> No father his son dearer. (L, III, 4, 171 ff.)

There is thus much affection between the true son and his father; but it is for a time clouded over by the rumor of the son's murderous thoughts. Both the pretended madness of Edgar and his rumored intention of parricide should be compared with the same traits, or hints of them, in Prince Hal.

Macbeth is richly supplied with fathers and sons. Banquo is slain by Macbeth's murderers but by his warning cry enables his son Fleance to escape and so assure the fulfillment of the prophecy that from him would descend many kings. Macduff flees into England, and Macbeth's murderers kill his son, along with his other children and his wife, whom he has left behind in Scotland; the death of his son is thus a part of Macduff's incentive in returning to kill Macbeth. But the most important figure among the fathers and sons as such is Malcolm, the son of the slain king Duncan. It is he around whom the rebels against Macbeth, the murderous usurper, gather and return to execute vengeance upon him. Malcolm enters the play just at the point where the murder of his father has become known; he and his brother Donalbain flee to avoid the death which they are sure also awaits them if they linger. They therefore become suspect, doubtless with Macbeth's encouragement, of themselves committing the murder of their father. In exile in England, Malcolm slowly gathers around him a band of adherents; but he does so with caution, as illustrated in his interview with Macduff, where he tests him out by pretending to be unfit to reign in Scotland. The charges which Malcolm brings against himself in this pretended indictment are such as were brought against Prince Hal by others. He speaks in particular of his lechery and avarice, but overwhelms Macduff, who thinks these endurable in a king, by denying that he has any of the virtues necessary to kingship:

> But I have none: the king-becoming graces,
> As justice, verity, temperance, stableness,
> Bounty, perseverance, mercy, lowliness,
> Devotion, patience, courage, fortitude,
> I have no relish of them but abound
> In the division of each several crime,
> Acting it many ways. Nay, had I power, I should
> Pour the sweet milk of concord into hell,
> Uproar the universal peace, confound
> All unity on earth. (M, IV, 3, 91 ff.)

The outraged Macduff, who has been struggling to remain loyal to Malcolm in spite of the previous self-description, at this repudiates him as unworthy to live. Convinced then of Macduff's integrity, Malcolm takes back what he has said, declaring himself innocent of the faults he has enumerated:

> I am yet
> Unknown to woman, never was forsworn,
> Scarcely have coveted what was mine own,
> At no time broke my faith, would not betray
> The devil to his fellow and delight
> No less in truth than life: my first false speaking
> Was this upon myself: what I am truly,
> Is thine and my poor country's to command. (M, IV, 3, 125 ff.)

Here again, in this reversal of the picture, we have a Prince Hal (but a purer and more attractive one) revealing his hidden qualities—not to his father, who is dead, but to a representative of his father who is ready to restore the son to the throne.

In the concluding three plays of our list, *Cymbeline, The Winter's Tale,* and *The Tempest,* the primary theme is the reunion of father and son, which is faintly reminiscent of *The Comedy of Errors* and even of *The Taming of the Shrew.* King Cymbeline recovers, after many years, his twin sons Guiderius and Arviragus, who previously have saved his life in battle. Leontes loses his little son Mamillius by death, but in a fashion recovers him in the person of Florizel, the son of his old friend Polixenes; and Polixenes himself, after disowning his son and causing him to flee for protection to the Court of Leontes, recovers him by following and becoming reconciled to him. Leontes evidently delights in the company of

Mamillius, and grieves profoundly over his death; and Polixenes says of his own son at the same stage of childhood:

> If at home, sir,
> He's all my exercise, my mirth, my matter,
> Now my sworn friend and then mine enemy,
> My parasite, my soldier, statesman, all:
> He makes a July's day short as December,
> And with his varying childness cures in me
> Thoughts that would thick my blood. (WT, I, 2, 165 ff.)

The feelings of Leontes are comparable, and the sight of Mamillius carries him back to his own boyhood:

> Looking on the lines
> Of my boy's face, methoughts I did recoil
> Twenty-three years, and saw myself unbreeched,
> In my green velvet coat, my dagger muzzled,
> Lest it should bite its master, and so prove,
> As ornaments oft do, too dangerous:
> How like, methought, I then was to this kernel,
> This squash, this gentleman. (WT, I, 2, 153 ff.)

And finally, in *The Tempest*, Alonso, the king of Naples, in grief because he believes his son Ferdinand drowned and wakened to guilt by the memory of the wrongs he had done to Prospero, goes wildly looking for his son:

> Therefore my son i' the ooze is bedded, and
> I'll seek him deeper than e'er plummet sounded
> And with him there lie mudded. (T, III, 3, 100 ff.)

But after due punishment he is permitted by Prospero to see his son alive, playing at chess with Miranda. The charming picture which the two lovers make reminds us of Florizel and Perdita. Both father and son are overjoyed at the reunion which they had ceased to expect.

Reviewing all the plays of Table 9, we notice that, although the relationship between father and son is not very intensively handled in the first six plays, there is implicit in four or five of them a kind of reproach against the son for failing to live up to the father's hopes or wishes in some way; this is not made distinctly a moral affair except in the case of Aumerle, but there is a lurking disappointment present with regard to Lucentio, Proteus, Romeo, and (though this will hardly bear urging) Antipholus—because of the grievous trouble he occasions Aegeon. From then on, from the first part of *Henry IV* through *Macbeth* and not even excluding the school-lesson incident in *Merry Wives* (interlude though it is), very serious reproaches and difficult demands are laid upon the sons by the fathers or by reason of their relations with their fathers, and the sons are in general under strong compulsion to justify their existence—to prove to their fathers or on behalf of their fathers that they are worthy of their love and their hopes. In the last three plays, there is little of this need for the sons to justify themselves; what reproaches there are seem to be rather on the side of the fathers; and the theme is principally the recovery by the fathers of sons who have been lost.

The impression reported above that with *Henry IV* there begins a phase of heightened interest in the fathers of sons receives additional support from a quantitative analysis of father weights. Taking each play as constituting a unit and determining the proportionate weight of the fathers of sons in each play by dividing the total weight of the twelve leading characters into the weight of the father (or fathers, in *Hamlet, Macbeth,* and *The Winter's Tale*), and then setting the plays *Comedy of Errors* to *King John,* inclusive, over against those beginning with the first part of *Henry IV,* one finds that the average weight of fathers in the second group is significantly greater than in the first. The F, based upon a square root transformation, is 6.51, where the figure required for significance at the 5 per cent level of confidence is 4.67.

In the light of this finding and the basis given for dividing the plays at *Henry IV* (namely, that here the topic of father-son relations first becomes dramatically serious), it seemed legitimate to inquire once more into the trend of weights for fathers of daughters previously examined and found statistically unreliable. When the set of plays was divided into halves and the father weights compared, it will be recalled, no significant difference appeared between the two periods, although the second period's average was indeed greater. But this division into halves is artificial, since it is based upon nothing better than a general supposition that there might be a temporal change. In studying the weights of fathers of sons the division was not arbitrarily made at the halfway point, but rather at *Henry IV*—because here was the first play to give central importance to that relationship. On the same logical grounds we should choose *King Lear* as the beginning of the second phase in the father-daughter relationship. When the division is made there, it turns out that the weights of fathers of daughters in *Lear* and the four plays following are quite decidedly higher than in the preceding eight plays. The F is 12.71, exceeding the 1 per cent level of confidence, for which the required value in this case is 9.65.

The general conclusion seems to be well justified that in the latter part of Shakespeare's career the father component in his personality, and the accompanying relations, come to a greater prominence. But there are two fairly distinct steps, rather than a gradual change: first, the elevation of the father-son theme to prominence in *Henry IV*, about 1597–98; and second, the elevation of the father-daughter theme in *King Lear*, about 1605–6. The psychological meaning of this alteration would presumably be that certain properties of fatherhood (such as authority and moral severity, for instance) rose to greater importance and affected his behavior or at least mood. Since the change was apparently somewhat abrupt, we might reasonably look for events in Shakespeare's personal history to which a causal significance might be assigned.

CHAPTER 6. BIOGRAPHICAL

1

THE ANALYTIC WORK of the three preceding chapters has led to a number of inferences regarding the personality of Shakespeare which may be gathered together here in a rough summary sketch, before venturing a few comments on Shakespeare's biography and other matters related to the evaluation of the man and his plays.

It has been emphasized at several points that there is no good reason for thinking of Shakespeare as eccentric or unusual in his general personality structure. Many of the most important topics in his plays have a broad human appeal; his mind seems to have run most on the primary human relationships and ancient human concerns; and, to speak a bit more technically, the components of his personality seem to have been of a predominantly human cast and to have been arranged in an orderly manner widely characteristic of human beings, as seen through their imaginative productions. It was remarked that he was perhaps more intimately and variously permeated with humanity, as expressed in the great number of delicately distinguished dramatis personae of his plays, than are the majority of his fellows; and that this fact suggested a more than ordinary sensitivity to his social environment and perhaps a corresponding finely modulated responsiveness to it, which should have proved ingratiating to his companions. Intelligence, wit, charm, emotional richness, dignity, and graciousness are so abundantly present in his writings that it is almost superfluous to mention them. Yet to imagine that he was some Ariel, above all human suffering and without his own particular difficulties, is to do him an injustice.

He was predominantly masculine, aggressive, subject to wide swings of mood, not especially romantic and growing less so with the years. In his aggressive masculinity there are considerable traces of strain. Specifically, the masculine aims have a way of running counter to the feminine components in him, which incline toward idealistic love and the domestic virtues, or, less idealistically, toward sexual pleasure untroubled by the strenuous ambitions which mark and often disfigure the male heroes of the plays; and it may be that there was a latent homosexuality, indicated by the occasional rise to dominance of the feminine components, as well as by his favorite dramatic trick of disguising heroines in male attire, which lends to them and their behavior an interesting sexual ambiguity. The diversity of the top-ranking male characters in the plays even suggests that Shakespeare may not have been able to settle down to a single conception of himself; and the dramatic stresses to which these components are subjected reinforce this impression. One feels perfectly confident, at least, that Shakespeare would not have made an ideal citizen of Plato's ideal republic, fixed immutably in one restricted role. The uncertainty about himself might very well have taken the form of such a question as, "Am I a conquering hero, or am I only a frail vessel of flesh corrupted by a too-feminine tenderness and sensuality?" The struggle against the tenderness and sensuality is present everywhere in the dramas, from Navarre's chaste Academy to Prospero's hermit island, but most emphatically in the Prince Hal series and in *Measure for Measure*.

There seems to be in him the feeling that it is his proper duty as a man to put away feminine traits and to justify his existence by vigorous and even ruthless action. There is a guilty feeling that he has not lived up to the requirements of his superego or conscience, or, more concretely, to the wishes of the father in him. Included in this guiltiness there is the reproach, quickly repudiated when it arises, that he has even desired to murder his father. Abstractly considered, this would mean that he wished to be relieved of responsibilities and conscientious scruples against the free enjoyment of his sensual impulses; but, concretely and historically, it would point to an attitude of hostility toward his actual father. More impressive than the feeling of guilt, however, is the reaction to it: the tendency toward grandly violent action, which, though more self-justifying than self-glorifying, is a bit of both. The sense of duty seems to move definitely in the direction of revenge. In opposition are the feminine elements—both the general inclination to sensual delight, and particular female images of mother or daughter or sweetheart, usually loving, and often innocent, hopeful, and idealistic.

Complicating the threefold motif of guilt, and reaction into violence, and opposition to the violence, there is a pervasive theme of treachery. Shakespeare seems to have labored under an almost or quite paranoid suspiciousness with regard to the trustworthiness of others, especially in sexual affairs. He suspects that other men have come between him and the women or woman he loves. This suspiciousness is periodically accentuated and regretted; and in regard to wifely infidelity there appears to be a constant struggle with his beliefs, tending toward the conclusion (whether wish-fulfilling or realistic) that there was no moral lapse except in his own jealous imagination. If the homosexual tendency is admitted, it would help to explain this particular paranoid vagary; for the latent homosexual, experiencing difficulties in his heterosexual relations (because of his attraction to his own sex), finds it natural to explain these difficulties to himself as due to the woman's inconstancy of affection—her fickleness—or to the actual intervention of a rival. That is to say, the homosexual revulsion from the woman is translated into a recoil of the woman into the arms of another man. The *Sonnets* are very much to the point; and so are *Venus and Adonis* and *The Rape of Lucrece* when taken together as two scenes from the same drama; but it is not necessary to appeal to them for either evidence or explanation, since the plays are sufficient in themselves. But it must be remembered that it is *latent* homosexuality to which we are referring, not overt, since overt homosexuality would tend to eliminate the possibility of serious jealousy in regard to a woman—at least in the form it assumes in Shakespeare. Furthermore, it must be admitted that the suspicion of wifely infidelity could have originated in perfectly real experiences. What militates against such an origin in Shakespeare's case is the peculiar development of the theme in the plays, as already explained.

Increasingly, as he grew older, he seems to have identified with his father, or certain aspects of him. This might imply an increasing sense of responsibility toward family and community, an increasing sense of authority, and perhaps a less restless masculine striving, since it would mean overcoming the tension between father and son by eliminating the differences between them. The identification would not be easy if the image of the father was one which Shakespeare could not wholeheartedly accept, and in those plays which deal most centrally with the father-son theme the difficulty is apparent.

Sensuality and self-indulgence seem to have grown more and more repulsive to him. At the same time it does not appear to have been easy for him to accept the spiritualized emotions by which the baser passions can be kept under control, perhaps because of the connection of this spiritualization with the feminine elements in him. Vigorous as his striving was to keep these elements in check, especially where they tended toward sensualism and homosexuality, he could not admit the loving-kindness of Christian charity without feeling threatened with overwhelming weakness. A kindly and forgiving attitude toward people is less likely to be misconstrued if it is accompanied by demonstrated power. Thus the situation in *The Tempest* is an ideal solution. Where power is so absolute that the destruction of all one's enemies is conceivable, loving-kindness appears gracious and magnanimous and not as the evidence of spinelessness. Shakespeare does not seem to have been easy in his mind about gentleness and tenderness unless they came as a relaxation from strenuous endeavor aimed at establishing beyond cavil his worth as a man. Even this formula leaves room for uncertainty. Prospero, powerful as he is, has to remain vigilant on his tiny island; and one wonders what will happen to him when he has drowned his book deeper than ever plummet sounded. Shakespeare at any rate protected his grave with a curse. But this is to anticipate.

2

The brief biographical résumé which follows is based upon the volumes of Halliwell-Phillipps, Lee, and Chambers.

In 1557 John Shakespeare, who had come to Stratford-on-Avon from nearby Snitterfield a few years before and was already a rising merchant in the town of his adoption, married Mary Arden, a favorite and perhaps the youngest daughter of the well-to-do farmer Robert Arden. Robert Arden had signalized his interest in Mary by settling two important pieces of property upon her in the will which became effective at his death in 1556, and perhaps by the conveyance of other property to her during his lifetime. Mary was one of eight children, all girls, and two of these, Joan and Margaret, were destined to figure prominently in her later history. To John Shakespeare and his wife were born eight children: Joan, in 1558; Margaret, in 1562; William, in 1564; Gilbert, in 1566; another Joan, in 1569; Anne, in 1571; Richard, in 1574; and Edmund, in 1580. The first two children, the early Joan and Margaret, died in infancy before William was born. William was therefore the eldest of the surviving children. It may be presumed on that account, and also because he was the first male child, that he occupied from the beginning a place of importance in the family. It may well have added to his natural value to his parents, after the two losses they had already suffered, that he survived the threatening plague which raged in Stratford during the early months of his life. His father was in such circumstances at the time that he was able to contribute substantially to the relief of the plague victims in the town.

William thus began life auspiciously. His father's prosperity continued to increase, and by 1568 he had risen to the highest office attainable in Stratford—that of bailiff. During his year of office he welcomed to the town on its behalf two companies of traveling actors, the Queen's and the Earl of Worcester's. In 1571, when Anne was born, he was chief alderman. But from about this time, though he continued for a while to be financially solvent, his fortunes began to decline, and in 1578 he was unable to make the contributions (though one of them was only fourpence for the relief of the poor) which his position on the town council demanded. In this same year, on November 14, he and his wife mortgaged property of hers at Wilmcote (traditionally supposed to be the estate of Asbies willed to her by her father, though Chambers doubts it) to Edmund Lambert, Mary's brother-in-law by marriage to her sister Joan, for the sum of 40 pounds. Less than a year afterward, the Shakespeares' little daughter Anne died, aged seven and a half, and was buried April 4, 1579. And on October 15 of the same year another piece of Mary's property, at Snitterfield, was sold for the sum of 4 pounds to Robert Webbe, a relative of the Alexander Webbe who had married her sister Margaret. All in all it was a desperate year. John Shakespeare's fortunes never revived; and the mortgaged property was never recovered, although personal gestures were made and legal action was entered into over a period of years in a futile endeavor to win back the Wilmcote property from Edmund Lambert, and later from his son John.

In the meantime William had probably attended the local grammar school from about his seventh year. Somewhere around 1577, however, he is supposed to have been removed from school and possibly apprenticed to his father, who was obviously hard pressed. William therefore, as an active partner in his father's business and certainly as a member of the family, should have been directly concerned with the transactions of 1578 and 1579 by which his mother's property was lost, and with the other financial embarrassments of his father. It is not quite certain what the nature of his father's business was, though it is known that he was some kind of tradesman, but it is suspected that butchering was a part of it, at least at this time; and one of the earliest anecdotes about the young William represents him as making fine ranting speeches whenever he killed a calf. The anecdote is from Aubrey, and is told very circumstantially as coming from the neighbors of the Shakespeares; but some critics, who seem to doubt that in 1681 Aubrey would have been aware of the existence of the "droll performance" called "killing the calf" which was still in the repertory of an 18th-century entertainer, according to a note in Chambers, think that the anecdote may have referred to William's early dramatic inclinations.[1]

In the fall of 1582 William was married to Anne Hathaway of Shottery, the daughter of a small farmer, though the records are so confused that it could have been an Anne Whateley of Temple Grafton. He was eighteen and she was twenty-six. The circumstances of the marriage contract are such as to make it probable

---

1. Hardin Craig, in *An Interpretation of Shakespeare*, p. 6, asserts categorically that Aubrey's story "has been disposed of as a mistaken reference to a rural game called Killing the Calf." Chambers, *William Shakespeare*, *1*, 17, wavers, saying: "Perhaps this really points to some early exercise of mimic talent. 'Killing a calf' seems to have been an item in the repertory of wandering entertainers." He footnotes: "Collier, i. 90, from *Account* of Princess Mary for Christmas 1521, 'Itm pd. to a man at Wyndesore, for kylling of a calffe before my ladys grace behynde a clothe.' J. Raine, *Priory of Finchale* (Surtees Soc.), ccccxli, cites a 'droll performance' called 'killing the calf' by an eighteenth-century entertainer."

that he was forced into the marriage, perhaps without the approval or knowledge of his parents. But "A kindly sentiment," as Chambers says, "has pleaded the possible existence of a pre-contract amounting to a civil marriage." [2] If we can do without the kindly sentiment, we can argue that hasty marriages to legalize the birth of a child were taken more matter-of-factly by the Elizabethans than by later generations. At any rate, a daughter was born to William and Anne six months after the recorded ceremony, and was baptized Susanna on May 26, 1583. Two other children, the twins Judith and Hamnet, were baptized on February 2, 1585. Shortly after this William is believed to have left Stratford.[3]

Various reasons, more or less speculative, have been given for his departure from his home town. His own financial condition is not likely to have been any better than his father's, and that is known to have been bad. A certain John Brown about this time obtained a writ of distraint on John Shakespeare's goods because of unpaid debts, and discovered that there were no goods to be distrained. In addition there is a substantial tradition, through some four different channels at least, namely, Davies, Rowe, Oldys, and Capell, that William came into conflict with Sir Thomas Lucy, possibly by deer stealing, possibly by writing ballads against him, and possibly by both, and found it convenient to leave the neighborhood. Finally, it has been argued that the marriage with Anne was an unhappy one. Both the poaching story and the inference of an unhappy marriage have been vigorously disputed by some. The denials, however, seem somewhat forced; and it is evident that they have sometimes been motivated by the wish to make a true-born gentleman out of Shakespeare.[4]

2. *Op. cit., 1,* 18.

3. It is not known exactly when Shakespeare left Stratford for London, or whether he first went to some other place; and it may even be that he was never away from Stratford for as much as a whole year. Thus Dover Wilson writes (*The Essential Shakespeare,* p. 43): "Many have believed that he made a regular practice throughout his career of returning to Stratford for the summer season."

4. The poaching story has been particularly hard hit, although it is based on several accounts emanating from Stratford itself in the 17th century, when local memories might be supposed to be reasonably good and nearly first hand. It has frequently been remarked that the stretch of human memory in such matters has sometimes been underestimated. I myself was recently surprised and delighted to get a story about Abraham Lincoln from a lady who had it by word of mouth from

Between 1585 and 1592, when a bitter reference by Robert Greene to a rival playwright who was "in his owne conceit the onely Shake-scene in a countrey" indicates the presence of William in London, there is no clear trace of his whereabouts. He may possibly have taught school for a while not far from Stratford. Much less possibly he may have done some soldiering abroad. Very probably he was in London working his way up in the theater. At any rate, from around 1592 and for twenty years thereafter he was actively engaged in writing and producing plays for the London stage, and he is known to have resided in several locations there. He steadily rose financially. Eventually he became an important stockholder in the Globe and Blackfriars theaters. In 1597 he was able to buy New Place, the second largest house in Stratford, and from that time on he continued to acquire property both there and in London. His fellow townsmen now found it expedient to appeal to him for financial aid. He is believed to have visited Stratford at least once before the purchase of New Place, to be at the funeral of his only son Hamnet, who was buried August 11, 1596, at the age of eleven and a half.

In London, as a member of theatrical companies supported by the nobility and the reigning monarchs, he was necessarily thrown into some contact with persons of the highest social rank. His early poems *Venus and Adonis* and *The Rape of Lucrece* were dedicated to the young earl of Southampton, and he is supposed to have received special marks of favor from him, such as a large gift of money. Dover Wilson speculates that during 1593 and 1594 Shakespeare resided at Titchfield, Southampton's seat, "in the capacity of a tutor," [5] thus explaining the tradition of a period of schoolmastering in the country, and putting him into intimate association with the earl, for whom he supposes he chiefly provided dramatic

---

an eyewitness (and earwitness) of perhaps ninety years ago. The account, which was like a thing of yesterday to her, brought ancient history suddenly very close to me. As to the motive of discounting records or whitewashing them in the interpretation, it is flagrantly evident in the arguments of the Baconians and other anti-Stratfordians, who obviously want their great author to have a first-rate pedigree (though not necessarily an upright character), and in milder form in such extravagancies as Halliwell-Phillipps' comparison of the famous second-best bed to a precious jewel.

5. *The Essential Shakespeare,* p. 64.

entertainment, particularly the play *Love's Labour's Lost,* which might have pleased a whole circle of the nobility around Southampton, including the earl of Essex, by its reputed caricaturing of Sir Walter Raleigh. There is evidence, at least, that Southampton received Shakespeare's attentions favorably, and the warm tone of the *Sonnets,* if they were meant for Southampton as Wilson and others believe, would witness to a considerable familiarity. But the *Sonnets* may have been addressed to Lord Herbert, or other persons indeed, and Lee would have us regard them as mere frigid conventionality. Shakespeare's relations with the nobility may have passed conventional bounds. It is argued by some, and as hotly denied by others, that for a time he had as his mistress Mary Fitton, a lady of the queen's Court fairly certainly known to have been the mistress of Lord Herbert. One might see in these associations with royalty and nobility, even in their most limited form, a further inducement to whatever social aspirations he already had, and connect them with his persistent suit for a grant of a coat of arms to his father, and thus also to himself, which apparently terminated in success by 1599.

As Shakespeare gained security financially and socially, he entered more vigorously, though not always amiably, into the affairs of Stratford. In 1597 he joined with his father in instituting lawsuit against his cousin John Lambert in another effort to recover the Wilmcote property alienated in 1578. The action proved as fruitless as the rest. In 1604 he sued Phillip Rogers for £1 15s. 10d. In 1608 he sued John Addenbrooke for £6, and, failing to collect, relentlessly took action against Thomas Horneby who had gone bail for Addenbrooke. In other dealings with his neighbors he displayed a comparable sharpness.

As time wore on he frequented Stratford more and more. His father died and was buried there September 8, 1601. Other family events besides were likely to have drawn him to Stratford. Three children were born to his sister Joan and her husband William Hart between 1600 and 1605. His daughter Susanna was married to Dr. John Hall, June 5, 1607. Another child was born to the Harts at the end of 1607, and early in 1608 a daughter to the Halls, making Shakespeare a grandfather. His mother died and was buried September 9, 1608. A few days later another child was born to his sister

Joan. All these were Stratford events. In London on the last day of December 1607 his brother Edmund, registered as an actor, was tolled to his grave "with a forenoone knell of the great bell."

About 1610 Shakespeare retired more or less permanently to Stratford, and probably lived there with his unmarried daughter Judith and his wife during the succeeding years. A brother Richard died in Stratford in 1613. Judith married Thomas Quiney on February 10, 1616. The marriage in some way violated ecclesiastical regulations and resulted in the excommunication of the pair. There are hints that her father also was displeased. In March of that year he completed the drawing up of his will, with its famous interlineation bequeathing to his wife "my second best bed with the furniture." He was probably already mortally ill. The story has it that he contracted a fever following a drinking bout with the poets Drayton and Jonson, which caused his death. Literally true or not, the anecdote reminds us, as does the will, that he maintained contact with his old London associates to the last. Death came, it is generally supposed, on April 23, 1616. Over his grave in Stratford church were placed, at his request, the energetic lines which have protected his remains ever since:

> GOOD FREND, FOR IESUS SAKE FORBEARE
> TO DIGG THE DUST ENCLOASED HEARE:
> BLESTE BE THE MAN THAT SPARES THES STONES,
> AND CURST BE HE THAT MOVES MY BONES.

3

It would be quite impossible to predict from this brief history that Shakespeare's plays would have the characteristics that they do have. Even with a full knowledge of his times, of the books that he read, and of the dramatic works of his contemporaries before us, I doubt that we could predict. The leap from historical data to psychic act is indeterminate, and its path is covered by darkness. But when we look back from the plays to the personal history the obscurity seems to grow less. It is not at all a case of plucking the heart of the mystery out of Shakespeare. But just as between one play and another there are likenesses of pattern, sometimes conspicuous, so between the plays and the personal history of their creator there are points and areas of similarity. At moments the conviction seizes us that we have discovered a causal relation, or that, at least, the same reality which is mirrored in the plays is also mirrored in the life story.

Two of the greatest of Shakespeare's tragedies were composed within a year or less of his father's death in 1601 and of his mother's in 1608. The exact dates are uncertain. Lee places them slightly after these deaths; Chambers, using the same scraps of evidence, places them slightly before. There seems to be general agreement that *Hamlet* was composed no earlier than 1601. E. C. Pettet thinks that something of the Midlands insurrection of 1607 is reflected in *Coriolanus,* "which, while exceptionally lacking in external dating-reference, is usually ascribed on grounds of style to 1607 or early 1608." [6] But J. G. McManaway notes: "G. B. Harrison contributes one new item: an allusion to Hugh Middleton's project for bringing clean water into London, work on which began in February 1609. Since this was a common topic of conversation, the play may have been written shortly before or just after this date." [7] Since Shakespeare was continuously productive, the near coincidence of these plays with the deaths of his father and mother might be passed over as not having any special significance, except for their content. But the content is such as to suggest that they were incited by either bereavement or the anticipation of it; for in no other of the plays is the relation between father and son so tragically in focus as in *Hamlet,* or that between mother and son as in *Coriolanus.*

Freud has laid great stress on the psychological implications of *Hamlet.* Accepting the statement of Brandes that it was composed shortly after the death of John Shakespeare, and noting that the play is indeed abundantly saturated with painful emotions consequent upon the death of a father, he attributes its prevailing mood to Shakespeare's recent bereavement. But he sees more than a significant mood in it: he sees in the action of the play the outlines of the Oedipus complex, which he supposes to have been reactivated by the current state of mourning. It is on this basis that Freud explains the inhibition of Hamlet's purposed revenge. That is, he

6. In *Shakespeare Survey 3*, p. 35.
7. In *Shakespeare Survey 3*, p. 30.

thinks that Hamlet, unconsciously wishing that his father were not in the way of his possessing his mother, is partially identified with the murderous and incestuous Claudius and therefore cannot think of killing him without at the same time contemplating suicide for himself, since the crimes of Claudius are no worse than those which he himself has obscurely intended. The interpretation is ingenious, and many would say overingenious. But it suffers, from a theoretical standpoint, from attributing Shakespeare's Unconscious to a dramatic figure, which, one would suppose, could only represent (along with the other dramatis personae), and not have, an Unconscious mind. For Freud Hamlet *is* Shakespeare. His repressed desires are therefore displaced on to Claudius, who carries them out; and he experiences guilt for Claudius' crimes, and wishes to spare his life if he spares his own. Freud supposes that the repressed wishes of Hamlet originated in Shakespeare's childhood, at an early age. Such a theory is undoubtedly attractive to anyone who has some knowledge of psychoanalytic principles and sympathy with the general point of view. Indeed, the results of the present analysis, which has not pretended to deal with repressed material, lend some color to Freud's interpretation. But the difficulty of being sure about such things is pointed up by a later interpretation by Frederic Wertham, a heterodox psychoanalyst: he finds, instead of an Oedipus complex, an Orestes complex, laying stress as he does upon the motive of revenge, aimed at the restoration of the father's damaged honor; and he illustrates his view by a case drawn from life, a young Hamlet-Orestes in the flesh.[8] In my own opinion Wertham's theory is nearer to the truth than Freud's, but it does not necessarily exclude Freud's. And lest even a double view of the play should do its complexity an injustice, there should be men-

8. Ernest Jones, in *Hamlet and Oedipus*, p. 98, states that Wertham in a personal communication to him admitted that his *Dark Legend* theory of an independently functioning mother hostility in Hamlet was "one-sided," and goes on to say: "Actually matricidal impulses, which are familiar to psychopathologists, always prove to emanate from the Oedipus complex." On the other hand, I too had a personal communication from Wertham, shortly after the publication of *Dark Legend*, in which he very vigorously argued against the opinion I had expressed that possibly the Oedipus complex could be regarded as the source from which what he called an Orestes complex could be derived. I am therefore uncertain about Wertham's evaluation of his own theory; but it merits consideration as stated, regardless of subsequent denial.

tioned here the theory put by James Joyce into the mouth of Stephen Dedalus in *Ulysses,* persuasively if ironically identifying Shakespeare with the Ghost and his dead son Hamnet with Hamlet. Did not Shakespeare himself take the part of the Ghost and make it the top of his performance as an actor? And who then could Hamlet be but the lost son, come back to punish Shakespeare's faithless wife in the person of Queen Gertrude? The argument is advanced with subtlety and in detail, although at the end Stephen, when his auditors are convinced, cynically laughs it off.[9] Yet it has merit—especially in view of the continually repeated motif of wifely infidelity in the other plays and the fact that the little boy Mamillius in *The Winter's Tale* (who by calculation, and taking Leontes' history as close to Shakespeare's, would be of about Hamnet's age and of his time of death; for Mamillius is 23 years younger than Leontes, while Hamnet was 21 years younger than his father; and the lapse of 16 years between Mamillius' death and his restoration in the form of Florizel corresponds closely with the length of time from Hamnet's death to the date of composition of the play)—that Mamillius, I say, is supposed by his father to peak and pine away because of sympathy with him in suspecting Hermione of adultery. But finally, it is possible to reconcile Joyce's theory with Freud's. At the level of Joyce the story is about Shakespeare's marriage; at the level of Freud, about his childhood family relationships, where the mother is desired as a wife. The theories meet in the figure of Gertrude. Shakespeare, then, as Hamlet *fils* partially brings to the surface the old Oedipal desires, and as Hamlet *père* looks back on his own unhappy marriage and calls for revenge. The beauty of the synthesis is marred only by the denial of some scholars that Shakespeare's marriage was unhappy.[10]

But all three of these theories about *Hamlet* have one thing in common: they all point to a close identification of Shakespeare with his father, either as his representative or his equivalent. The evidence of other plays of the period, especially of both parts of *Henry IV* and their sequel *Henry V,* points in the same direction.[11]

9. Pp. 185–211.

10. For example, Dover Wilson in *The Essential Shakespeare,* p. 43: "In any case—to nail one more slander to the counter—there is no ground whatever for imagining that his married life was an unhappy one."

11. See above, pp. 149 ff.

Neither do the scraps of biographical information offer any contradiction. There is, for instance, the matter of the application for
a coat of arms for his father. Set against the background of the
family history, the action looks like a part of a general effort by the
elder Shakespeare and his son to restore the fallen old man to his
former position of prestige in Stratford, and indeed to elevate both
son and father simultaneously. The business of becoming a gentleman, along with his father, was serious enough with Shakespeare
to elicit a gibe from Ben Jonson. (But how could a bricklayer's son
appreciate what it was to be the son of a ruined bailiff of Stratford?) The one anecdote that we have about the father leaves a
pleasant impression of him and of his relations with his son. Arch-
deacon Thomas Plume, writing about 1657, noted: "Sir John Mennis saw once his old Father in his shop—a merry Cheekd old man—
that said—Will was a good Honest Fellow, but he durst have crackt
a jeast with him at any time." [12] To be sure John Mennis, if he is
the one born in 1599 in Kent, could scarcely have had any such
memory; but his brother Matthew, who was born in 1593, as Chambers says, might have, and Plume may have confused the names.
The anecdote is not material to our argument, but, for whatever it
is worth, is in harmony with it. We ought to weigh rather more
seriously the fact that Shakespeare as his father's eldest son was
his chief legal successor; and association with his father in business
for several years, which is probable, should have helped to bring
his father's affairs close to his heart. Even the circumstances of his
early childhood—the prior death of two children, the threat of the
plague, and the rising tide of his father's prosperity—could have
worked toward a sympathetic relation between them. The biographical data increase the probability that *Hamlet* should be regarded as a mourning piece.

But there is more than general emotion in the play. There is a
specific plot; and this plot has a coherency with the family history
which deserves more than casual notice. In the play the cause of
the father's death and the queen's disgrace is Hamlet's uncle
Claudius, his father's brother. Now, John Shakespeare did not die
at the hand of a brother: that would be entirely too pat; but his
brother-in-law, Edmund Lambert, is the chief villain in the series

12. Chambers, *William Shakespeare*, 2, 247.

of events marking the financial and social decline of the Shake-speares. Edmund Lambert's capture of the valuable Wilmcote property by mortgage in 1578, his refusal to surrender it in 1580 when an offer was made to pay back the original loan, the tenacity with which he and his son held on to it in the face of litigation, all look unpleasant enough. That this loss of property was followed a year later by the sale, at perhaps less than its true value, of another piece of Mary Arden's property to Robert Webbe, likewise related by marriage, could not have made it look any pleasanter. And in the midst of this period of acute financial crisis occurred the death of William's sister Anne. Within the space of a year, then, tragedy descended upon the Shakespeare family in concentrated form; and standing at the beginning of this year of suffering, like a true dra-matic villain, was the unmerciful brother-in-law—not quite Clau-dius, but near enough. It is a curious and perhaps meaningful ap-pendage to these events that on May 3, 1580, the last of the Shake-speare children was baptized Edmund. One can detect in this a gesture of appeal to Edmund Lambert, leading up to the fruitless negotiations in the autumn of the same year for the return of the mortgaged land. The mere clustering of these names and dates and events does not make Edmund Lambert the prototype of Claudius; it does not even make him a villain. Apparently he did nothing but resolutely adhere to his legal rights, and he could hardly have been to blame for the death of the little girl. But, as all of us know, fami-lies do not view such matters logically and dispassionately. There is nothing psychologically improbable in supposing that even the little girl's death found its way into the feelings of resentment which we have every reason to believe were built up against the uncle.

An occurrence outside the family which perhaps should be bracketed with these events is the drowning of Katherine Hamlett in the Avon on December 17, 1579, which, as Chambers says, "may have given a hint for Ophelia's end." [13] The incident gains fur-ther significance from being closely associated in time with events which provide a pattern suitable for generating *Hamlet* in the mind of Shakespeare, whether they actually did so or not. Earlier in the same year, in June, there was another drowning in the Avon, a little farther upstream; and, oddly, the name of the victim was

13. *Ibid., 1*, 25.

William Shaxsper, the son of a Warwick shoemaker. The year 1579 was definitely one of portents in and around Stratford.

If the details of the present comparison between *Hamlet* and Shakespeare's biography are put aside as unacceptable, it still remains a plausible idea that the wrongs suffered by his father entered into the composition of the cruelly wronged king of the tragedy. One reason for maintaining this proposition is just the considerable rise in importance of father-son combinations in the plays shortly before *Hamlet,* at about the time (October 1596) that Shakespeare succeeded in first getting a grant of a coat of arms for his father. If we could take Prince Hal's confession of grief over the sickness of his father in the conversation with Poins in the second part of *Henry IV* as referring to an illness of Shakespeare's father (who died three or four years later), we should be in a position to contend very seriously that the grief which pours out in *Hamlet* was already beginning to well up. Regardless of that, I think it psychologically very possible that in *Henry IV* we have something like a debate going on in Shakespeare's mind over the question of which was his real father—a dignitary of Stratford, a kingly kind of figure in his way (especially in the eyes of the small child that Shakespeare was when his father was at the height of his glory as bailiff), a gentleman whose "late grandfather for his faithfull & valeant service was advanced & rewarded by the most prudent prince King Henry the seventh of famous memorie," [14] one worthy of a coat of arms "Gould, on a Bend Sables, a Speare of the first steeled argent. And for his creast or cognizaunce a falcon his winges displayed Argent standing on a wrethe of his coullers: supporting a Speare Gould steeled as aforesaid sett vppon a helmett with mantelles & tasselles"; [15] or, on the other hand, a merry-cheeked old fellow who was careless about the garbage at his door, who improvidently had let his own good fortune and reputation and that of his wife go to wrack and ruin, and whose white hairs ill became his proneness to jest and inordinately to frequent the taverns in the company of a Fluellen or Bardolfe or Sly? [16] Prince

14. *Ibid.,* 2, 19.

15. *Ibid.*

16. Fluellen, Bardolfe, and Sly are Stratford names, as well as names of characters in Shakespeare's plays. Cf. Chambers, *op. cit., 1,* 25: "It is intriguing to

Hal rejected Falstaff and accepted the austere King Henry. The choice was also Shakespeare's; and in the succession of grim tragedies which follow, on down to the relaxation of *Pericles,* we perhaps see how painful it was to live with such a father image at one's psychological core.

In *Coriolanus,* which was written in or around 1608, the year of the death of Shakespeare's mother, the primary human relationship explored is that between a mother and her son. Coriolanus is his mother Volumnia's ideal of a fighting man, as he ought to be, since he has been from childhood under her martial instruction. Volumnia herself is a woman of vigor and stern courage, devoted to her son but not indulgent. Though he is her hero, he is also her child forever, and for all his military valor and terrifying independence as a warrior he is helplessly under her sway. At the crisis of his revenge on the city of Rome for banishing him, and after turning back other delegations, including one headed by his old fatherly friend Menenius, he gives in to the pleadings of his mother and spares the city which he intended to destroy. In this battle it is the mother who wins; and, as Coriolanus prophetically warns her, her victory is his ruin.

In this play, then, the state of mourning or anticipation of bereavement does not produce the same result as that found in *Hamlet.* There the emphasis is on the wrong done the father, though in consequence to be sure the son is involved in a "sea of troubles"; here, in *Coriolanus,* the emphasis is on the wrong done the son. The wrong has several aspects: Coriolanus is unable to gain the love of the Roman citizens in spite of his achievements in war; he is banished by them; he is thus cut off from his wife and child, as well as from familiar surroundings; and when he is at the point of destroying his opponents and regaining at one blow his position of power in the city and access to his wife and child, he finds himself unable to carry through his aim. Behind all these failures is his mother; for it is she who has cultivated in him the intolerable patrician pride which alienates the Roman citizens, it is she who

find a Fluellen and a Bardolfe in the same list of recusants as Shakespeare's father." Should we let our fancy carry us further, and note that the name John Falstaff, literally taken, is the exact opposite of John Shakespeare, signifying a spear no longer shaken but disgracefully fallen?

deprives him of his revenge, and it is she who continually stands between him and any intimacy with his wife. Most succinctly, the cause of Coriolanus' defeat is that he cannot love; and the reason for his inability to love is his mother, who opposes sexual tenderness. The mother's attitude is vigorously expressed in the very first lines she speaks—pointedly addressed to her daughter-in-law:

> If my son were my husband, I should freelier rejoice in that absence wherein he won honour than in the embracements of his bed where he would show most love. (C, I, 3, 2 ff.)

There are great differences of character between Coriolanus' mother and Hamlet's. Hamlet's mother has all the feminine weaknesses—"Frailty, thy name is woman"—Coriolanus' has none; Hamlet's mother is sexually highly charged, lascivious indeed in his judgment, Coriolanus' might well be a votaress of Diana. In one respect, however, they are alike: they both exercise a considerable restraint on their sons' relations with other women. Volumnia does it by freezing up the sources of passion, Gertrude by voluptuously attracting her son and making her rival seem pallid in contrast. Ophelia and Virgilia, incidentally, are also in their turn alike —both mild unassertive creatures who could not possibly charm the sons out of themselves with the love magic of a Cleopatra.

The wronged father, involving his son in the problem of setting things to rights in a disjointed world; the wronging mother, who defeats the son she idolizes: these are the two contrasting mourning pieces of *Hamlet* and *Coriolanus*. Actually, of course, no information is available on the character of Shakespeare's mother. As a woman of property, she might have had an outlook on life tempered by practical concerns; as an Arden, whose ancient arms her son wanted to impale with his father's, and as the wife of a bailiff of Stratford, she might have been a woman of some pride; as a mother who bore eight children and lived to an advanced age, she must have had a sound constitution. None of these suppositions contradict the impression received from *Coriolanus*, but neither do they yield certainty; and we cannot say whether Mary Arden was cast in the Roman mold of Volumnia or not. Nor do we have even the slight degree of external evidence regarding her relations with her son which we have for John Shakespeare, in Plume's anecdote.

It must not be overlooked, however, that Mary Arden came of socially higher stock than John Shakespeare and possessed some little wealth and status at a time when her husband was still endeavoring to attain them; and finally we know that he both rose and fell, and by bad luck or imprudence lost his own gains and his wife's inheritance. Observation of other women placed in the same circumstances is enough to suggest that whatever traits of pride Mary Arden originally had would not have been diminished by her reverses, and like Volumnia she might very well have urged ambition on her son—who, according to tradition which Chambers even in his guise of "an arch-skeptic and a sardonic anti-romantic" [17] does not reject, was punished and degraded by Sir Thomas Lucy and, like Coriolanus, banished from his home town.

I have spoken of Volumnia as the wronging mother. There is, of course, only one point at which Coriolanus actually reproaches her: it is when she prevents him from carrying out his revenge on his fellow citizens. His whole life is brought to a standstill by her opposition there, and his subsequent death at the hands of the assassins is almost gratuitous. If we ask what this opposition might correspond to in the real life situation of the author, I think that we should reply that Shakespeare's mother by some kind of influence, direct or indirect, mitigated his hostility toward those who had wronged him or stood for those who had wronged him back in Stratford. We do know that Shakespeare prosecuted some Stratfordians for the recovery of debts, that he was not cordial in response to an appeal to help the town to prevent the enclosure of the town commons, that he was one of those excessive maltsters and engrossers of corn in a time of local famine against whom it was complained in 1597 that they were "wycked people . . . more lyke to wolves or cormerants than to naturall men" even though "in estymacion of worshipp," [18] and that he had a reputation for scathing satirical wit in such instances as the early verses against Sir Thomas Lucy and the later ones directed against the moneylender Thomas Combe. It is certainly imaginable that he enter-

17. The phrase is from Dover Wilson, *The Essential Shakespeare*, p. 3.
18. Chambers, *op. cit.*, 2, 100. See also Pettet, "*Coriolanus* and the Midlands Insurrection of 1607," in *Shakespeare Survey 3*, pp. 34–42, for a discussion of the possible repercussions of local popular revolt on Shakespeare.

tained more comprehensive thoughts of hostile action than he undertook—against the Lamberts, let us say—and that his mother in some way got him to hold his hand, which in his later years had grown financially strong. Speaking without historical reference, all we can say about *Coriolanus*, of course, is that it psychologically represents the control of strong vengeful impulses by a cluster of forces, particularly centered in Volumnia, combining a civilized (as contrasted to a barbaric) pride with maternal sentiment.

A considerable difficulty in taking Shakespeare's mother as a contributor, through the imagination, to the characters of both Queen Gertrude and Volumnia is that the two fictional mothers are so extremely different. Psychologically speaking, if we positively knew that their origin was the one suggested, we could handle the discrepancy by calling upon the notion of ambivalence; for we know that the same person may appear to us in both a bad and a good light, one set of qualities being emphasized at the expense of others which do not fall into harmony with the emotions present within us at the time. We do not positively know their origin. It may be pointed out, however, that it is not customary to dwell upon the worst aspects of those whose death we mourn. In *Hamlet* the image of the father, in the memory of his son contrasting him with Claudius (and in spite of the Ghost's confession of grievous sin), shines with brightness:

> So excellent a king; that was, to this,
> Hyperion to a satyr. (H, I, 2, 139 f.)

In *Coriolanus* the image of the mother is likewise exceedingly noble. The father and mother images, then, are appropriate to the supposed occasion. But at the time of *Hamlet* the occasion did not require the glorification of the mother. Furthermore, the emotions of the time seem to have carried the author's thoughts back to much earlier years, when his mother was still young enough to be bearing children and consequently more easily to be seen in sexually garish colors. But in *Coriolanus* his thoughts seem to run on a more recent time, a time when his mother was old and he was beginning to make his way back into the affairs of Stratford, armed with success and money and the gravity of full maturity. His mother, at these two chronological levels, could have looked very different to him; and the difference encountered in the two plays is of the general order that on this basis we should expect.

Unless the imagination necessarily involved in any interpretation has completely led us astray, then, we have discovered in Shakespeare a double image of both the father and mother capable of setting up powerful tensions in his personality system.

4

There is another conjunction of dates which the usually cautious Chambers thinks may be more than casual. He assigns the composition of *King John* to the winter of 1596–97. The poet's young son Hamnet, buried on August 11, 1596, would accordingly have been dead shortly before this play was completed, and Chambers suggests with appropriate scholarly hesitation that the story of young Arthur in the play owes its tenderness and emotional impact to Hamnet's death. If Chambers is right, the Arthur episode affords us valuable insight into the charm for Shakespeare of his young son, the strong attachment of the mother to him, and the storm of grief which his death released in her. It is not only in Constance's description of Arthur that we learn how beautiful and attractive he is; in the softening of the executioner Hubert by his gentle pleadings we have even more convincing evidence. As for the effect of Hamnet's death on his parents, we may have some indication in the angry grief of the manly Faulconbridge, who is anything but sentimental, as well as in the tormented outcries of Constance. Whether these scenes were actually written immediately after Hamnet's death, or some two years earlier (as supposed by Lee—though the more recent opinion of Harrison agrees with Chambers [19]), their most logical point of reference, as far as we know Shakespeare's biography, is his son; and they argue for an attitude of deep tenderness. Even the thoroughly hardened King John is ultimately overwhelmed with guilt at the thought of being instrumental in causing the child Arthur's death.

The brief sketch of the little Mamillius in *The Winter's Tale*, and the still briefer one of Coriolanus' son, indicate the same kind of

19. See J. G. McManaway, in *Shakespeare Survey 3*, p. 26, on the dating of *King John*.

tenderness; and in *The Winter's Tale* we again have the son's death, the overwhelming grief of the mother, and the reaction of guilt in a cruel man, this time the father himself. One should infer from these facts that Shakespeare valued his son highly and felt responsible to some degree for his death. One obvious cause for such possible feelings is that Shakespeare was absent from home much or all of the time during the years preceding the boy's death, emotionally neglecting his family if not willfully, and perhaps willfully. Shakespeare's capacity for tender feeling toward boys and young men is abundantly proved by the *Sonnets*, and by combinations in the plays of older men of the world, such as Antonio, Falstaff, and Parolles, with younger friends such as Bassanio, Prince Hal, and Bertram. It is a signal feature of *The Merchant of Venice* that Bassanio demonstrates a greater devotion to his friend Antonio than to his betrothed Portia; and it is characteristic of Falstaff and even the less pleasant Parolles that they speak of their young friends as sweethearts. If it were possible to date the *Sonnets* after 1596 (but this is debatable),[20] it would be appropriate to see in them a compensation for the loss of young Hamnet in affection for some other young man. It is a leading theme of the *Sonnets* that the young man should beget heirs, "That thereby beauty's rose might never die," and it must have been a painful reflection to Shakespeare, after the death of Hamnet, that he had no male heir to continue his name. He did have a godson, to be sure, the poet William Davenant, who was so pleased with the connection that he was not above countenancing the widely circulated rumor that he was Shakespeare's natural child; and Robert Davenant, his older brother, told Aubrey that Shakespeare, on visits to the Davenant home, "gave him a hundred kisses"—which at least reveals something about his feeling for children.

There are features of some of the other plays which may have a

20. Leslie Hotson (*Shakespeare's Sonnets Dated*) would place the *Sonnets* as early as 1589. This seems extraordinary in view of their content, which would indicate that the author was certainly maturer than a young man of twenty-five. Furthermore, Hotson's evidence, at the very most, can only set a lower limit to the time of their composition, not an upper limit. For critical comment, see Clifford Leech, *Shakespeare Survey 4*, p. 148. McManaway, in *Shakespeare Survey 3*, p. 31, states that Chambers prefers 1595–1600, "because of new evidence that links Shakespeare to plans for a marriage between William Herbert and Elizabeth Carey."

touch of the lost Hamnet. In *Twelfth Night,* which Chambers puts around 1600 but later commentators put a year or two after that, one of the characters is a young man, Sebastian, who is the twin brother of the heroine, Viola; this brother is supposed by Viola to have been drowned at sea, and it is one of the happy surprises of the play that he turns up alive. One of the happy experiences in *The Tempest,* too, is that after the sea storm Alonso finds his son Ferdinand alive; and it is Ferdinand, snatched magically from a watery death, who is paired with Prospero's daughter Miranda as her lover. Not only so, but in at least one passage a father takes his son-in-law as a duplicate of his own dead son; this is in *The Winter's Tale,* where Leontes so regards Florizel. In these incidents, particularly the one in *Twelfth Night,* we have before us what could have been imaginative efforts to recover the dead boy, of whom his twin sister Judith must have been a constant reminder.

Any speculation on Hamnet is inevitably bound up with questions regarding his mother. I have already dwelt on the theme of wifely infidelity running through the plays, or, more correctly, the lover's or husband's suspicion of infidelity, which reaches a culmination in *The Winter's Tale,* where the Hamnet theme also seems to be present. In reflecting on this infidelity theme it is hard to resist the conclusion that Shakespeare's marriage was a troubled one. It began unpropitiously; it apparently was virtually broken up three years later by his departure from Stratford and prolonged absence thereafter; and there is no indication in his will that he held his wife dear. The notorious interlineation about the second-best bed has had its apologists, notably Halliwell-Phillipps; but we are told in addition that Shakespeare took positive legal measures to hold her inheritance from him to a minimum. In Lee's words: "Her right to a widow's dower—i.e., to a third share for life in freehold estate—was not subject to testamentary disposition, but Shakespeare had taken steps to prevent her from benefiting, at any rate to the full extent, by that legal arrangement. He had barred her dower in the case of his latest purchase of freehold estate, viz. the house at Blackfriars. Such procedure is pretty conclusive proof that he had the intention of excluding her from the enjoyment of his possessions after his death." [21] The legal action referred to occurred in 1613. The mildest interpretation which Lee can put upon

21. P. 488.

the facts is that "Probably her ignorance of affairs and the infirmi-
ties of age (she was past sixty) combined to unfit her in the poet's
eyes for the control of property, and, as an act of ordinary pru-
dence, he committed her to the care of his elder daughter." [22] On
this interpretation, there may have been a reconciliation, or, indeed, not even the necessity of one. It should be remarked, however, that Anne Shakespeare was two or three years short of sixty
at the time of the Blackfriars transaction, and that, though she was
eight years her husband's senior and in spite of the imagined "in-
firmities of age," she survived him by more than seven years; and
the other fragments of evidence, when combined with the infidelity theme in the plays, are not favorable to the extreme view that
the marriage was sound to the core. There is the important fact, of
course, that Shakespeare did not remain away from Stratford all
his life; his retirement there in his last years would have made a
reconciliation possible and desirable if any was needed. But the
final legal arrangements are not encouraging, and the curse on his
gravestone seems to have prevented the burial of his wife beside
him.

On the other side of the relationship, what little evidence there
is favors the view that one would extract from the plays, namely,
that it was Shakespeare and not Shakespeare's wife who discovered
flaws in the marriage, if anyone did. Lee cites a local tradition
crediting her with wishing to be buried in his grave, and states
that her epitaph proves that her daughters genuinely loved her.
The tradition, given in Chambers, was transmitted in a letter from
a Mr. Dowdall, April 10, 1693, after visiting Stratford, seeing
Shakespeare's grave and the inscription over it, and talking with
the clerk. The relevant section of the letter runs: "the clarke that
shew'd me this Church is aboue 80 y^{rs} old; he says that this *Shake-
spear* was formerly in this Towne bound apprentice to a butcher;
but that he Run from his master to London, and there was Rec^d
Into the playhouse as a serviture, and by this meanes had an op-
pertunity to be w^t he afterwards prov'd. he was the best of his
family but the male Line is extinguished; not one for feare of the
Curse aboues^d Dare Touch his Grave Stone, tho his wife and
Daughters Did Earnestly Desire to be Layd in the same Graue wth

22. *Ibid.*

him." [23] The epitaph which Lee speaks of as expressing the affection of the daughters for their mother does indeed do so, and beyond that suggests that her character was one of ideal Christian goodness. Unfortunately, it is hard to estimate the degree of mere convention in such a testimonial. The inscription, partly in English and partly in Latin, is given by Chambers as follows:

*H*EERE LYETH INTERRED THE BODY OF ANNE WIFE
OF WILLIAM SHAKESPEARE WHO DEPARTED THIS LIFE THE
6ᵀᴴ DAY OF AVGVST : 1623 · BEING OF THE AGE OF · 67 · YEARES

> Vbera, tu mater, tu lac, vitamque dedisti.
> Vae mihi: pro tanto munere saxa dabo?
> Quam mallem, amoueat lapidem, bonus angᵉlus orem
> Exeatᵛᵗ, christi corpus, imago tua—
> Sed nil vota valent. venias citò Christe; resurget
> Clausa licet tumulo mater et astra petet.[24]

The Latin verses may be roughly translated:

> Mother, your gifts were rich—the milk, the life that you gave me.
> O in sorrow must I settle that debt with a stone?
> Rather would I implore a merciful angel to move it,
> That from the depths, like Christ, you in the flesh might arise.
> But that prayer avails not. Come quickly, O Christ, and receive her!
> Loose our mother from death: give her the star-filled skies.

5

An aspect of Shakespeare's life which has received much attention because of the availability of records is his shrewd financial enterprise. He was unquestionably successful. Lee estimates that his average annual income after coming to London, in the years before 1599, was about £150, an amount said by Lee to be the equal of £750 at the end of the 19th century; and he estimates that for the last fourteen or fifteen years of his life his earnings were about £700 annually. Chambers accuses Lee of immense exaggeration, but he agrees that Shakespeare's income was quite respectable. Shakespeare became a property owner in Stratford and also in London. He was not averse to litigation, nor did the smallness of the sum or personal ties with the debtor deter him. He on the other

23. Chambers, *William Shakespeare*, 2, 259.
24. *Ibid.*, p. 9.

hand was not always prompt in the payment of his own debts. In London he evaded the tax collector for several years, and, when caught up with, paid two incomplete installments on back taxes and perhaps no more. His wife borrowed 40s: from her father's old shepherd sometime before 1595: in 1601, when the man died, the debt was still unpaid and the will directed that it should be collected from Shakespeare and distributed among the poor of the town. There can be no doubt that Shakespeare was a thoroughly practical man of business, astute in acquiring and unsentimental in managing his estate. A mystery is sometimes attached to this because he was a poet. Poetry and business traditionally do not mix. But he was a success in both lines. In business he was far superior to his father. Both started out with little and throve in their affairs; but the son never faltered as the father did in his upward career, and he was eventually able to restore the Shakespeare name to a place of dignity as well as provide handsomely for himself. As a dramatic poet he was supreme.

There is in truth a kind of paradox here. Absorption in dreams from which plays are constructed would hardly be expected to contribute to a ready interest in business matters and the requisite promptness in dealing with them. The awkwardness of the combination has misled some into believing that Shakespeare was merely a clever theatrical craftsman, a dexterous mechanic of stage effects, caring nothing for his work except as a way of making money. The plays themselves, however, with their powerful emotional appeal and their exploration of the dark margins of experience, are a sufficient rebuttal of that thesis. I think it must be admitted that Shakespeare threw himself into the work of composition as passionately and wholeheartedly as any writer ever did. At the same time it is clear that he was no improvident bohemian. The mystery begins to vanish when we inspect the content of his writings. All through, an attitude toward money is expressed which is entirely consistent with the author's financial activity. Money is not treated by him as a luxury or an enigma, but as an instrument of power which one does well to get and guard. Some of his principal dramatic characters value it highly. In *The Comedy of Errors* Antipholus of Syracuse protects his money against threatened confiscation and runs into numerous adventures because of its fancied loss. In *The Tam-*

ing of the Shrew Petruchio is frankly in pursuit of it, regarding marriage as nothing but a means to that end. In *The Merchant of Venice* Antonio is an enterprising profit-maker, and the most important male character in the play, Shylock, is so notoriously money-minded that his name has become a byword for greed and sharp practice. In *Henry IV* much of the horseplay and humor pertains to money, Falstaff and his companions are thieves outright, and Falstaff applies his cunning eloquence to beating the hostess out of what he owes her. In *Othello* Iago rings the changes on the theme. In *Timon of Athens* money is the cause of Timon's popularity, its lack the cause of his downfall, and its reacquisition the means by which he takes his revenge. In *The Winter's Tale* Autolycus has a rogue's love of money, which he steals; and even the child Mamillius, when asked whether he would take eggs for money, answers, to Leontes' delight: "No, my lord, I'll fight." (WT, I, 2, 162)

Timon of Athens is of special interest. At the beginning of the play Timon is revealed as a man so liberal that he despoils himself for the sake of his friends and so lacking in petty caution that he will not listen when his steward tries to warn him that his resources are exhausted. The moment he realizes that his money has run out, he confidently turns for assistance to the old friends whom he has bountifully entertained and showered with gifts. One after one they refuse to help him, on transparent excuse after excuse, and as his creditors besiege him he suddenly discovers that he has been a prodigal fool who has not a single genuine friend in the world; or so it seems to him, for he is now so blinded by hatred of mankind that he cannot distinguish the loyalty of his steward from the fair-weather love of the rest. Ruined, he takes to the woods and cuts himself off from human society; but there, while digging for roots to eat, he finds a cache of gold, and with this weapon in his hands he cynically uses it to reinforce the desires of criminals, prostitutes, and soldiers, urging them on to the destruction of man and all his works. In particular, he finances Alcibiades in his campaign of revenge against the city of Athens which has ostracized them both, and presses him to set no bounds to his slaughter.

This play and *Coriolanus* have a common pattern. In both, a magnanimous hero falls from popular favor and seeks revenge against his native city. But the cause of banishment is different in the two cases: Coriolanus is driven out because of his pride and tyrannical designs; Timon, because of his inability to pay his debts. Possibly *Coriolanus* derives historically from Shakespeare's supposed treatment at the hands of Sir Thomas Lucy, who, according to tradition, drove him from Stratford for poaching on his preserves: on this view (which admittedly rests on disputable evidence), Coriolanus, the hunter of men, is a dramatically inflated William Shakespeare, the young Robin Hood of Stratford, noted for his prowess as a hunter of deer and rabbits. In *Timon of Athens*, however, we have something more like another reminiscence of his father's unhappy story. Just as Timon is the center of a vivid social life, so perhaps was John Shakespeare when he was alderman and bailiff of Stratford, welcoming troupes of actors and openhandedly entertaining the little town, "emporiolum non inelegans," where he was the most eminent figure; and just as Timon after his financial collapse finds his creditors pressing him hard and no friends to help him, so Shakespeare's father found his creditors unrelenting (as late as 1592 pursuing him to the church door) and relatives, like Edmund Lambert and Robert Webbe, eager to complete his ruin. And if we equate the father with Timon, then Shakespeare himself, once more the banished deer hunter blown up to the size of a great warrior, takes his place in the drama as Alcibiades, with his own revenge and the old man's both at heart. In the end Alcibiades is generous; and apparently Shakespeare, too, did not pursue his advantage as a substantial property holder in Stratford in any grandly vengeful spirit, though some spite may have emerged at times.

Both plays were written in roughly the same period, about the time of the death of Mary Shakespeare. They are contemporaneous with a time when Shakespeare's financial strength was approaching a maximum, and when, because of events like the death of his mother, the marriage of his daughter Susanna, the birth of a granddaughter, appeals for aid from the town, and the growth of his real-estate holdings, he was being drawn back into all the life of his native place, after his exile. Under such conditions, and with the memories of the family tribulations reawakened by the near or recent death of his mother, it is credible that he should have pro-

jected his old bitterness into plays where a man is set against a city,
as he and his father had been, longing for revenge. The particular
relevance of *Timon of Athens* to the point now under discussion
is that it pivots upon the theme of money and that it has plausible
connections with Shakespeare's own financial enterprise.

Perhaps the traditional opposition between the dreaming of
poets and various practical concerns, like money-making, could
be resolved in this way: It is the nature of their dreams rather than
the fact that they dream which makes them impractical, when they
are. After all, the builders of great fortunes, the giants of finance,
probably also dream, though not tenderly. Shakespeare's dreams included those desires—for money, for revenge—which in a competi-
tive, litigious, money-making society could very well be brought to
fulfillment on the plane of public reality.

But Shakespeare's dreams went farther than his activity in the
real world possibly could; and in that very fact we have an important aspect of his mind.

It is as though Shakespeare had looked at some of his near-at-
hand experiences through a telescope and so magnified them that
their gigantic scale makes them unrecognizable as belonging to
any ordinary world. By turning the telescope around we bring the
projected images back to their original size and begin to understand them—in the prosaic everyday way of understanding. Coriolanus, the mighty and terrible, is reduced to the valiant scamp
William, the butcher's apprentice; Rome, to the village of Stratford.
Or Athens becomes Stratford, and magnificent Timon turns into
the little bailiff who welcomed the strolling players of the Queen.
And proceeding thus through other scenes: wars and rebellions become village quarrels; the France of Constance against the England
of John becomes the Stratford of Anne, grieving over her dead son,
against the London of William; great Antony and Cleopatra become the world-conquering playwright and some capricious fascinating mistress, like Mary Fitton; the Forest of Arden is seen to be
just what its name implies, though lions roam through it; the family
wars of the kings of England are indeed family wars, as bitter if
not so grand; and the powerful magician Prospero alone on his
island with Miranda—and with his imagination and his base desires—is the master of the stage gone into retirement and living in

relative seclusion with Judith, his unmarried and possibly admirable daughter.

I would not insist on these examples in detail (and they cannot be proved), but I believe they illustrate the truth of a general principle. An elevation of persons from humble to high station, a shift of scene from a village to a world-renowned capital, a heightening of the emotional pressure by endowing private relationships with international consequences, a darkening or brightening of the atmosphere by a howling storm or by music and moonlight sleeping sweetly on a bank—and the affairs of the most ordinary individual take on a universal significance and remain true to life while seemingly remote from the particular concerns of any living man, the writer himself most of all. If the poet helps himself to a story from Plutarch or Boccaccio, and here and there adapts their very words to his dramatic purposes, it is only to achieve a greater objectivity, a greater sharability, in the treatment of things which at bottom are very personal. The use of a time-tested framework may actually give the writer greater freedom to express what is most burningly near him; the general dimensions being already solidly there and easily appreciated by his audience, he needs only to fill in where he likes and add the touches which give vital significance to the whole.

The tendency to magnify personal joys and personal sufferings into something involving the world at large is not restricted to dramatists. It is found in everyone. The very appearance of the earth and sky may be altered by one's current mood, and quite grandiose phantasies are common enough. Many a small-town girl identifies herself with some famous actress and imagines her own face and name on the billboards. Many a boy is a football or baseball hero in his imagination. And even in a democratic country where the hierarchy of rank is played down, one may dream of being a president or dictator or of having intimate conversation with one. For example, a young woman who adores her father dreams of entertaining President Franklin Roosevelt, a father ideal; another, with unsatisfied sexual desires which she is trying to restrain, dreams that Hitler accosts her in the street and spits on her. The blending here of universal self-glorifying tendencies with the dreamer's contemporary historical world (for these dreams are dated, as one can see) is typical. When such phantasies become complexly worked out, and the distinction between them and one's publicly recognized circumstances become lost or blurred, then the individual who has them begins to be regarded as a serious psychiatric case. But by allowing them to expand to the utmost and then converting them into a dramatic composition, one becomes a triumphant artist, like Shakespeare.

In Shakespeare's case, however, as I hope I have shown, there were special reasons why he should compose dramas marked by grandeur. As the locally degraded son of a locally degraded father, and yet endowed with unusual talents, he would naturally desire to assert his superiority in the face of a skeptical world. To a certain extent the dramas are compensatory. But a further inducement to grandeur was supplied by the times themselves. He lived in a society in which there was a very exalted hierarchy of hereditary power, and the players' companies were sustained by noble and royal patronage. In that world the kingly dreams of Shakespeare were at home.

6

The guiding assumption throughout this study of Shakespeare has been that his plays reflect his personality. To many readers, doubtless, the question which has been most seriously neglected is whether, after all, this assumption is not fatally compromised by the knowledge that Shakespeare was working within a set of stage conventions and on the basis of literary sources which he used freely and sometimes literally.

First, it must be replied that there is nothing in the conception of personality, as I understand it, which excludes the conventional and the derivative. Personality is in part a conventional thing itself —is cut to the pattern of the times, stuffed with contemporary events and postures—and a man of the theater like Shakespeare may have his personality affected by the conditions of his occupation. It was he who wrote of his nature being subdued "To what it works in, like the dyer's hand." One often notes a certain so-called artificiality in theater people: they do not step immediately out of their roles on leaving the dressing room; and in the eye of most perceivers, playing the ordinary roles of the ordinary good citizen, these denizens of another world, where the calculated gesture and the aesthetic intonation are *de rigueur,* seem slightly preposterous. The judgment is no juster than Plato's or Philip Stubbes', but it points to the effects of an occupation on the manifest personality. In accepting the stage conventions of his time, as well as in modifying them (as he did), Shakespeare reveals their initial congeniality with what he was, and allows them to enter into his outer structure at least. But something more ought to be said. When we look back on the plays of the Elizabethan-Jacobean era, we notice that some of the playwrights were more woodenly wrapped up in the conventions than he. Shakespeare appeals to us still as virtually a contemporary; he seems to speak in a voice truly human, while some of his fellows and immediate predecessors seem to be speaking through a mask, frozen in a rigid posture, fixed like the stiff conventional figures of a medieval woodcut. He seems less time bound than they. In the limited meaning of personality as personal charm, he has it and they do not. But this is not the meaning of the term as I have been trying to use it. In this broader meaning they are personalities as much as he, but they are more restricted personalities: his emotional richness, flexibility, variety of motive, sense of individuality surpass theirs. And therefore as we leave the Elizabethan-Jacobean conventions behind, he goes along with us, living and understandable still, while the others require a very special effort of appreciation. From our point of view his personality is less trussed up in that epoch's rather barbaric clothes (in the Carlylean sense); and in our expanded universe, where the human individual is more humbly informal than in those strutting days when man, sinful though he was, yet stood at the very center of his tiny stage, Shakespeare seems to be breathing and moving still almost like the sans-culottes that we are.

As to the matter of literary sources, I should emphasize Shakespeare's freedom of choice; not his absolute freedom, since the nature of his personality at the time of choosing would in my opinion be determinative, but his freedom relative to that. If he had invented the stories of *Coriolanus* and *Hamlet* outright, they would have been no more expressive of his personality than they are, Plutarch and Saxo Grammaticus and all. To find in history and previously written fiction the patterns which appeal to one is much the same as generating these patterns out of the imagination *de novo*. And then there is always modification. Suppose we take the infidelity theme traced in detail in an earlier chapter through the four plays of *Much Ado About Nothing, Othello, Cymbeline,* and *The Winter's Tale.* What are the sources detected by the scholars? For *Much Ado:* the *Chaereas and Kallirrhoe* of Chariton, the story of Timbreo and Fenicia from Bandello's *Novelle,* Ariosto's *Orlando Furiosa,* and Castiglione's *Il Cortegiano;* for *Othello:* Giraldi Cintio's *Ecatommiti;* for *Cymbeline:* a story from Boccaccio's *Decameron,* Tasso's *Gerusalemne Liberata, The Mirrour of Knighthood, The Rare Triumphs of Love and Fortune,* Apuleius' *Golden Ass,* Johnson's *Tom of Lincoln,* and Holinshed; for *Winter's Tale:* Greene's *Pandosto,* Sidney's *Arcadia, Amadis de Gaule,* the *Odyssey,* Lyly's *Woman in the Moon,* and Marston's *Pygmalion's Image.* An immense hodgepodge! What scholar, after immersion in all that, would have been able to predict that the theme of infidelity and guilt in Shakespeare's four plays would have run so clear and strong to the bitter-strange termination in *The Winter's Tale?* It is evident from simply glancing at the titles of the sources that any sort of unity of theme would have to depend on an active selection and fusion by a reader with his own purposes on the alert. If we consider the debt of *The Winter's Tale* to Greene's novel alone, we notice something very interesting: Greene supposedly invented his story outright, and there is in its sorrowful plot more than a hint of a connection with his own guilt about the wife he had neglected. *Pandosto* was written about 1588. Greene died about four years later, in 1592. His last piece of writing was a letter to his wife, whom he had deserted and not seen for six years. *Pandosto,* taken together with his *Francescos Fortunes* of 1590 ("Wherein is discoursed the fall of Loue, the bitter fruites of Follies pleasure, and the repentant sorrowes of a reformed man."), which Dyce thinks autobiographical in part, points to a state of mind in Greene not totally unlike that inferred for Shakespeare.[25] In adapting *Pandosto* to his uses, then, Shakespeare was employing a literary source which had emerged from experiences in the much less stable, much more dissolute, Greene which reverberated his own. I do not wish to press the

25. Cf. Alexander Dyce's introduction to his edition of Greene's *Dramatic Works,* listed in the Bibliography.

parallel very hard. I merely wish to indicate by a possibly valid example how it could happen that one author might profit from the writings of another in the construction of a drama capable of absorbing his innermost energies. The common vein of emotion is what is important, and not the fact that the book happens to be in print. Shakespeare, I am contending, was no mere copyist of other men's writings taken at random; but used them, when he did, because they appealed strongly to interests which were already awake and clamoring for attention. It should be noted that the philosophical idea of perpetual recurrence was congenial to him and to his practice of rifling other men's minds, as appears from Sonnet 59:

> If there be nothing new, but that which is
> Hath been before, how are our brains beguiled,
> Which, labouring for invention, bear amiss
> The second burthen of a former child!

I must also comment on the difference between the historian's use of sources and the poet's. For the historian the sources have intrinsic value as evidence, and must be handled reverentially, with proper acknowledgments, since he is acting as a collector of data and needs to fix the legitimacy of his materials; but for the poet the only value of sources is to be a stimulus or support to his own emotions and ideas, and if he gains a richer texture in his writing by their use, so much the better. The deliberate use of quotations in Eliot's *The Waste Land* is a modern instance of the practice. And who but Eliot himself, put on the defensive, would deny that the poem is a very personal, Eliotish vision, even though it also expresses the weary disillusionment of a whole generation?

7

Eyebrows may be raised over the decided emphasis I have given to early experiences of Shakespeare's as a vital point of origin for the content of the plays. In doing so I have been expressing, no doubt, a common psychological bias which will be found in the thinking of students of animal learning as well as in the doctrines of the psychoanalysts. Nevertheless, the aspects of Shakespeare's life which I have dwelt on most do not belong to that earliest period of the first half-dozen years which the psychoanalysts think so fruitful of later developments. My reason is just that Shakespeare is not available to furnish us information on that period; and the scanty records which we do have are principally from a later time —his later childhood and manhood. I have no aversion to the theory that the very earliest experiences are highly important to the individual's future personality; but those experiences which are common to childhood seem hardly worth noticing when the aim is to discover the origin of peculiarly individual traits, and, on the other hand, it hardly seems fair to attempt to supply appropriate incidents where the only clue we have lies in the trait itself which we wish to explain—and we cannot do more than this in the case of a long-dead author if the records on tap do not help us. But neither do I wish to imply by my emphasis that nothing subsequent to childhood is of any importance. There are doubtless thousands of topical allusions scattered through the plays of Shakespeare (and speckling his personality, as it were), and of some of these we can be very certain. Furthermore, it seems to me very likely that much deeper effects of graver current events in the London of Shakespeare's maturity could theoretically be detected in him. I will cite here two instances of such effects which have some scholarly approval.

There is the matter of Essex. Shakespeare's connection with Southampton, if nothing else, would have made the events of 1599–1601 leading up to Essex's execution for treason and Southampton's imprisonment more than ordinarily important to him, quite apart from the concern that any intelligent Londoner might have felt. Dover Wilson has argued seriously that Hamlet is a portrait from the life of the earl, who, like the melancholy Dane, was "a bundle of contradictions, to explain which baffled even the subtlest of his contemporaries." [26] Wilson's reasons for making the equation are primarily two: Shakespeare's interest in human character, which could be plentifully gratified by Essex; and his concern (almost that of a political mentor) for the welfare of England. But if one wants to equate Essex with Hamlet, there is no need to stop with their similarity of character and the need Shakespeare may have felt to expound the relations between persons and politics. Essex's whole history may be brought into the argument; and it is a history

26. *The Essential Shakespeare*, p. 103.

which Shakespeare, if he was indeed intimate with Southampton and the Essex circle, should have known by heart. It begins, as far as the parallel with *Hamlet* is concerned, with Essex's father. Walter Devereux, the first earl of Essex, died September 22, 1576, aged thirty-six, when Robert his son and heir was nine years old, a delicate but precocious boy. He died at Dublin, of a dysentery, while undertaking to settle an Irish rebellion on behalf of Queen Elizabeth. His wife, born Lady Lettice Knollys, was a cousin of the queen's, and at that time "a lady of great beauty, courageous personality, and quick, tart speech." [27] She was not with her husband when he died in faraway Ireland. "She was at Kenilworth for the celebrated revels; the attentions of the Earl of Leicester were conspicuous, and when Essex died scandalmongers said that he had been poisoned." [28] Suspicion attached to Leicester, the powerful favorite of the queen. Not only were the immediate circumstances favorable to the rumor, but the reputation he already had of having murdered his first wife many years before was ready to support it, as well as the fact that a second wife had recently left him in apparent fear of coming to a similar end. It further embellished the scandal of the elder Essex's precipitate demise that on September 21, 1578, virtually the second anniversary of his death, his charming widow was married to his supposed murderer. By this ceremony the earl of Leicester became the stepfather of the young earl of Essex, a brilliant and thoughtful child of eleven, then a student at Cambridge. The boy continued at the university until 1581, when he took his Master's, and afterward for a while lived in quiet studious retirement. He was urged by Leicester to come to Court. "Essex disliked his stepfather, and at first refused, but in the end he yielded to the persuasions of his mother." [29] In 1584 he was presented to Queen Elizabeth. He soon became her favorite, succeeding to his stepfather's position, and his passionate life from then on was inextricably bound up with hers, ending, after many fluctuations from extreme affection to furious indignation, in his beheading as a traitor February 25, 1601, the queen having refreshed herself the evening before at Whitehall by witnessing a play presented

27. G. B. Harrison, *The Life and Death of Robert Devereux, Earl of Essex*, p. 1.
28. *Ibid.*
29. *Ibid.*

by Shakespeare's company. As for Essex's mother, who is rumored to have poisoned her second husband around September 1588 (afterward marrying his Master of Horse without unnecessary delay), the evidence points toward a strong and continuing affection between her and her son. It takes little imagination to see in the fortunes of the House of Essex a foreshadowing of *Hamlet,* which appeared on the stage shortly after the death of the second earl. Though the connection cannot be proved, it can easily be suspected. What if it was truly there? Must we then discard the previously advanced theory that *Hamlet* goes back into Shakespeare's boyhood for some of its roots? I believe not. The complex character of Essex and his darkly glamorous story would rather come as a further incitement and historic support for Shakespeare's own bitter revelations. Indeed, I should like to argue that the concentrated and mysterious power of the drama of *Hamlet* owes much to the knotting together in one entangled whole of the stories of both Shakespeare and Essex. Once again, none of this can be proved: it can only be noted that there is a triple resemblance—between *Hamlet* and certain conspicuous features of the lives of the dramatist and the earl; but it may be added that it is exactly this kind of collocation of the personal and the outward historical, of past and present, which is the usual origin of phantasies, as Freud clearly states in his essay on "Der Dichter und das Phantasieren." And in general I should say, in agreement with Freud, that the early life of the dramatist is—not the sole originating source of his plays, but —a very important source, perhaps the most important in giving the main directions to his interests in later years, and so capable of giving special meaning to certain events on the world's great stage—such as the tragic affair of the earl of Essex, who was not only "the observed of all observers," but particularly close at hand for Shakespeare in more ways than one.

It is in the same light that I view the interesting revelations of Hotson in regard to Justice William Gardiner, that undoubted rascal.[30] The satirical portrait of Shallow in *The Merry Wives of Windsor* has traditionally been taken as a gibe at Sir Thomas Lucy. Hotson, because of what he found out about the unpleasant Justice of the Peace Gardiner, who was related by marriage to the Lucys

30. Cf. *Shakespeare versus Shallow.*

and had luces quartered on his coat of arms, prefers to see Shallow as a portrait of Gardiner. The case is well made out; and he finds also a source for the inane Slender of the same play in Gardiner's nephew and henchman, William Wayte, who in 1596 registered a legal complaint against Shakespeare and others and asked the court's protection from their threats of violence against his life. That Gardiner and Wayte would have been suitable models for Shallow and Slender seems indisputable, and the emotional condition of Shakespeare at the time after the death of his son three months before and after the troubles of the playmakers and especially of Francis Langley, owner of the Swan, with Gardiner would also seem to be suitable for carrying out the job. But why this perfectly reasonable argument of Hotson's should require us to forget the old legends in regard to Sir Thomas Lucy and the deer poaching escapes me. Encountering another Lucy in the repulsive form of Gardiner, a London Lucy to recall the old Lucy of Charlecote, and this one too threatening his livelihood, would have been the ideal situation for provoking a satirical attack on the Lucy tribe— and giving him or them a dozen louses, not just the three that Gardiner had acquired, but the whole set to be found on a Lucy tomb in Warwick. The legal action of 1596 and the quarrel on which it was based would have been an occasion in the present for developing a revenge phantasy already alive but dormant, and would furnish another illustration of the principle of convergence of past and present in the work of the imagination. Incidentally, as Hotson does not overlook, the Wayte document forces a revision of the notion that sweet Master Shakespeare was always and entirely "gentle."

The question regarding the contribution of contemporary events in maturity to the development of dramatic phantasy is related, of course, to the question about literary sources. In both cases I have sided with those like Abercrombie and Madariaga,[31] who insist that Shakespeare above everything else was an artist, with an artist's magisterial attitude toward the stuff he worked with. In addition, I have argued that the dominant influence in his handling of whatever materials he used was the set of personality trends

31. Cf. Lascelles Abercrombie's "Plea for the Liberty of Interpreting" in British Academy Lectures, *Aspects of Shakespeare;* and Madariaga, *On Hamlet.*

issuing from the obscurity of his childhood experiences—insofar as personality trends are due to the historical circumstances of the individual at all. I have thus taken up a commonplace psychological position. But it must be admitted that we are not able to estimate even roughly the proportionate contributions of the various kinds of experience to any given outcome in the personality or phantasy of Shakespeare or any other individual. We are inclined to grant priority to what is prior, on the doubtful principle of *post hoc, ergo propter hoc.* Always, in problems of genesis, we are on unsure ground. We can speculate, we can come to plausible and even useful conclusions; we cannot prove.

CHAPTER 7. CRITICAL
RECONSIDERATIONS

1

THE EXPLORATION OF one man's imagination has here been taken as an exploration of his developing personality. The terms of the analysis have chiefly been the dramatis personae, and the chief analytic task has been the isolation and description of certain configurations of relationship among these persons. Such analytic and descriptive work, whether in these terms or others, would appear to be the necessary prelude to any further designs which the student of Shakespeare (as a personality) might have.

Other analytic terms than the dramatis personae might easily have been chosen, of course, and made the basis for a systematic and quantitative analysis. Caroline Spurgeon has led the way in showing the possibilities of using Shakespeare's imagery in the study of his personality, and E. A. Armstrong has pushed the method farther by an intensive examination of certain clusterings of images.[1] Yule's statistical study of literary vocabulary points to another approach which has not been fully exploited in regard to Shakespeare.[2] It is clear that in order to be systematic and quantitative in the extraction of information from Shakespeare's plays which might be relevant to questions about his personality it is not necessary to utilize the particular analytic terms which I have chosen. The choice of these terms rather than others is bound up with general theoretical views, and in particular with a conception of personality which gives central importance to persons and personal relationships. Any statements about Shakespeare based on such material, or on any particular variety of material, are obviously limited by the nature of the material and the method by which it was gathered. Furthermore, inferences in regard to the origin and

1. Cf. Spurgeon, *Shakespeare's Imagery and What It Tells Us,* and Armstrong, *Shakespeare's Imagination.*
2. *The Statistical Study of Literary Vocabulary.*

the behavioral manifestations of a personality known through analysis of the imaginative output presuppose a knowledge of the laws connecting phantasy with the milieu and the person; but our knowledge in this respect is sadly deficient. Before going into the problem of inference, however, I should like to consider briefly two questions bearing upon the task of description merely—specifically, the description of Shakespeare's dramatis personae.

There is, first, the general question of procedure. The usual method is just to read the plays, react emotionally to the characters, and then set down one's impressions. The more one reads the plays the more knowledgeable one becomes. One may at the same time be seduced into oversubtlety. One begins reading between and behind the actual lines and straying off into speculations about the past adventures of Falstaff, the number of Lady Macbeth's children, the academic career of Hamlet at Wittenberg, the exact status of Ophelia's virginity. This is dangerous. It is a danger which cannot be entirely avoided, being implicit in language itself; for one must be prepared to leap from the tiny platform of the written or spoken word into its circumambient meaning if one is to profit from verbal discourse at all. Still, it is a danger. The inevitable margin of error may perhaps be reduced if one is systematic in one's reading and careful in marshaling the evidence. One may tabulate what the characters say, what they do, and what other characters say and do about them; and one may throw this information into a common language by stating in terms of a prepared list of traits what properties each character manifests.[3] This procedure can be further refined by having the job done by a whole committee of judges and correcting for individual biases by using the average opinion. In this manner the number and nature of the traits possessed by all the characters in which one is interested may be ascertained; and if one then wants to compare the characters to determine the extent of their likeness or unlikeness, it can be done by mathematically working out the amount of trait overlap between them. It was such a method that I used in my study of the novels of Charlotte and Emily Brontë. The method is laborious, however, and I have not attempted to use it in studying Shake-

3. Such lists may be found in Allport and Odbert, *Trait Names, A Psycho-Lexical Study,* and in Cattell, *Description and Measurement of Personality.*

speare's characters. Instead, I have relied on impressions, supported to some extent by a systematic canvassing of pertinent comments by the characters on themselves, and to a lesser extent by the comments of other characters, and have, in view of the imprecision of my data, employed only very broad categorizations of their traits. Greater refinement could have been achieved by a more minute examination of the data just mentioned, and by special methods such as the examination of the types of images clustered around given characters, in the manner very interestingly suggested by Morozov.[4] There are still other possibilities of methodical, repeatable procedures which may occur to the reader.

But there is, secondly, the question of special bias, introduced by the cultural changes differentiating, let us say, Eisenhower's United States from Elizabeth's and James' England. It is a question which has received a great deal more attention from modern Shakespearean scholars than from psychologists, who are much less aware of the sweep of history. Putting aside the innumerable minor troubles caused by words which are now obsolete or whose meanings have shifted slightly, by grammatical forms, literary and topical allusions, stage conditions, and symbolical conventions now out of fashion, and so on and on, there remains the major problem of adjusting our reading of a Shakespearean play to the whole cosmological, political, and religious framework of that period, in many ways very different from ours. One of the great services rendered by scholars like Edmund Chambers, Dover Wilson, and Hardin Craig is that they have continually reminded the modern reader of this problem and have furnished the necessary information for spanning the centuries which lie between us and Shakespeare. It seems clear from their evidence that an Elizabethan-Jacobean audience would not have taken everything in a play of Shakespeare's in quite the same way that we are likely to do, whether as readers or theater goers. True enough, the scholars themselves do not entirely agree as to what reactions Shakespeare intended or managed to get from his audiences when he brought a Shylock or Harry of Monmouth or Jack Cade on the stage; but they are sure that there is a difference between then and now. And in

4. Mikhail M. Morozov, "The Individualization of Shakespeare's Characters through Imagery," in *Shakespeare Survey 2*, pp. 83–106.

regard to the heroines, a good deal has been said about the havoc that is wrought by replacing his boy actors with flamboyantly romantic female stars. There can be little doubt, once we reflect on the differences between the times—the religious, political, philosophical, and even sanitary differences—, the differences between the Elizabethan and modern stage, the differences of belief and value and custom and focal social problems, that there must indeed have been different reactions from the audience. On such grounds it has been argued by some that Shylock was not really a profound psychological study but a stock Jew devil; that every gesture and word of great King Henry aroused unquestioning patriotic fervor; that merciless behavior, if only it were directed against conventional enemies such as a Jew or a Frenchman, would not have been so construed. Let us pin down the issue by taking one possible example. Suppose that it was indeed Shakespeare's intention to present a riproaring stage devil in the person of Shylock, and that furthermore his audience's reaction, conditioned by earlier plays like Marlowe's *Jew of Malta* and by the recent shocking conspiracy of the Jew Roderigo Lopez against the life of Elizabeth, proved his success. Color is lent to such an interpretation, in fact, by the very words of the title in the First Quarto, beginning: "The most excellent Historie of the Merchant of Venice. With the extreame crueltie of Shylocke the Iewe towards the sayd Merchant, in cutting a iust pound of his flesh." [5] Now, assuming that this or something like this is a true account of the facts for the sake of the argument, the crucial question is whether we today are justified in seeing in Shylock the suffering outcast, the heartbroken as well as pursebroken father, and so on, which modern acting and criticism and our own special sensitivities in a prejudice-conscious culture have accustomed us to. Is a characterization of Shylock in such terms true or false? Are we reading into his lines more than we ought? The question is a part of the more general question whether, without special information, we can transcend cultural boundaries in making judgments of persons.

The question is important and difficult. On the general level, it can be partially resolved in the following way. If our judgment has to do with the normalcy or acceptability or even just the function

5. Chambers, *William Shakespeare, 1,* 368.

of a trait within a particular society, then we must know that society. Lying may be cultivated as a virtue among the Spartans, murder as a religious duty among the Thugs; epilepsy and schizophrenia may be regarded as sacred diseases, putting one in touch with the Divine, within certain tribes; the dread of contamination by ritually prohibited foods may be a sign of cultural normalcy in an individual rather than a symptom of a merely private obsessional neurosis. But if our judgment has to do simply with the presence of a trait, and not with the question whether it is widespread or valued or disvalued in a given context, then it is not necessary to know the society to which the individual belongs. For the sake of clarity I put the statement absolutely, although I know that it requires some qualification. In particular, it needs to be qualified if we are dealing with expressive traits like smiling as opposed to outright acts like killing. A smile may be ironical; killing, scarcely so. Yet even killing, it must be admitted, may fulfill different purposes and affect the observer in different ways. Both the attention-getting quality of an act and its significance will vary with the observer. Nevertheless, I think it is easier to come to agreement on the presence or absence of a trait, when one does not know its social background, than it is to elucidate its social value. I confess that the distinction I am trying to make here is not really an absolute one, and that a very long discussion would be required to relieve it of crudity; but a single illustration may help to make it clear what I am driving at. Both a naïve layman and an expert physicist, if of reasonably normal hearing, would be likely to notice the chattering of a Geiger counter, if they were in the same room with it, and could agree that it was indeed making a noise; but they would not equally appreciate what the noise was referring to. The case of the lay reader and the Elizabethan expert confronted by a Shakespearean character is similar: they may agree that the character is expressing hatred or love or even some ironical mixture, if they are sensitive readers, but disagree as to what the reaction of Shakespeare's audience would have been or what Shakespeare as a playwright was trying to do to his audience. There should be less disagreement about the function or value of the trait within the confines of the play itself. To the extent that the play can be taken as a self-contained world, the evaluation of any element in it is simply dependent on its interconnections with the other elements in it. To the extent that the context of the special theater and social cosmos within which Shakespeare worked is necessary to fill out the contours of the play world, the interpretation of the elements must be deficient, apart from a knowledge of that context. I am of course contending that, in the main, a common human nature unites us with Shakespeare and allows us to resonate with fair accuracy to the emotional tremors which are set up in his characters; and that there is a level of description on which it is possible for readers of very diverse backgrounds and sophistication to come to essential agreement.

There is, however, a problem peculiar to Shakespeare in that his characters are especially complex and lively. They strongly engage our emotions and can be seen in different ways. It is a part of Shakespeare's distinction from his fellow playwrights that this is so. His characters seem to be capable of an endless unfolding as we examine them, and some of the disputes regarding their true nature result from this very richness. I would not say that this richness lies entirely in the eye of the beholder; Shakespeare himself put into his characters a power of enticing and surprising us beyond the scope of a Ben Jonson or even a Webster. But disputation based upon this fact is theoretically separable from, and should be separated from, another form of disagreement. Henry the Fifth is a first-rate test case. Is he the model of a good king? Is he human knighthood in flower? For Sir Sidney Lee, yes. For Harold Goddard, no. Dover Wilson says that when he saw the play given in Stratford during the first week of the first World War he found it intensely exciting, and, presumably, gratifying; and during the second World War, as we all know, it had another great career in technicolor. I think that some of the answer to the disputes over Henry is contained in this fact—the fact that he is capable of arousing enthusiasm in wartime. Given the attitude of intense patriotism in the reader or audience, of England right and the enemy wrong, Henry rises to the occasion as the glorious sun that he says he is. But if he is contemplated in a more peaceful season, and without any prepossessions in favor of English royalty, he is seen to be a rough-hewn powerful savage whom we should like to keep at a distance behind the bars of an ancient time. "How then do we like him?" asked Hazlitt, and proved by his answer that he did not deserve to be knighted.

> We like him in the play. There he is a very amiable monster, a very splendid pageant. As we like to gaze at a panther, or a young lion, in their cages in the Tower, and catch a pleasing horror from their glistening eyes, their velvet paws, and dreadful roar, so we take a very romantic, heroic, patriotic, and poetical delight in the boasts and feats of our younger Harry, as they appear on the stage, and are contained in lines of ten syllables; where no blood follows the stroke that wounds our ears, where no harvest bends beneath horses' hoofs, no city flames, no little child is butchered, no dead men's bodies are found piled on heaps and festering the next morning—in the orchestra! [6]

But suppose that we actually do thirst for blood? In my opinion, the chief obstacle to coming to agreement about some of the Shakespearean characters lies not in different degrees of ignorance about Elizabethan-Jacobean times but in certain powerful sentiments in the minds of the judges. The critic's favorite set of ideals, the enthusiasms of the moment, and so on, are likely to sway the balance, when a pronounced value judgment is called for. There is less biasing by such factors when the characters under examination are merely samples of Man or Woman in the generic sense than when they are the banner bearers for a sect or nation to which the reader owes allegiance or enmity. In the latter case, the impartial study of traits is overwhelmed by a flood of societal emotion, and the only happy survivors are those who can go with the flood.

2

Our inferences from any given set of data are limited by the fullness and precision of the data, and by our knowledge of lawful connections. My principal concern in this study has been to apply a method for the extraction of data. The method is admittedly somewhat stiff and crude, and the data accordingly somewhat blockish. But it is not the blockishness of the data which I find myself stumbling over at this point—the point of making inferences—but rather the ignorance of laws.

One direction in which we might want to move from the data at hand is toward the description of behavioral traits in Shakespeare such as a companion of his might have observed; and another di-

6. Pp. 145 f.

rection is that of explaining the existence of his dramatis personae and their dramatic interrelations by reference to events in his personal history of an external or internal nature and by reference to laws of personality development. In neither direction can we move with perfect freedom and in utter confidence. Indeed, we can only grope.

In the preceding pages some inferences have indeed been risked, but it remains to examine the inferential task a little more formally, especially with regard to psychoanalytic practice. And first let us examine the nexus between biographical or historical events and personality as revealed in the imagination.

One possibility to consider is that the personality, and hence its expression in the elements and tensions of the imagination, is simply a kind of mirror held up to the contemporary stream of events in the external world, so that we should search in Shakespeare's plays for a duplication, total or selected, of the immediately prior course of history—that is, history which might also be recorded in some other way. No doubt there are topical allusions in the plays, and no doubt the known frequency of these will increase as knowledge of Shakespeare's environment increases. Examples are the legal collision between Shakespeare and William Wayte, the underling of Justice Gardiner, which may have made its contribution to *The Merry Wives of Windsor,* and the excitingly tragic fortunes of the House of Essex, which may have entered into the composition of *Hamlet,* as, with some certainty, we know they entered glancingly into the Chorus of *Henry V,* in the words:

> As by a lower but loving likelihood,
> Were now the general of our gracious empress,
> As in good time, he may, from Ireland coming,
> Bringing rebellion broached on his sword,
> How many would the peaceful city quit,
> To welcome him! (HV, V, Prologue, 29 ff.)

One observes in regard to such examples, however, that it is not sheer duplication that we have to deal with, but rather a special reaction of the author to the event. Thus, it is not Shakespeare's legal scrap with Wayte and Gardiner which emerges in the play, just so, but a fanciful story which involves the supposed dramatic replicas, Slender and Shallow, in such a way that they appear ridiculous. The originals are held up to scorn and Shakespeare gets his revenge, or so Hotson thinks, without any direct reference to the real legal action. We see that the event, the historical occasion in the recent past, far from being merely repeated, is woven into the texture of Shakespeare's drama, functioning there on Shakespeare's terms rather than on its own. Reflection on such matters leads to the conclusion that contemporary historical events enter into the personality system only at the price of conforming to the demands of that system. It is like the entrance of a new person or group into an already established group: some disturbance will occur, some alteration of the receiving group, but on the whole the established patterns and tendencies of the group will prevail, and the new elements will be assimilated into the old organization. In this connection it has often been pointed out that the topical allusions in Shakespeare's plays are very much at home there; they do not stick out like a sore thumb, and they function dramatically so well that they seem to lose little of their effectiveness by a reader's ignorance of what they refer to. There is a charming story about an encounter between Shakespeare as an actor and Queen Elizabeth, which, true or not, illustrates his capacity for sweeping the extraneous deftly into the main currents of his own creative endeavors. "One evening," says Richard Ryan,

> when Shakspeare himself was personating the part of a King, the audience knew of her Majesty being in the house. She crossed the stage when he was performing, and, on receiving the accustomed greeting from the audience, moved politely to the poet, but he did not notice it! When behind the scenes, she caught his eye, and moved again, but still he would not throw off his character, to notice her: this made her Majesty think of some means by which she might know, whether he would depart, or not, from the dignity of his character while on the stage.— Accordingly, as he was about to make his exit, she stepped before him, dropped her glove, and re-crossed the stage, which Shakspeare noticing, took up, with these words, immediately after finishing his speech, and so aptly were they delivered, that they seemed to belong to it:

> > 'And though now bent on this high embassy,
> > Yet *stoop* we to take up our *Cousin's* glove!'

> He then walked off the stage, and presented the glove to the Queen, who was greatly pleased with his behaviour, and complimented him upon the propriety of it.[7]

7. Chambers, *op. cit.*, 2, 300 f.

Personalities of the quality of Shakespeare's pass through their world as if their course were determined and their meaning given by factors lying outside the momentary environment. To a lesser degree, I should say, the same holds true for all personalities.

But what are these influential factors lying outside the environment of the moment? And where are they to be found? The prevailing psychological disposition of our times has been to look to childhood and infancy for an explanation of the relatively stable, coherent, and assimilative personality of the adult. Especially is this true, though not exclusively, of the psychoanalysts, and it is over and over again illustrated in their treatment of Shakespeare. Though there are individual psychoanalysts, like Ernst Kris, who have dealt with Shakespearean plays without dwelling heavily upon the infantile determinants,[8] this has not been the orthodox and, one might say, distinctive, psychoanalytic tendency. When Freud in that fateful note in *The Interpretation of Dreams* explained Hamlet's indecision by the Oedipus complex, and through Hamlet peered at his creator, he was setting the fashion; for the Oedipus complex to which he referred was the emotional entanglement of the small child with his father and mother, and, in Freud's view, it was by the death of Shakespeare's father that the buried and undying complex was raised powerfully from the Unconscious and Shakespeare became in effect a child again, regressing to the age of three or four or five emotionally and conationally. The personality of the thirty-seven-year-old master of the British stage, at the height of his mastery, is thus regarded as predominantly the personality of the little child he once was. Now, to make such a discovery about Shakespeare is to say that, as for every other male child in our society (for such was Freud's view), the chief personality configuration was that in which the father is an enemy, the mother a desired sexual object, and the child (the ego) is murderous toward the father and lustful toward the mother. The personality of Shakespeare is thus stripped down to its primitive universal skeleton, and becomes indistinguishable from that of any other male. One of the main quarrels of the critics of psychoanaly-

8. Cf. Kris, "Prince Hal's Conflict," *Psychoanalytic Quart.*, 17 (1948), 487–506; also, Hanns Sachs' discussion of *Measure for Measure* in his book, *The Creative Unconscious.*

sis is that by such a reductionistic analysis the real problems—those relating to the currently acting personality—are left behind; and though this complaint is only partly justified, since there is much more to psychoanalysis than such reductionism, it cannot be ignored as trivial. To the extent that the reduction of Shakespeare to Oedipus makes clear the continuity of the individual life in its emotional aspects from childhood to adulthood, all is well—at least for those of us who can accept the Oedipus complex as a reality; but the reduction is largely empty of predictive power, as can be seen by turning the proposition around and attempting to deduce from the fact of an Oedipus complex in childhood the fact of a Shakespeare producing *Hamlet* in manhood. But apart from this criticism (which can equally well be directed against any formulation of the personality that I know of), and apart from the doubts which beset some in regard to the sexual lustfulness of the child, there is the fundamental uneasiness over the apparent dismissal of any significant distinction between the adult and the child.

That the example of Freud has not seemed radical enough to some of his followers is demonstrated by the work of Ella Sharpe, who reduces Lear, and, by implication, Shakespeare at the time of Lear, to a violently jealous child, screaming in misery and losing control of his bowels in a regression to the earliest period of infancy. The Shakespeare who produced Lear, and precisely in the moment of producing Lear, thus becomes an angry incoordinated baby, wildly thrashing about and defecating into his diapers. (It must be parenthetically remarked that for the psychoanalyst—and for normally loving and realistic parents, for that matter—there is nothing essentially nasty or wicked about infantile defecation.) Here once again the idea of continuity, the idea of the maintenance in the adult of the possibilities of infantile behavior, is quite acceptable to many who are not psychoanalysts; but it must be questionable even to a psychoanalyst whether the continuity argued for in this case is very useful in characterizing the Shakespeare who produced Lear, or the Lear whom he produced. It is not only that a vast stretch of time, in terms of individual human life, lies between infant Shakespeare and the man of forty who is the greatest poet in the world, but also there is a vast difference of powers, techniques, environment, and, very possibly, goals. One may be willing to grant that the Oedipus complex and infantile impatience lie beneath much that is human, and that protoplasm lies beneath that, and chaos beneath all, and yet not be willing to grant that the problem of distinguishing between chaos and Shakespeare at the peak of his career is nothing, or that it is solved by referring to the hypothetical rage of an infant. It is one thing to say that the capacity for crying out against the world which Shakespeare manifests in Lear is the same as the notorious capacity of the very young baby, and quite another thing to say that their crying out relates to the same sufferings and can be appeased by the same means. To be sure, there are philosophical levels of analysis on which one may want to do just this, and be able to do so persuasively; but, so the complaint runs, there is entirely too much of this reduction of the complex to the simple, of the present to the past, of the adult to the infantile, in the writings of psychoanalysis. I especially speak here for the idealistic reader of Shakespeare who finds in his works, and accepts as valid, moral striving, psychological penetration, and some of the finest and most delicate sentiments known to man— not to mention an all-embracing, exquisitely sensitive, masterful artistry. To such a reader, neglect of these things, or a perfunctory bow to them followed by a headlong rush into other matters, is little short of cynicism. One may argue, if one wishes, that science is above all mere moralistic judgment, especially when it is based on squeamishness; but if the judgment implies that the scientist is neglecting the very phenomena he should be dealing with it cannot be ignored. Some evidence of a changed attitude among the psychoanalysts toward these concerns is found in recent articles by Lee (formerly Levey) and Kris.[9]

Combined with the familiar criticism of psychoanalysis as tending to reduce everything to the infantile (a too sweeping criticism if applied to every psychoanalytic document, as witness, for instance, the elaborate case studies by Freud),[10] there is commonly a distrust of the means by which the psychoanalysts reach their

9. Kris, *op. cit.*, where other references will be found; and H. B. Levey, "A Theory Concerning Free Creation in the Inventive Arts," *Psychiatry*, 3 (1940), 229–93. Both these authors criticize their brother analysts for their neglect of aesthetics, and Kris takes them to task for their cavalier disregard of literary scholarship.

10. Freud, in contrast to many of his followers, resorts to technical jargon and omnibus explanations with surprising infrequency. An example of the down-to-earth realism and subtle complexity of his case reporting is his "Notes upon a Case of Obsessional Neurosis," in *Collected Papers*, Vol. 3.

conclusions. Thus, to refer to Sharpe once again, the transition from the elements she picks out of *King Lear* to her conclusion that Shakespeare was displaying his infantile knowledge of sexual functions is effected by very obscure reasoning.[11] To one versed in the esoterica of psychoanalysis and thoroughly sympathetic to the cause, the obscurity is not troublesome; but it is to any scientific methodologist. Where is the evidence? What is the logic? Such questions, to be sure, come up with reference to many kinds of interpretation of Shakespeare which are innocent of psychoanalysis. But they rise acutely in regard to psychoanalytic interpretations, because psychoanalysis professes to be a science. We may choose to grant that there are other avenues of approach to truth than science, and even that these other avenues are better; still, it is not well to confuse intuition, or creative thinking, or prophetic insight, with that approach which emphasizes orderly procedure and the sticking by certain rules of collecting data and treating them, which has seemed, whether illusion or not, to have opened up some of the secrets of nature during the past three hundred or so years in the Western world. My point is that, though it is not necessary to be scientific in order to be useful to mankind, it is a disservice to everyone concerned, including the psychoanalysts, to present as evidence what does not look like evidence, and as logic what looks like inspired mystification, and ignore the rules of orderly method which we expect in every other science.

Is it possible at all, by proceeding scientifically, to discover the necessary antecedent conditions of a personality state? To be more precise, is it possible to discover a state of affairs not itself a personality state which is necessary for the production of a given personality state, or to discover a personality state from which some subsequent personality state is necessarily derived? The causal or predictive linkage is what is desired. Since the present frame of mind of scientists is more congenial to prediction than to study of causation (though the two concepts have much in common), the question should perhaps be limited to the form: Is it possible to predict from a given state of affairs, or a given personality state, what a subsequent personality state will be; or, contrariwise, to predict (that is, say without prior knowledge) from a given per-

11. See above, pp. 43 ff.

sonality state what personality state or state of affairs will be found to have preceded it?

I think it may be assumed that, at the best, we should be able to answer any particular question of this type only in terms of degrees of probability. Nevertheless, it is not uncommon to see the adjective "invariable" used by psychoanalysts with reference to some purported connection between a previous and a subsequent state. Even if we substituted for this unfortunate word the more humble phrase "highly probable" we should still be in danger of having to do with an overstatement. In fact, in the present condition of our knowledge about personality, I think we cannot claim any highly probable predictions in this area, except in some peculiarly banal instances. We can, for instance, take a universal or nearly universal characteristic of early childhood and connect it with certainty or high probability with any subsequent state whatsoever. That is, given some particular personality state we can say that the universal characteristic of early childhood must have preceded it; or, if we like, that the state grew out of it, or was a causal consequence of it. But this is the same kind of proposition of which complaint has already been made. For if we turn it around, we see that it is not really very helpful. If anything is universal in childhood, then whatever follows it may be taken as a consequence of it, if one please, but cannot in its specific quality be predicted, unless it is the only thing that follows it or unless it is known to follow it in a certain percentage of cases—and the prediction, under either alternative, should be qualified by a statement of its probability. Thus it may be true that Shakespeare was as much entangled in the Oedipus situation as any man ever was, and yet it would not be predictable, except as one chance in many billion, that he would write any play at all, and not at all predictable that he would write *Hamlet* (since that is unique in world literature and unique in the history of Shakespeare), and only vaguely predictable that as a grown man he would have exhibited clearly in any way the personality state represented in *Hamlet*. Put more formally, the Oedipus complex or any other personality state of early childhood is a class of facts from which a number of very different consequences may flow; it is, symbolically, an A with implicates a, b, c, . . ., and we cannot from knowledge of it alone predict whether implicate a or b or c or some other will actually appear. However, if the list of implicates is finite and known, it would be possible from noting an implicate (i.e., some subsequent state) to assert meaningfully that A had previously occurred. But if A, the previous state, is universal, this assertion, though absolutely certain, would be minimally informative, since it could be made without any knowledge of a particular subsequent state: *any* subsequent state, whether an implicate of A or not, would allow us to say that A had preceded it, since A is universal. If, on the other hand, A is not universal, such an assertion based upon an implicate of A would be informative. What we are seeking, then, in an inquiry about the personality of Shakespeare or anyone, is an assertion of this latter kind. Such assertions are rarely if at all possible in psychology or psychoanalysis at present. But the kind of assertion desired can be illustrated. Freud, at the beginning of his therapeutic career, was led to believe that hysteria was the product of sexual assault in childhood; he later abandoned this absolute position, but it still may be true that the presence of certain kinds of hysterical symptoms, especially symptoms carrying traces of sexual defensiveness, should be taken as indicating early sexual assault. Again, the hypothesis has been developed on the basis of the theories of Abraham and others that early weaning will incline the child toward a lasting pessimism because of the frustration of oral pleasure seeking; and a modest correlation has actually been found between adult pessimism, operationally defined, and brevity of the nursing period.[12] It must be admitted that brevity of nursing is not therefore fixed as the sufficient cause, and would not be if the correlation were higher; it may merely reflect the general attitude of the mother toward her child, which may be more truly determinative, especially since it can operate over the whole growing period; still, it seems to have been demonstrated that adult pessimists in our culture have a slightly greater chance than adult optimists to have been subjected to early weaning. It is this type of relationship between personality state and prior event or personality state which we should like to have in order to make predictions.

12. Cf. Frieda Goldman, "Breastfeeding and Character Formation," *Jour. Personality, 17* (1948), 83–103; *19* (1950), 189–96.

The ventures which I myself have made in the preceding chapters to attach personality state to prior conditions—for example, attributing some features of the personality state appearing in *Hamlet* to the Lambert affair and the attendant circumstances—have rested upon two principles of unknown value: (1) that the prior conditions should have been such as to arouse or be capable of arousing strong emotions at the time of their occurrence, and (2) that there should be some perceptible resemblance between the dramatic structure of these conditions and the dramatic structure of the play in question. These principles are surely inadequate, whether taken separately or together, but they appear stronger when taken together; in any case, I have used them as guides, not guarantors. The trouble with both principles is that they cannot operate decisively unless the personality is passive; and I am persuaded that the personality is not passive, but is a dynamically interacting whole which transforms its own past, whether this past is *ab initio* in itself or originates outside. In brief, I think of the personality as creative. Such a point of view does not interfere with making *descriptions* of personality states, but it does interfere with making predictions from one state to another, on the basis of the two principles given. To arrive at the stage of making predictions of some known degree of probability from one personality state to another requires a thorough knowledge of the dynamic processes, or at least a knowledge of the usual sequence of states within the dynamic system for a number of classes of such states. But we do not at present have such knowledge, and the study of Shakespeare which I have undertaken is to be regarded as only a small step in that direction. A study of personality states in series in a large sample of personalities, done according to some such method as the one adopted here, might eventually produce a body of knowledge about personality which would enable us to set up normative patterns of sequential development, so that we finally could assert with some known degree of probability what personality state could be expected to precede or follow a given personality state. I think that only a very ambitious program methodically carried out could have any hope of success, and the risk of comparative failure is great. My reason for skepticism is, as I have said, that I regard personality as a dynamic creative system of great complexity: its complexity alone would make for difficulty; but even more would its creative nature.

In spite of this postulated creativity, it is true that in the present analysis of Shakespeare's plays, as well as in other analyses of Shakespeare and other authors, there do appear to emerge certain developmental sequences that proceed in a single direction. As striking an example as any is the jealousy theme in the plays *Two Gentlemen of Verona, Much Ado About Nothing, Othello, Cymbeline,* and *Winter's Tale*. But the existence of a theme developing in a certain direction is no guarantee of either its continued existence or its continuing development in the given direction. At least there is nothing in our present state of knowledge to guarantee it. One of the most provocative questions we can ask is why there should be intermissions in the sequence, or exacerbations of it. Only a great deal more research can tell us to what extent empirical laws can be found.

There is no more entertaining game than speculating about the causes of the existence of a personality state in an author. The literature on Shakespeare is replete with these speculations. The most convincing are those which have appealed to common human passions as the cause, and known or plausibly guessed-at events in his personal history. Thus, despite all the contempt rained on Frank Harris, he does make out a fascinating case for the contributions of Mary Fitton to the products of Shakespeare's dramatic genius. Dover Wilson, likewise, nearly or wholly persuades us that Shakespeare's relations with patrons and friends among the nobility, especially Southampton and Essex, contributed their share. I mention these as just two examples out of many. In both cases the convincingness of the argument rests partly on the fact that numerous details in the plays correspond with the known or conjectured details of Shakespeare's day-by-day experience, and these details are combined with some dominant passion—sexual love and jealousy by Harris, ardent friendship by Wilson—to give them meaning and force. The psychoanalytic attempts have suffered, in comparison, by appealing to stranger motives, not to say grotesque ones, and by failing to be as circumstantial in matching details, or, if circumstantial, largely by way of obscure symbolisms.

There is, however, a different point of view to be considered. I may introduce it by quoting some highly suggestive words from Yeats. "I have often had the fancy," he says in *Ideas of Good and Evil,*

> that there is some one Myth for every man, which, if we but knew it, would make us understand all he did and thought. Shakespeare's Myth, it may be, describes a wise man who was blind from very wisdom, and an empty man who thrust him from his place, and saw all that could be seen from very emptiness. It is in the story of Hamlet, who saw too great issues everywhere to play the trivial game of life, and of Fortinbras, who came from fighting battles about "a little patch of ground" so poor that one of his captains would not give "six ducats" to "farm it," and who was yet acclaimed by Hamlet and by all as the only befitting King. And it is in the story of Richard II., that unripened Hamlet, and of Henry V., that ripened Fortinbras.[13]

From the point of view adopted by Yeats one sees the personality developing from within outward rather than from without inward as the result of the impingement of a series of historical events. The theory makes the personality its own cause, and is close to Leibniz and Jung. It is the antithesis of mechanistic and cultural theories. The two can, nevertheless, meet. Let us assume an unfolding of personality from immanent cause and an encounter between it and a particular social configuration providing, at an early age, a chronic problem of ethics; in its subsequent unfolding certain aspects of the personality's development might be seen as continued attempts to deal with the problem. In Shakespeare's case, for example, we could see the problem of jealousy as such a problem, beginning in childhood with his displacement in his mother's affection by his brother Gilbert and by the succeeding children; later, by the displacement of his father and hence of himself as the owner of family property by his uncle Edmund Lambert, emotionally accented by the death of his sister Anne and the immediately following birth of his ill-named brother Edmund; later still, by his displacement in the sexual love of some woman, some Dark Lady, by some man he had trusted, perhaps his patron; and so on, through his life. The jealousy theme could therefore be important for Shakespeare both because of his "Myth" and because of particular events in his life history; and either a different "Myth" or a different set of experi-

13. Pp. 112 f.

ences could have given an entirely different direction to his personality development. There is no way at all to settle the rightness or wrongness of conceptions of this kind by empirical research. All that empirical research can do is to establish.what the sequences are, and by the accumulation of cases establish the probability of such and such relations. This descriptive task can be undertaken without any prepossessions in favor of any theory of personality. It is likely, however, that the emphasis given to the purely descriptive task will owe something to the nature of the personality theory favored. For a theorist of Yeats' party (as I suspect I am), the description is in itself rewarding, since it informs one of the "Myth." For a psychoanalyst, however, if one may judge from the usual procedure in writing up Shakespeare, the emphasis tends to fall on explanation; a given trait or symptom is isolated which has the earmarks of a mystery, this mystery is built up by showing that nonpsychoanalytic investigations have failed to solve it, and then the criminal motive is cunningly tracked to its lair. This manner of proceeding, which has an undeniable fascination of the Sherlock Holmes variety, may have originated in one of the early principles of psychoanalysis, subsequently overlaid by a far more complex network of ideas—the principle, namely, that behind every neurotic symptom one should look for the one, crucial, secret, traumatic event.

3

The other phase of our general inferential problem concerns the nature of the relationship between personality structure (as revealed in imagination) and observable behavior traits. One would like to know what personality configurations go with what traits. Essentially, the inquiry is about correlations and is not infeasible; but it is an inquiry which has scarcely been begun.

Although, as far as any established knowledge goes, it is quite possible that a man in the frame of mind for writing *Love's Labour's Lost* might be behaviorally the picture of gloom, and the writer of *King Lear* the most cheerful of companions, on a common-sense basis it seems improbable; and it is on this basis—which assumes a direct correspondence between the mood of an imaginative production and the behavior of the author—that biographers like

Brandes, Masson, Wilson, and others, have ventured to trace a sequence of mood states in Shakespeare, from the lightheartedness of the early plays through the depression and cynicism of the great tragedies and bitter "comedies" on to the religious conversion or recovery of poise in the late romances. Doubtless the scheme is too simple, but it makes good sense. It rests of course on something profounder than the distribution in time of the so-called comedies and tragedies. Sometimes a comedy, as Shakespeare demonstrates, can be a bitter thing; while a tragedy can be a high-spirited display of aggressive blood and thunder. The mood of a play is something more than its plot, and it is to mood that these biographers are especially referring when they trace out in Shakespeare's plays his emotional career. In general, however, mood and plot go together; the effect on the reader is peculiarly disturbing when they do not.

Yet, even if we grant that the mood of a play represents the mood of the author, we may have other questions. Granted that a mood exists, can we know how this mood is connected with the author's actions, or his tendencies to action, in the world? Into what kinds of situations would the mood seem to fit best? It is common observation that not every mood is uniformly pervasive: a man may be gloomy and surly at home, and cheerful and obliging at the office. The mood is often geared to a particular situation. We should like to know, therefore, whether for a given mood manifested in phantasy there is some given social arrangement in the external world which is especially likely to bring it out into the open. One way of answering this question is to pick out some one from among the many characters of the imaginative drama, note the relation between his actions and the mood of the piece, and thence conclude that Shakespeare (or other author) would act in that mood as this character does, and with reference to the same kind of situation. This is the procedure of Masson, for example, when he says that Shakespeare, during his early dramatic period up to about his thirty-third year, was in the Romeo-Proteus-Biron mood—"a mood compounded of the passionate impetuosity, the all-for-love recklessness" of these characters.[14] Not only is the mood of these plays identified with Shakespeare's prevailing mood, but it is attached to him as a person oriented toward certain kinds of action—im-

14. *Shakespeare Personally*, p. 147.

petuous love-making in particular. Now Masson does not abide by this conception of Shakespeare entirely; he in effect takes into account the apparent complexity of the mood, and possible contrary tendencies, by going on to remark, in this regard, that "through this time the prudential in Shakespeare's character was singularly large and strong." [15] The evidence on which he bases this qualifying statement is the known fact that Shakespeare was steadily increasing his worldly possessions at this very time; but he might also have noted that this manifest prudentiality was not really out of keeping with the plays, if only we will throw into the balance certain other elements besides Romeo and the others he mentions which are likewise found in the plays. I am here insisting once again that, if we are to get any real illumination from the plays, we must consider them as wholes, involving many characters and many relationships, rather than as simply the vehicles for displaying a single character to whose views, actions, and emotional state the author is exclusively committed. But the crux of the question is whether we can actually go from observing the dramatis personae and their relations with one another in a given play to making definite statements about the actions of the author, granting that these actions are in some way a function of the configurations we see in the play. Masson is cutting through this complexity when he says that Shakespeare in the Romeo-Proteus-Biron period was in the adventurous, reckless mood of these characters, and would have been found acting in their manner so far as opportunity would permit. Frank Harris puts the proposition more simply and more strongly still. Both accounts are persuasive, and when one is absorbed in reading them it is hard to doubt; but it is necessary to doubt—not only because the two accounts differ but also because of their partiality for certain single characters, sometimes of quite minor rank, such as Jaques in *As You Like It*. If the principle of wholeness which I have insisted on has merit, from which we should deduce that Shakespeare's behavior would be a resultant of the total array of forces represented in a play rather than a direct copy of the activity of any one character, then we should not expect him to appear in concrete social settings as quite the impetuous young man that Romeo was: there was the Mercutio in him,

15. *Ibid.*

the Tybalt and Capulet, and the Nurse too, among others. We should attempt to conceive of this whole combination as squeezed together into an apparently single man (but internally complex), and then ask ourselves what might come out of it. Shouldn't we expect the behavior of such a man to be dazzlingly varied? In the period of *Romeo and Juliet* there might have been a dominant note of somewhat melancholy romanticism, and various strange undertones of irascibility, calculating worldliness, and gross country foolishness. Shakespeare was surely as complex as the plays he wrote, and probably a great deal more, since there are always realities which a writer cannot express.

We can only speculate, however, until the necessary correlational work has been done. Scarcely any progress has been made in that direction, though the efforts of Freud and his disciples are of first-rate importance as a beginning. We have only tantalizing glimpses of possible laws. An example of our predicament is afforded by an experiment briefly reported in the recent literature.[16] A set of stories based upon the Thematic Apperception Test pictures was assembled from a group of schoolboys chosen for their outstanding normalcy of behavior, and these stories were then circulated for diagnosis among a number of clinicians familiar with such stories and with the psychiatric classifications. Working from the stories alone, the clinicians classified a large proportion of these normally behaving boys as definitely pathological. It is evident from this example that lawful connections between behavior and phantasy are not well established.

In an ambitious study published under the title *Adolescent Fantasy*, Percival M. Symonds has reported on a large number of stories collected from adolescents in response to a set of pictures somewhat resembling those of Murray's T.A.T. series. One of the questions raised by Symonds concerns the relationship between the stories and the observed behavior of his subjects in other situations. His answer is not very elaborate or logically rigorous, but the upshot of it is that no dependable relationship could be discovered. In trying to evaluate this result one must certainly not overlook the

16. Beverly Cox and Helen Sargent, "TAT Responses of Emotionally Disturbed and Emotionally Stable Children: Clinical Judgment versus Normative Data," *Jour. Projective Tech., 14* (1950), 61–74.

conditions under which the stories were obtained. The stories were in reaction to pictures which were forced upon the experimental subjects, not freely chosen by them; and the pictures for the most part express a somber mood and dramatic situations which must have had fairly definite meaning for the artist himself. The pictures, to the degree that they are attended to as objects to be described, surely limit the range of response of the subject who is examining them. Some of the reported looseness of connection between behavior and stories told must be due to nothing more profound than the fact that a random collection of boys and girls were endeavoring to characterize a set of pictures limited in mood and theme. Though these pictures are doubtless more ambiguous than a written story might be, we might consider as a kind of limiting case what the results would have been if the same random collection of adolescents had been asked to read, or even summarize after reading, a series of short stories. One would certainly expect to find, under these conditions, a greater uniformity in the stories produced than in the behavioral characteristics of those who read or summarized them, and would not expect any positive correlation between persons and stories, unless the stories had been chosen to conform to the main trends of adolescent life. The pictures have some ambiguity, to be sure, but they are more than a little restrictive. Take a test case. Symonds writes:

> The following story, told by Julia (case 25), illustrates the same tendency even more strikingly. [He is referring to a supposed tendency to disguise the phantasy life by the outward behavior.]

>> Mary Jane came from a poor family; goes to high school. Is bright in school. Likes to read; enjoys activities in school. Is taking academic course. Would like to go to college if family can afford it. After school in afternoons walks through country paths; sits beneath a tree, thinking of life plans. (Julia, case 25—story 28)

> The girl who tells this story is in real life an example of flaming youth. Sixteen years old, Julia has long red hair and wears bright clothes and flashy jewelry. Actually she is not very bright in school and does mediocre work. She is spoiled and undisciplined and has her mind on boys and dancing. But this story shows another side of her nature—a wistful, shadowy, serious wish self to which she retreats in fantasy. This is an-

other example which shows the fantasy life and the real life representing opposite trends.[17]

Now, on comparing the girl's story with the brief sketch of her character, one must admit that there is an evident contrast. But the crucial question is whether the heroine of the story, whom she has endowed with certain thoughts and traits, really does represent her own innermost, though buried, wishes. If the story were spontaneous, one would be inclined to go along with Symonds. A great deal of the mystery of the storyteller's dual personality vanishes, however, when we turn to the back of Symonds' book and locate the picture which was the basis of her remarks. One sees a sober, if not depressed or fatigued, young woman, alone in a shadowy landscape—which suggests a deserted beach rather than a forest, but which is obviously a part of the great outdoors; resting on her left thigh, she props her weight somewhat wearily on her left hand, her body turned front three-quarters toward the observer and her face slightly averted; her tight-fitting dress is simple and without ornament, and conspicuously displayed on the ground in front of her are two books and a notebook, strapped together in typical high-school fashion. That in this picture the extroverted young playgirl described by Symonds should see a bookish, solitary, and poverty-stricken figure is not surprising. The fact certainly does not justify the conclusion that "a wistful, shadowy, serious wish self" hides behind her brazen exterior; for we have no indication at all that she identifies herself with the girl in the picture. The picture was, after all, thrust upon her by the examiner; it did not rise up in a dream or daydream out of her own depths.

Where objective material like these pictures in the Symonds collection is used as the precipitation point for phantasies, it is important to separate the contribution of the picture to the outcome. For example, very few of the stories told by Symonds' forty adolescents are cheerful, though many of the adolescents are; and this agrees with the fact that the pictures on the whole are a somber, morbid lot. One must subtract the morbidity of the pictures from the precipitate in order to arrive at a just estimate of the story-

17. Pp. 112 f.

teller's performance. In the case of the T.A.T. series this need has been realized and partially met in a recent study,[18] but this type of investigation could be greatly expanded, and probably must be if results from the use of the test are to be clarified. I suspect that failure to allow for the impact of the material itself is a main source of the distrust of the T.A.T. as a clinical instrument which has lately been expressed by Sanford. In the foreword to a *Manual* published by Betty Aron in 1949, he says: "I think we must admit that the usefulness of the T.A.T., in a practical way, is no greater today than it was in 1937. This last point may be illustrated in this way. In the OSS Assessment School where the aim was to make a diagnosis in dynamic terms of the total personality, one that would include 'deep' trends, and where the interests of practicality swept all others aside, the T.A.T. was given up after a very brief trial." [19] He adds that, as a clinician, he has no use for the instrument, and knows of no one in similar practice who does. But if the clinical usefulness of the test is limited or nonexistent because of the masking effects of such factors as the expressive qualities and content of the pictures, whose exact contribution to the elicited stories is unknown, then also its usefulness for the theoretical inquiry into the relation between phantasy and behavior in general is limited. It is to be hoped that this limitation will in time be overcome. The attention given to the simple, basic problem of describing and scoring the stories in the publications of Tomkins, Stein, and Aron is in itself a hopeful sign.

4

The remarks which I have been making in this chapter have been highly critical of various attempts, not omitting my own, to utilize imaginative material in the study of personality. I should like to conclude on a more positive note.

Great issues like those of personality cannot be settled by a few precise measurements or a few crucial experiments. Breadth of view is necessary, patience with vague preliminary formulations, tolerance of confusion and guesswork. To insist at an early stage

18. L. D. Eron, Dorothy Terry, and Robert Callahan, "The Use of Rating Scales for Emotional Tone of TAT Stories," *Jour. Consulting Psychol.*, 14 (1950), 473–8.
19. *A Manual for Analysis of the Thematic Apperception Test.*

of inquiry that nothing but faultless methodology will be accept-able is, in such a case, a prelude to withdrawal from the main busi-ness. One must be willing to bungle along and muddle through, and, above all, respect intuition, even if it threatens to expose the limitations of a favorite technique. Every technique or method is necessarily limited: it is a special point of view, which cannot af-ford to pretend that it reveals everything, and which may have to admit that it reveals little or nothing. One's aim may be wrong. Nevertheless it is important, I think, that we are now at a stage at which we are ready to try out defined methods, rudimentary meas-urements, and testable hypotheses. It is equally important that we should not surrender the concept of personality, if a particular ap-proach fails to bear fruit, nor surrender ourselves to dullness and picayunishness. Personally, if I had to choose between poetic in-tuition and sharable scientific methodology, I should unhesitantly choose the former, whether it was in the matter of understanding Shakespeare, the universe, or my next-door neighbor; but I hope that the choice is not necessary, since it seems clear to me that human beings have the possibility of functioning in both ways without detriment to either—that, in fact, it is self-destructive (in-dividually and for the race) to attempt to sacrifice the one mode of thinking to the other.

We need, however, to get as clear as possible about the limits of usefulness of certain methods of approach to personality. As sci-entists we must be concerned about the sort of generalizations which a method permits, and about the accuracy and informative-ness of its predictions. No method can take care of everything. But we can and must ask what questions a given method can answer, and then put these questions rigorously to appropriate material. Up to now there have been only tentative beginnings with those variants of the general method which stems from the idea of per-sonality projection. We must have bolder, more comprehensive, more hardheaded investigations. The present study points to one way of proceeding, but I am very far from arguing that this is the only way, or that even within its limits all has been faultlessly done.

I am especially hopeful of the benefit which there may be in the drawing together of psychological and literary interests. They have a common stake in the enterprise of understanding Man. While the laboratory has its contribution to make to this end, as well as the consulting room, I think that our main resource in the future, as in the past, is in study of the creations of the human mind under the natural conditions of social interaction on the wide stage of the world. Among these creations there is none more interesting than imaginative literature, and none closer to the heart of the human mystery.

APPENDIX A. ON THE USE OF
THE TERM SOUL

THE TERM SOUL has long been out of fashion in American psychology, in spite of the implications of the term psychology. The reason for its abandonment, however, is not that it has been proved useless by a thorough examination of the phenomena with which it has in the past been associated. The reason is simply the fear of theological and philosophical embroilment.

In flight from the Church and Metaphysics, psychologists abandoned term and concept both, and tried to restrict themselves to methods and areas of investigation which would keep them safe from the embarrassing memory of what they had left behind. But with the emergence of the new interest in personality the problem of the soul has arisen again. Not that the term is ever used—but the problem is discussed! One of the most curious manifestations at present is the widespread concern with self and role. The self (which might be taken as equivalent to soul, if one were not warned) is said to be a role, or a set of roles, or the result of playing roles, in society; and it is usually left unclear what it is that takes or plays the role. Or it may be said that originally there is no self, but that a self is gradually formed by a kind of accretion; or it may be that it is a conception of a self rather than an actual self that is thus formed. For example, a recent textbook of social psychology states on the first page of the first chapter: "All that is distinctly human in the behavior of man results from his participation in organized social life. It is only within such social processes that he acquires a mind and a conception of self." [1] Later on there is a chapter devoted to self-consciousness, and the first words are: "Man is not born with a self, or with consciousness of self. Each person becomes an object to himself by virtue of an active process of dis-

1. Faris, *Social Psychology*, p. 3. The author is a sociologist; but his views do not distinguish him from psychologists at large, and are particularly congenial with those of Norman Cameron.

covery. The material for building a conception of self is acquired in the process of interaction with other persons. The self is defined in the reactions of others." [2] The writer's shifting back and forth between self and consciousness of self makes all the obscurer what the supposed process is by which a self (or is it a consciousness of self?) is acquired. A leader in the field of abnormal psychology makes very similar statements. Others could be cited to the same effect.

It was my original impulse to use the term self where I have used soul, but in view of the current usage I could not do so without some risk of being misunderstood. By soul I do not mean self-consciousness, or a social role, or an aggregate of bodily sensations and social roles. I mean a unitary, unanalyzable principle of life which is present in the phenomena of consciousness and which is the basis for the awareness of personal identity. As far as I understand Leibniz, I mean what he means when he uses the term. At least I mean what he says in the following passage:

> You next ask my definition of *soul*. I reply, that *soul* may be employed in a broad and in a strict sense. Broadly speaking, *soul* will be the same as life or vital principle, *i.e.* the principle of internal action existing in the simple thing or monad, to which external action corresponds. And this correspondence of internal and external, or representation of the external in the internal, of the composite in the simple, of multiplicity in unity, really constitutes perception. But in this sense soul is attributed not only to animals, but also to all other percipient beings. In the strict sense, *soul* is employed as a nobler species of life, or sentient life, where there is not only the faculty of perceiving, but in addition that of feeling, inasmuch, indeed, as attention and memory are added to perception. Just as, in turn, mind is a nobler species of soul, *i.e.* mind is rational soul, where reason, or ratiocination from universality of truths, is added to feeling. As, therefore, mind is rational soul, so soul is sentient life, and life is perceptive principle.[3]

While the term self, or even ego, might have suggested to the reader one of the current peripheralistic theories, it is unlikely that the term soul will. The unpopularity of the term has at least preserved it from confusion with an evanescent social role; under its archaic form there is still a naked and pristine substantiality.

2. *Ibid.*, p. 149.
3. In Russell, p. 266.

APPENDIX B. ON ROLFE'S COUNT

W. J. ROLFE, in his edition of Shakespeare, publishes a count of
the lines spoken by each of the characters.[1] Disregarding strictly
enumerative errors in my count and differences of a textual nature, I think it is evident that Rolfe was estimating part lines and
lines of prose according to a different standard from that which I
adopted. Table 10 compares his count with mine for those characters which I have assigned to first rank. With four exceptions, his

TABLE 10

CHARACTER	COUNT OF LINES	
	McCurdy	*Rolfe*
Gloucester	1078	1161
Antipholus S.	270	279
Petruchio	577	585
Valentine	380	393
Biron	638	627
Romeo	613	618
K. Richard	754	755
Bottom	245	279
Bastard	518	522
Portia	568	589
Hotspur	558	566
Falstaff	553	719
Benedick	383	474
K. Henry	989	1063
Brutus	809	727
Rosalind	599	749
Viola	326	353
Hamlet	1382	1569
Falstaff	379	488
Troilus	543	541
Helena	473	479
Duke	847	880
Iago	1061	1117
K. Lear	682	770

1. Rolfe (ed.), *Complete Works of William Shakespeare.*

TABLE 10 (*continued*)

CHARACTER	COUNT OF LINES	
	McCurdy	*Rolfe*
Macbeth	689	705
Antony	818	829
Coriolanus	865	886
Timon	826	863
Pericles	580	603
Imogen	605	596
Leontes	674	681
Prospero	629	665

count is larger. The chief discrepancies are for Falstaff and Hamlet, and in both these cases, especially in the case of Falstaff, a fair amount of prose is involved.

The absolute number of lines spoken is of less concern for our purposes than the relative number. It is especially important to determine whether there is any serious disagreement between Rolfe's data and mine in this respect. I think it is fair to say that the disagreement is not serious.

There are two cases out of thirty-two where following Rolfe's count would result in a reversal of position for first- and second-ranking characters: Proteus would stand above Valentine, Falstaff (of *1 HIV*) above Hotspur. According to my own count, as Table 1 shows, the weight difference between these characters is not large. We may go into the question more deeply by considering the whole set of twelve ranks for the thirty-two plays. There are four plays in which the ranks by the two counts are identical; at the opposite extreme is *The Tempest,* where Rolfe's count would place five of the characters in different positions. In terms of the correlation coefficient, the agreement of ranks by the two counts ranges from 1.00 to .87, with an average of .97. Table 11 along with Table 1 of the text will show that in the most extreme instance—that of *The Tempest*—the order is not greatly disturbed, especially in view of the narrow range of percentage weight differences involved, if Rolfe is followed.

Finally, a comparison may be drawn between the summed character weights for the twelve ranks obtained by the two counts. In Table 12 I present the series of average weights resulting from my count (the harmonic properties of which have been pointed out

TABLE 11

The Tempest

Order

McCurdy	Rolfe
Prospero	Prospero
Ariel	Ariel
Caliban	Caliban
Ferdinand	Stephano
Antonio	Gonzalo
Gonzalo	Antonio
Miranda	Miranda
Stephano	Ferdinand
Sebastian	Sebastian
Trinculo	Trinculo
Alonso	Alonso
Iris	Boatswain
(Boatswain	Iris)

in the text) and the series resulting from Rolfe's, when Rolfe's figures are inserted in Table 1 without changing the position of any of the characters. There are differences, but I doubt that any of them are statistically significant. One may guess that a perfectly accurate line count, according to my previously stated rules, would produce a series closely similar to what I have already described, and an order of characters not greatly different from that which I have utilized in my analysis.

TABLE 12

Average Character Weights

Count	
McCurdy	Rolfe
100	100
63	58
52	46
40	37
35	32
30	26
25	22
21	19
18	16
15	13
12	11
10	9

BIBLIOGRAPHY

MOST of the items listed are directly referred to in the text. A few others are included because of their special influence or usefulness in the development of this particular book, though not mentioned in footnotes or otherwise. No attempt has been made to present an exhaustive bibliography of any phase of the subject.

ALLPORT, G. W., AND ODBERT, H. S. "Trait Names: A Psycho-Lexical Study," *Psychological Monographs,* Vol. 47 (1936), No. 211.
ARMSTRONG, E. A. Shakespeare's Imagination:'A Study of the Psychology of Association and Inspiration. London, Drummond, 1946.
ARON, BETTY. A Manual for Analysis of the Thematic Apperception Test. Berkeley, Berg, 1949.
AUDEN, W. H., AND MacNEICE, L. Letters from Iceland. London, Faber, 1937.

BARTLETT, F. C. Remembering. Cambridge University Press, 1932.
BARTON, D. P. Shakespeare and the Law. Boston, Houghton Mifflin, 1929.
BERGLER, EDMUND. The Writer and Psychoanalysis. New York, Doubleday, 1950.
BRADLEY, A. C. Oxford Lectures on Poetry. London, Macmillan, 1950.
BRANDES, GEORGE. William Shakespeare. London, Heinemann, 1899.
BRITISH ACADEMY LECTURES. Aspects of Shakespeare. Oxford, Clarendon Press, 1933.
BUTLER, PIERCE. Materials for the Life of Shakespeare. Chapel Hill, University of North Carolina Press, 1930.

CATTELL, R. B. Description and Measurement of Personality. Yonkers-on-Hudson, World Book Co., 1946.
——— Personality, A Systematic Theoretical and Factual Study. New York, McGraw-Hill, 1950.
CHAMBERS, EDMUND K. William Shakespeare: A Study of Facts and Problems. 2 vols. Oxford, Clarendon Press, 1930.
——— Sources for a Biography of Shakespeare. Oxford, Clarendon Press, 1946.
COX, BEVERLY, AND SARGENT, HELEN. "TAT Responses of Emotionally Disturbed and Emotionally Stable Children: Clinical Judgment versus Normative Data," *Journal of Projective Techniques, 14* (1950), 61–74.
CRAIG, HARDIN. An Interpretation of Shakespeare. New York, Dryden, 1948.

DAVIES, W. R. Shakespeare's Boy Actors. London, Dent, 1939.
DOWDEN, EDWARD. Shakspere: A Critical Study of His Mind and Art. New York, Harper 1880(?).
DYCE, ALEXANDER (ed.). Dramatic Works of Robert Greene. 2 vols. London, Pickering, 1831.

ERON, L. D., TERRY, DOROTHY, AND CALLAHAN, ROBERT. "The Use of Rating Scales for Emotional Tone of TAT Stories," *Journal of Consulting Psychology, 14* (1950), 473–8.

FAIRBAIRN, W. R. D. "Endopsychic Structure Considered in Terms of Object-Relationships," *International Journal of Psycho-Analysis, 25* (1944), 70–93.
——— "Object-Relationships and Dynamic Structure," *International Journal of Psycho-Analysis, 27* (1946), 30–7.
FARIS, R. E. L. Social Psychology. New York, Ronald Press, 1952.

FIEDLER, F. E., AND SIEGEL, S. M. "The Free Drawing Test as a Predictor of Non-Improvement in Psychotherapy," *Journal of Clinical Psychology*, 5 (1949), 386–9.
FREUD, SIGMUND. Gesammelte Schriften. 12 vols. Vienna, Internationale Psycho-analytische Verlag, 1924–34.
——— The Interpretation of Dreams. New York, Macmillan, 1933.
——— Collected Papers. 5 vols. London, Hogarth, 1949–50.

GALTON, FRANCIS. Inquiries into Human Faculty and Its Development. London, Macmillan, 1883.
GARMA, ANGEL. "The Traumatic Situation in the Genesis of Dreams," *International Journal of Psycho-Analysis*, 27 (1946), 134–9.
GARRETT, H. E. Statistics in Psychology and Education. New York, Longmans, 1940.
GODDARD, HAROLD C. The Meaning of Shakespeare. University of Chicago Press, 1951.
GOLDMAN, FRIEDA. "Breastfeeding and Character Formation," Parts I and II, *Journal of Personality*, 17 (1948), 83–103, and 19 (1950), 189–96.
GRANVILLE-BARKER, HARLEY. Prefaces to Shakespeare. 2 vols. Princeton University Press, 1947.
GRANVILLE-BARKER, HARLEY, AND HARRISON, G. B. (eds.). A Companion to Shakespeare Studies. Cambridge University Press, 1934.
GRIFFIN, W. J. "The Use and Abuse of Psychoanalysis in the Study of Literature," *News-Letter of the Conference on Literature and Psychology of the Modern Language Association*, Double No. 5–6 (1951), 3–20.

HALLIDAY, F. E. Shakespeare and His Critics. London, Duckworth, 1949.
HALLIWELL-PHILLIPPS, J. O. Outlines of the Life of Shakespeare. 2 vols. London, Longmans, 1887.
HARBAGE, ALFRED. Shakespeare's Audience. New York, Columbia University Press, 1941.
HARRIS, FRANK. The Man Shakespeare and His Tragic Life-Story. New York, Harris, 1921.
HARRISON, G. B. The Life and Death of Robert Devereux, Earl of Essex. London, Cassell, 1937.
——— Introducing Shakespeare. New York, New American Library, 1947.
HAZLITT, WILLIAM. Characters of Shakespeare's Plays. New York, Wiley & Putnam, 1845.
HOEL, P. G. Introduction to Mathematical Statistics. New York, Wiley, 1947.
HOTSON, LESLIE. Shakespeare versus Shallow. Boston, Little, Brown, 1931.
——— I, William Shakespeare. London, Cape, 1937.
——— Shakespeare's Sonnets Dated, and Other Essays. London, Hart-Davis, 1949.
HUME, DAVID. A Treatise of Human Nature. 2 vols. London, Dent, 1939.

JONES, ERNEST. "The Oedipus-Complex as an Explanation of Hamlet's Mystery: A Study in Motive," *American Journal of Psychology*, 21 (1910), 72–113.
——— Hamlet and Oedipus. London, Gollancz, 1949.
JOYCE, JAMES. The Portable James Joyce. New York, Viking, 1947.
——— Ulysses. New York, Random House, 1934.
JUNG, C. G. The Integration of the Personality. New York, Farrar & Rinehart, 1939.

KELLEY, T. L. Fundamentals of Statistics. Cambridge, Harvard University Press, 1947.
KITTREDGE, G. L. Shakspere. An Address Delivered on April 23, 1916 in Sanders Theatre at the Request of the President and Fellows of Harvard College. Cambridge, Harvard University Press, 1924.

KLEIN, MELANIE. "Notes on Some Schizoid Mechanisms," *International Journal of Psycho-Analysis,* 27 (1946), 99–110.
KRIS, ERNST. "Prince Hal's Conflict," *Psychoanalytic Quarterly,* 17 (1948), 487–506.

LEE, SIDNEY. A Life of William Shakespeare. New York, Macmillan, 1931.
LEIBNIZ, G. W. Philosophical Writings. London, Dent, 1934.
LEVEY, H. B. "A Theory Concerning Free Creation in the Inventive Arts," *Psychiatry,* 3 (1940), 229–93.
LUNDHOLM, HELGE. God's Failure or Man's Folly. Cambridge, Mass., Sci-Art, 1949.

MADARIAGA, SALVADOR DE. On Hamlet. London, Hollis & Carter, 1948.
MARLOWE, CHRISTOPHER. The Plays. London, Dent, 1926.
MASSON, DAVID. Shakespeare Personally. New York, Dutton, 1914.
McCURDY, H. G. "Literature and Personality," *Character and Personality,* 7 (1939), 300–308.
———— "Literature and Personality: Analysis of the Novels of D. H. Lawrence," Parts I and II, *Character and Personality,* 8 (1940), 181–203 and 311–22.
———— "A Note on the Dissociation of a Personality," *Character and Personality,* 10 (1941), 35–41.
———— "The History of Dream Theory," *Psychological Review,* 53 (1946), 225–33.
———— "A Study of the Novels of Charlotte and Emily Brontë as an Expression of Their Personalities," *Journal of Personality,* 16 (1947), 109–52.
———— "A Mathematical Aspect of Fictional Literature Pertinent to McDougall's Theory of a Hierarchy of Sentiments," *Journal of Personality,* 17 (1948), 75–82.
———— "Literature as a Resource in Personality Study: Theory and Methods," *Journal of Aesthetics and Art Criticism,* 8 (1949), 42–6.
McDOUGALL, WILLIAM. Outline of Abnormal Psychology. New York, Scribner, 1926.
McNEMAR, QUINN. Psychological Statistics. New York, Wiley, 1949.
MURRAY, HENRY A., et al. Explorations in Personality. New York, Oxford University Press, 1938.

NEWTON, ISAAC. Optics. In Isaaci Newtoni Opera Quae Exstant Omnia, edited by Samuel Horsley, Vol. 4. London, Nichols, 1782.
NICOLL, ALLARDYCE (ed.). Shakespeare Survey: An Annual Survey of Shakespearian Study and Production. First 4 vols. Cambridge University Press, 1948–51.

PAVLOV, I. P. "Letter addressed to H. S. Langfeld in 1929," *American Psychologist,* 2 (1947), 210–11.
PLATO. The Dialogues, translated by Benjamin Jowett. 2 vols. New York, Random House, 1937.

ROLFE, W. J. (ed.). Complete Works of William Shakespeare. 40 vols. New York, American Book Co., 1870–1909.
RUSSELL, BERTRAND. A Critical Exposition of the Philosophy of Leibniz. London, Allen & Unwin, 1937.

SACHS, HANNS. The Creative Unconscious. Cambridge, Mass., Sci-Art, 1942.
SCHÜCKING, L. L. Character Problems in Shakespeare's Plays. New York, Holt, 1922.
SHAKESPEARE, WILLIAM. Students' Handy Shakespeare, edited by H. N. Hudson. Vols. 1, 3, 5. New York, Dana Estes, 1881.
———— Comedies, Histories, and Tragedies. 3 vols. London, Dent, 1927.
———— The Complete Works of William Shakespeare, edited by W. G. Clark and W. A. Wright, with Complete Notes of The Temple Shakespeare by Israel Gollancz. (Reprint of the 1911 revision of the Globe Edition.) New York, Cumberland, n.d.
———— The New Variorum Shakespeare, edited by H. H. Furness and J. Q. Adams. 23 vols. Philadelphia, Lippincott, 1871–1944.

SHARPE, ELLA FREEMAN. "From *King Lear* to *The Tempest*," *International Journal of Psycho-Analysis*, 27 (1946), 19–30.

—— "An Unfinished Paper on *Hamlet: Prince of Denmark*," *International Journal of Psycho-Analysis*, 29 (1948), 98–109.

SISSON, C. J. "The Mythical Sorrows of Shakespeare," *Proceedings of the British Academy*, Vol. 20. London, Humphrey Milford, 1934.

SKINNER, B. F. "A Quantitative Estimate of Certain Types of Sound-Patterning in Poetry," *American Journal of Psychology*, 54 (1941), 64–79.

SMART, J. S. Shakespeare: Truth and Tradition. London, Edward Arnold, 1928.

SOPHOCLES. The Text of the Seven Plays, edited by Sir Richard Jebb. Cambridge University Press, 1914.

SPURGEON, CAROLINE. Shakespeare's Imagery and What It Tells Us. New York, Macmillan, 1936.

STEIN, M. I. The Thematic Apperception Test: An Introductory Manual for Its Clinical Use with Adult Males. Cambridge, Mass., Addison-Wesley, 1948.

STOLL, E. E. Art and Artifice in Shakespeare. Cambridge University Press, 1933.

—— From Shakespeare to Joyce. Garden City, Doubleday, 1944.

SYMONDS, PERCIVAL M. Adolescent Fantasy: An Investigation of the Picture-Story Method of Personality Study. New York, Columbia University Press, 1949.

TILLYARD, E. M. W. Shakespeare's History Plays. New York, Macmillan, 1947.

TOMKINS, S. S. The Thematic Apperception Test: The Theory and Technique of Interpretation. New York, Grune and Stratton, 1947.

VAN TESLAAR, J. S. (ed.). An Outline of Psychoanalysis. New York, Modern Library, 1925.

WENDELL, BARRETT. William Shakespere: A Study in Elizabethan Literature. New York, Scribner, 1895.

WERTHAM, FREDERIC. Dark Legend. New York, Duell, Sloan, 1947.

WILSON, J. D. Life in Shakespeare's England. Harmondsworth, Middlesex, Eng., Penguin Books, 1944.

—— The Essential Shakespeare: A Biographical Adventure. Cambridge University Press, 1948.

WYATT, FREDERICK. "The Thematic Apperception Test; the Theory and Technique of Interpretation, by Silvan S. Tomkins. A Book Review," *Journal of Projective Techniques*, 14 (1950), 321–5.

YEATS, W. B. Ideas of Good and Evil. London, Bullen, 1914.

YULE, G. UDNY. The Statistical Study of Literary Vocabulary. Cambridge University Press, 1944.

ZIPF, G. K. Human Behavior and the Principle of Least Effort. Cambridge, Mass., Addison-Wesley, 1949.

INDEX

All dramatic characters from Shakespeare are identified by their specific plays, indicated by abbreviated titles in parentheses. For a list of abbreviations see p. ix.